THE WORLD OF MEGALITHS

JEAN-PIERRE MOHEN

Facts On File

New York • Oxford • Sydney

This book is the result of twenty years of interest in megaliths and personal experience of the constructions and the civilization that gave birth to them, gained from the excavations at the Bougon necropolis. I am grateful to the many people who have contributed to my overall understanding of these impressive monuments:

Jean-Pierre Adam, Martin Almagro, Gérard Bailloud, Patrice Birocheau, Bruno Bréard, Jacques Briard, Colin Burgess, Aubrey Burl, Claude Burnez, Jean Clottes, André Coffyn, David Coombs, Jean Courtin, Ahmad Hasan Dani, Glyn Daniel, Roger de Bayle des Hermens, Henri Duday, Christiane Eluérè, George Eogan, Jacques Gachina, Alain Gallay, Dr Gaudron, Georges Germond, Ierre Roland Giot, José Gomez, Xavier Gutherz, Ian Hodder, Eric Huysecom, Vitor and Susana Oliveira Jorge, Roger Joussaume, Lilli Kaelas, Hiline Kalb, Ian Kinnes, Ian Lanting, Jean Leclerc, José Lecornec, Charles Tanguy Le Roux, Jean L'Helgoucah, Gilles Loison, Catherine Louboutin, Frances Lynch, Eric Maheiu, Claude Masset, Guy Mazière, Jacqueline Mohen, Fernando Molina, Bernard Pajot, Jean-Pierre Pautreau, Yuri Piotrovski, Renan Polles, Sergio Rapu, Colin Renfrew, Raymond Riquet, Gérard Sauzade, Chris Scarre, Antonio Carlos Silva, Marta Strómberg, Jacques Tarrete, Bal Krishen Thapar, Guy Verron, Jean-Louis Voruz.

Christine Le Meignen, Catherine Theffor and Odile Tissier helped to prepare the text and the documentation.

Casterman's editorial team were actively involved in the preparation and design of the book.

I would like to express my thanks to all these people.

First published in the United States 1990 by
Facts on File, Inc.

Original edition published in French
(Le Monde des Mégalithes)
Copyright © 1989 by Casterman, Tournai

For information contact:
Facts On File, Inc.
460 Park Avenue South
New York NY 10016

Library of Congress Cataloging-in-Publication Data.

Mohen, J. P.
[Monde des mégalithes. English]
The world of megaliths/Jean-Pierre Mohen.
p cm
Translation of: Le monde des mégalithes.
Includes bibliographical references.
ISBN 0–8160 2251 8
1. Megalithic monuments. 2. Neolithic period.
I. Title
GN790.M7413 1990   89–16972
930.1.4—dc20   CIP

Photographs taken for this book at the Musée des Antiquités Nationales, Saint-Germain-en-Laye are by Jean-Michel Labat.

Translated by Helen McPhail in association with First Edition

Printed in Portugal

Facts On File books are available at special discounts when purchased in bulk quantities for businesses, associations, institutions or sales promotion. Please contact the Special Sales Department of our New York office at 212/683–2244 (dial 800/322–8755 except in NY, AK or HI).

Picture credits

Pages 10–11
Dolmen on the Kurd-Dagh, on the Syrian-Turkish border.
(Photo © Roger-Viollet)

Pages 68–69
Stonehenge.
(Photo © F. Dalgety/Explorer)

Pages 156–157
The Sleeping Lady,
Hal-Saflieni hypogeum, Malta
(Photo © R. Estall)

Pages 220–221
Gavrinis.
(Photo © M. Sharp)

Pages 282–283
Tamuli, Sardinia.
(Photo © M. Polles)

Jacket illustrations:

front, Drawing of Stonehenge by Luc Chaufoureau; back, Easter Island, photo © Annebicque/Sygma.; front jacket flap, photo © Annebicque/Sygma.

Contents

4 Monumental Daring *page 94*

Megalithic architecture reached its peak during the second half of the fourth millennium: the imposing mass of the tumulus, the use of more and more massive blocks of stone, and the intricacy of their deployment, reflected the defiance of the builders, in the face of the material, its weight and their intention to create permanent monuments. Within a single site monuments proliferated, were enlarged, divided, and superimposed on each other. The climax of this intense creativity was the great complex of Stonehenge, which was developed continuously over more than a thousand years.

5 The Spread of Megalithic Construction *page 128*

In the third millenium the megalith builders met another challenge: that of great numbers. Dolmens, mounds, cromlechs and menhirs multiplied and spread across great tracts of Europe. At the same time, however, their designs lost the creative inspiration that had pervaded the work of the preceding millenium. This was mass megalithism. Only the British Isles with their superb circles of standing stones, and the Mediterranean islands with their abundant rock-cut tombs, or hypogea, stood out.

THE SECRET OF THE BUILDERS

6 The 'Master of the Stones' *page 158*

Nothing was left to chance during megalithic construction. First came the search for stones worthy of the undertaking, with the right type of grain and texture, faults, weight, resonance, colour, and brightness. Next came the transport of the megaliths perhaps for 20 or even a 100 kilometres in spite of their huge mass, 350 tonnes for the broken Great Menhir at Locmariaquer, 180 tonnes for one of the stones of Antequera in Spain. Yet the secrets of these early builders were simple: ropes, logs and manpower!

7 Ancestral Society *page 188*

Neolithic people tamed their surroundings for farming and animal domestication. They set up their megaliths in open country, cleared for the purpose if necessary, and well away from their dwellings. The group was united by the cult of ancestor-worship, with bones carefully preserved in megalithic mounds. Sometimes the ancestors were just a few individuals, sometimes several hundreds. The Hal Safliéni hypogeum in Malta contained 7,000 bodies.

THE SACRED WORLD OF MEGALITHS

8 Ceremonial Centres *page 222*

Were megaliths no more than graves? They had wider importance, providing an effective focus of religious practice carefully orientated on the great celestial axes. Bones selected as relics, trepanned skulls, skeletons riddled with arrows, offerings of great diversity bear witness to the rituals practised there. Art, the main means of expressing spiritual belief, flourished especially in Brittany, Portugal, and Ireland. Almost all the many statuettes, the statue menhirs, and the richly decorated stones represented female figures.

9 The End of the Megaliths *page 270*

At the end of the third millenium, the introduction of new agricultural techniques, and above all of metalworking, unsettled the megalithic societies. The practice of collective burial associated with the cult of the dead vanished, and the cult of the ancestors gave way to the princely figure who was henceforward buried alone with his ornaments and his weapons. Gradually the great sites were abandoned. Only in the Mediterranean islands were the great stones still used for a while for fresh constructions. Thus the world of megaliths came to an end, and with it the first civilization of peasant Europe.

Introduction

The 'great stones' were for a long time shrouded in legends and fantasies. Looking like thousands of prehistoric monsters stranded on plains and moorlands, all these cairns, stone tables, alignments, fairy chambers, and giants' working bear witness, as we now know, to one specific period in our past. It is nearly 7,000 years since these rough monuments began to spread across the Atlantic regions of Europe; it was the first time in the history of humanity that such immense masses of stone had been brought together. The whole of western Europe, from Portugal to Scandinavia, was soon scattered with these massive monuments often visible from great distances. Great fingers of granite or limestone were set up, alone, in circles, or in rows, forming spectacular markers for a whole civilization.

The most extraordinary feature of megalithism is not the use of these enormous blocks of stone, but their widespread distribution both in space and in time. Megaliths have been found from Ireland to Madagascar, and as far away as Korea and Colombia. Experiments have proved that the extraction, transport and erection of the great stones can be achieved reasonably easily. Jean-Pierre Mohen's own experience shows that nothing in these operations presents insurmountable technical problems. He tells us that the manipulation of megaliths is within the capabilities of any farming society and it was indeed almost always farming societies, lacking even an awareness of metals, that built these monuments.

There are further searching questions to be asked. Why was so much labour and effort expended? Obviously there must have been pressing reasons, reason that are deeply and permanently engraved on human consciousness, since archeologists can trace their effects over nearly 3,000 years. In focusing attention on megalithic society and religion and assembling all the documentation which might help to explain them, Jean-Pierre Mohen explores hitherto little-known territory, and his conclusions offer some remarkable advances in our understanding of the entire civilization. This book, therefore, is more than a synthesis, and index of knowlege: some mysteries have been explained, although others remain unanswered, the natural fruits of any advance in knowledge.

Enigmas and theories are much loved they offer so many opportunities to fantasize! But if we must forget fairies, we may be able to create other dreams, and better ones. With its beliefs, it ceremonies, and the social structures it attempted, this pre-metalworking farming world takes on a new life, and we can begin to perceive their religions as well as their monuments. And though it may be true that one of the great functions of science is to feed our dreams, the advances made by megalithic researchers over the last three decades have done more than banish myths and legends they have brought us an abundant harvest of images based, at last, on reality.

SITES

AND

LEGENDS

The Silent Giants

'Speak to me! Why can't you speak!' cried Father Mahé, canon of Vannes, to the megaliths around him in 1825. Recalling his plea nearly ninety years later, Father Millon added mischievously that although the stones were silent, scholars were loquacious on their behalf. And not only scholars. Some of the opinions voiced were of an extravagance that amounted to 'megalithomania', as John Michell rather fancifully came to call it, and their eccentricities illuminate the thinking that lay behind the archeological studies of the time.

At first the names attached to the 'great stones' were drawn from legend and from time to time acquired importance in practice or belief; some of these oral traditions still survive, coloured by fantasies that have nothing to do with historical accuracy. But in the climate of the eighteenth-century cult of reason and curiosity about the past, antiquaries began looking at megaliths in detail. They drew them, they gathered together the remains – particularly bones – that lay nearby, and they scoured ancient texts for references that might be relevant; their conclusions were sketchy, however, and their interpretations varied and often fantastical. Archeological methods adequate for research into these megalithic monuments were not developed until the second half of the nineteenth century, and so to this day certain famous sites, such as Stonehenge or Boscawen-Un in England remain a focus of lively popular beliefs.

At the beginning of this century the ethnologist Georges Guénin carried out a survey on this theme in Brittany, but unfortunately never published his results. At the same period Paul Sébillot published an important collection of place-names and oral tradition concerning French megaliths, followed by Leslie Grinsell in 1976 with a similar collection relating to Great Britain. A few examples taken from different countries indicate the poetic richness of popular expression and its mythic or religious range.

The history of these stones, many of which are very large indeed, was often associated with supernatural beings, the only ones believed capable of setting them up. Extra-terrestrial creatures were supposed to have constructed the platform at Baalbek, while a fourteenth-century manuscript attributed the building of Stonehenge to the giant Merlin. In 1532, Rabelais described in his satirical masterpiece *Gargantua and Pantagruel* how and why Pantagruel built the dolmen of Pierre Levée at Poitiers:

> He came to Poitiers to study, and profited much thereby: at which place, seeing that the students were sometimes at leisure and did not know how to pass the time, he took pity on them; and one day took from a big rock called Passelourdin a great stone of seventy feet square and fourteen spans thick, and placed it firmly upon four pillars at the centre of a

Saint Genevieve, the patron saint of Paris (background), watching over her sheep gathered within a circle of standing stones. This sixteenth-century painted wooden panel is one of the oldest pictures of a megalithic monument. It links Christianity and pagan religion. The stone circle no longer exists.

(Musée Carnavalet, Paris. Photo © J.-L. Charmet)

field; so that those same scholars, at such times when they knew of naught else to do, could pass their time by climbing onto this very stone and feasting there, with flagons, hams and pies, and mark their names upon it, and now it is known as the Raised Stone.

This monument, shown in a 1561 engraving in Georgius Hovenaglius' *Civitates Orbis terrarum*, still stands today, although it was broken in the eighteenth century and is undoubtedly somewhat less imposing now than as described by Rabelais.

Pantagruel's father Gargantua is also mentioned quite often in this area. In Brittany the quartz menhir at Saint-Suliac in Ille-et-Vilaine is known as Gargantua's Tooth, and a standing stone near Fort de la Latte in the Côtes-du-Nord is called Gargantua's Finger. Legendary ogres are often evoked in England and in the Finistère region of France. Megaliths are also frequently known as 'giants' tombstones' – the giant at Brennilis-en-Loqueffret (Brittany) was so big that he had to be folded up nine times to get him into his grave!

Sometimes dwarfs, gnomes, or imps with magic powers replaced these giant builders, or were associated with them. In Johan Picardt's engraving, published in 1660, they are depicted building a long megalithic monument in the Netherlands province of Drenthe. It was believed that the Indian megalithic tombs of Sorapoor, the Deccan, and Malabar, were inhabited by dwarfs before the days of human-

Gods, Devils, Giants, and Fairies

kind: because they were turbulent and disruptive creatures, their king turned them into monoliths. Fairies too made their homes in megalithic tombs, in such places as Saint-Saviour in Guernsey and some of the rock-cut tombs of Sardinia. They consoled the dead and ensured local prosperity as long as they were respected by the human population. They are familiar figures in this context: they were responsible for the standing stones, and sometimes used the most narrowly tapering stone as a distaff. Some monuments were named after them, such as the Roche aux Fées at Essé, where the fairies transported the red schist stones in their aprons from an outcrop at least four kilometres away. One of the rocks was dropped on the way, and became the Rumfort menhir. Many legends describe fairies scattering great stones at random during a game of quoits, or simply because an apron-string broke – and, like the dwarfs, they exist within or near the megaliths, dancing and tumbling, filling them with their complete and secret life. The Devil himself might have built megaliths, including the menhir known as La Tremblais at Saint-Samson-sur-Rance in Brittany. Wizard-like devils gather round the Pierre du Rendez-vous at Vaumort on the Sabbath. Some monuments feature in epic cycles; the quest of Arthur's Knights of The Round Table for the Holy Grail led them through the forest of Brocéliande near Paimpont where Jacques Briard has traced 'Merlin's Tomb', a long funerary chamber, as well as the 'Hotié-Viviane', a megalithic coffer where the fairy Vivian lived, and a cromlech, within whose magic circle she imprisoned her lover Merlin, rendering him totally invisible.

As in ancient mythology, petrification was regarded as divine punishment. In France the lines of standing stones at Langon, at Saint-Just, and in the south of the Ille-et-Vilaine *département*, are known as Les Demoiselles, young girls turned to stone because they went dancing in the fields on a Sunday afternoon instead of going to church. The same fate befell a Bristol clergyman and his curate who failed to take a service; they, and the musicians and dancers at the fair they went to instead, were turned to stone. The crowd of great stones at Néant-sur-Yvel in Morbihan, Brittany, are called the Jardin aux Moines, and are revelling monks turned to stone by St Méen. At Carnac, in the same *département*, God saved St Cornelius as he fled from pursuing Romans by turning three thousand legionaries into stone, forming the lines of menhirs – a tale that was still recounted by children to visitors until quite recently.

Popular tradition places megaliths in the world of magic, as animate beings whose form of life differs from that of humans: more secretive, deaf, and slow, and perhaps also not continuous. Some stones grow like trees, getting bigger year by year: the Pontivy stone in

The giant Merlin building Stonehenge, as depicted in a fourteenth-century manuscript preserved in the British Library in London. This is the oldest known picture of Stonehenge and illustrates clearly the legend which is the earliest form of megalith interpretation.

(Photo © British Library/ Casterman Archives)

the Morbihan area of Brittany was only as big as a walnut when God planted it in the earth. The Peiro Ficado at Malvès in south-west France, more than 5 metres high, is said to have been no taller than a man in 1850, and the nineteenth-century inhabitants of Trie-Château, in the Oise region of the Ile de Paris, believed that the Trois Pierres dolmen had emerged like a plant out of the ground.

Other stones have the power of movement, animated by fairies, the Devil, or some other supernatural being. The Saint-Martin-d'Arcé menhir turns round at the stroke of midnight, and that at Culey-le-Patry in Normandy rotates several times during the night, stopping only at the first cock-crow. At Bégadan in the Gironde and at the Pierre Folle at Saint-Priest in the Massif Central all the stones dance when midnight strikes. Some of these mobile stones favour Christmas night: the menhir at Gerponville in Normandy and the Pierre Frite near Aillan in the Yonne area of Burgundy revolve three times on the spot at the moment when the priest reads from the Gospels. The Pierre de David at Cangy, the Pierre de Minuit at Pontlevoy, the stone at Ham, and the turning stone at Gouvix all do the same; while the Pierre des Demoiselles at Mesnil-Hardray raises itself to let out a file of white-clad girls who dance in a circle. At the instant that the Mass begins the Virgin appears on the highest flat stone of the Pierres Folles at Nohant-en-Graçay, with the other flat and upright stones dancing round.

The stones' circular movement is connected with dancing and music, particularly with bells ringing. The slabs of the dolmen at Tauzac begin to dance when the bells call worshippers to Midnight Mass, the Pierre Levée at Brétignolles revolves when it hears the bells of Saint-Nicholas-de-Brem, and the Pierre Folle at Montguyon turns round three times at the sound of the angelus. Sometimes a crowing cock regulates a megalith's movements: at Chermignac in Charente-Maritime the dolmen slab jumps three times when the cock crows on Christmas morning. It is the first cuckoo-call in spring, however, which sets the menhirs turning at Perron, at Culey-le-Patry, and at the Pierre Tournante near Avranches in Normandy. There is a singing dolmen at Méré, in the Yonne, and the Ancresse dolmen in Guernsey is known as 'the ringing rock'. Others sound the twelve strokes of midnight, such as the largest stone of the Forges cromlech at Montguillon, that of the Rennefraie alignment, and the Pierre-Bise at Boissy-le-Sec. At Ham the stone that grows sighs and groans, also at midnight.

Some stones are even more active – they move about, sometimes to bathe in the sea, as at Carnac, or to drink. The menhir of La Bouëxière quenches its thirst once every century, at midnight precisely on Christmas night. So do the megaliths at Plouhinec; drinking their fill in the river at Intel, they leave their treasures uncovered – but unattainable, for their movements are too swift. In any case, it brings bad luck to try to check the accuracy of legend by observing the feats of the invisible powers – one bold individual managed to spy on the Pierre Levée at Jugon on the night when it went to drink from the river Arguenon, but he was never seen again.

Megaliths have been the object of some popular and very personal practices and ceremonies, often concerning love, fertility, or health. Some megaliths are connected with divination and witchcraft, and may be the confidants of girls seeking husbands. At Carnac young girls would undress and rub their navels on the stone as they repeated their wishes. Others would lift their skirts and rub their stomachs against the Pierre-de-Chantecoq in Eure-et-Loir, or one of the upright Roche-Marie stones near Saint-Aubin-du-Cormier. The women of Saint-Samson-sur-Rance would sit astride the leaning La Tremblais menhir by night, in order to find themselves husbands within the year.

To ensure handsome children husbands would rub their naked stomachs against each side of the Kerloas menhir at Plouarzel in Finistère. Women fearing infertility would go alone to certain standing stones, in Eure-et-Loir, in Brittany, in the Landes, or in the Pyrenees. At Le Mans a woman longing for a child would dip her finger into a deep cup-shaped hollow in the menhir beside the cathedral. Childless women went to Nohant-Vicq to suck a morsel of red sandstone from the flat stone of a dolmen which was still visible in 1789, dedicated to St Greluchon. Another widely practised custom was to walk three times round a stone, or form a ring round it. At the foot of the Plomb du Cantal in Auvergne young bridegrooms from La Noulède would walk round the menhir, while in another village the whole wedding

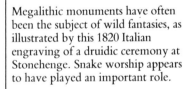

Megalithic monuments have often been the subject of wild fantasies, as illustrated by this 1820 Italian engraving of a druidic ceremony at Stonehenge. Snake worship appears to have played an important role.

(Bibliothèque des Arts Décoratifs, Paris. Photo © J.-L. Charmet)

party would join in this form of fertility dance. Near Carnac, older couples without children would dance round a stone and ask for an heir, and in the Landes parents would carry their new-born babies nine times round the Pierre de Gribère, near Sabres, to ensure their sturdiness.

Alliance with the unseen powers of the stones opened the way to magical practices and to the blacker kinds of witchcraft. At the trial of Gilles de Retz in 1440 one of his accomplices, Étienne Cornillaut – known as Pontou – admitted that he had gone by night with a friend 'to invoke a certain demon who had hidden treasure in his power . . . in a field with large standing stones'. There, he claimed, was a magic circle marked out with a cutlass dipped in blood!

Perforated stones also sometimes became the object of superstitious beliefs and activities. Young children were passed through the hole of one such stone at Tolvan in Cornwall in order to purify them, in a ceremony that complemented their baptism. Sick children could be cured if they crept into the hole in the stone at Tobernavean, near Sligo in Ireland. In India, Mircea Eliade has identified similar standing stones with curative powers; in the Caucasus, the hole in such a stone is characterized as a mouth giving voice to oracular pronouncements and messages from buried ancestors, sometimes in the form of dwarfs, as at Tzarskaya. In the 'passage graves' of the Paris basin the perforation was called 'the soul's opening', and allowed the spirits of the dead to come and go. A 1660 engraving shows a sibyl uttering her prophecies at the entrance to a megalithic corridor beneath the tumulus in Drenthe in the Netherlands; again, the small opening takes on the approximate shape of a mouth through which the divination was heard. Victor Hugo turned to this source of inspiration in 1854 as 'the mouth of the shadow', linking it to one of Jersey's megalithic tombs:

A prophetic vision of archeological tourism! In the satirical magazine *Punch* (issue dated 30 August 1899); the English caricaturist C. Harrison imagined various ways of making a profit out of the great site.

Stonehenge's annual 'druidic' ceremony, on the day of the summer solstice. The sequence of rites and prayers dates only from the last century, and is based on literary allusions to ancient druids and some cosmic observations.

(Photo © Robert Estall)

> Man's dreams take him down into the universal pit.
> I wandered by the dolmen overlooking Rozel,
> Where the cape reaches out in a peninsula.
> The ghost was waiting; the quiet sombre being
> Took hold my head, in his spreading hand,
> Bore me to the rock's peak, and spoke:
> Remember that all know his law, his aim, his way:
> That all space, from stars to smallest mite, listens;
> That all acknowledges creation ...
> (*Les Contemplations*, VI:XXVI, ce que dit la bouche d'ombre)

All the megaliths mentioned here are seen as extraordinary places, standing on the boundaries between the visible and the invisible, where people of ancient times would pray or bring gifts – generally modest offerings to the immaterial spirit of the stone. Young girls wishing to marry within the year would leave a silver coin on the Colombiers menhir, and at Long-Boël they put scraps of wool or charms into cracks in the menhirs. According to Paul Sébillot in 1820, similar offerings were slipped into cracks in the dolmen at Guérande in Loire-Atlantique. Young men would drive nails and pins into the Pierre Frite menhir in Seine-et-Marne before their marriage, and oil and flowers were placed on megaliths in the Cahors region, in south-west France. Elsewhere children offered fruit, pieces of bread, or simply stones symbolizing bread and meat.

At least two types of object were much sought after near megaliths for their protective properties: polished axe-heads and stone arrow-heads. The axe-heads were known as 'thunderbolts' or 'thunder-stones' and the arrow-heads, less frequently identified, were known in Hainault as 'fairy tips'. They were – naturally – the weapons of giants and fairies who had retreated underground; but the belief that polished stones descended with flashes of lightning from the sky was also very widespread throughout western Europe, and they were valued as talismans against lightning-strikes. For this reason it is not surprising to find them embedded in the walls of religious buildings, as at Trévron in the Côtes-du-Nord, or in the foundations of houses, as in Morbihan, the Yonne, Anjou, the Gironde, and the Pyrenees. Axe-heads have also been found under the hearth in houses in Morbihan and the Yonne. Such stones, whether axes or arrow-heads, protected both inhabitants and their flocks from various illnesses: at Quimperlé polished axes could cure rabies, epilepsy, and typhoid fever. In the Corseul area a polished stone was offered to the dying for their last kiss, and one old man there even stipulated that one should be placed in his coffin. Perforated Neolithic stones might be worn as a necklace, and around Vannes they were held to have been beads from saints' rosaries. Megaliths were also thought to conceal many other treasures, particularly quantities of gold or silver coins. Indeed the standing stone set in the cemetery wall at Pontivy reveals treasure of this sort when it goes to drink from the river Blavet. At Plédran a great pile of gold is buried under the stone known as the Fuseau de la Fée Margot. The Golden Calf was buried under Peyre Longue near Dax, after being worshipped there in olden times, while another Golden Calf was hidden beneath the Terrier de la Fade at Anglade. Such riches, however, may be no more than glimpsed by humans – they are too well protected by devils, evil spirits, and other beasts of fantasy, quite apart from the megaliths themselves.

Megaliths compel the respect of the passer-by, even from those who are ignorant of their origins, or who do not believe in their powers. If any great stone structure is destroyed, popular tradition immediately denounces the sacrilege. A twelfth-century Guernsey noble who pulled down a cromlech to build his castle was cursed by the populace and hounded by ill-luck until his death. The pioneering antiquaries of the eighteenth century could not approach such sacred stones or dig at their base without offending against such beliefs. Around 1800 the inhabitants of Vert claimed that if the Pierre Piquée were pulled down, a flood would pour out of its foundations and would drown the whole of the Beauce; and the menhir at Saint-Samson-sur-Rance near Dinan must not be moved because France would be flooded by the sea. Anyone who ventured to demolish a megalithic monument would be dead within the year, according to oral tradition in the Indre, and anyone digging at the foot of the Ardillières dolmens would discover the road to hell, and be swallowed up without hope of return.

Megaliths could also withstand assault: at Plouréour-Trez quarrymen's tools lost their edge on cromlech stones, which set them-

The Conversion of Idols

The text in the engraving reads: *La pierre leuee demie lieue de Poictiers.* along the top; *chemin vers Bourges* at the left; *Poictiers* at the right; *GEORGIVS HOVFNAGLIVS Aº 1561*; *OBERTVS GYFANIVS BVRANVS PAEDAGOGVS 1561*; *ROBERTVS VAN HAFTEN 1561*; *IOANNES A BLOMEDAEL 1561*; *GVILHELMVS MOSTAERT 1561*; *Georgius Braun Colin 1580*.

The Pierre Levée at Poitiers, idealized in this sixteenth- century engraving, became famous when in 1532 Rabelais used it as Pantagruel's great banqueting table for students bored by their studies.

(Musée des Antiquités Nationales, Saint-Germain-en-Laye.
Photo © Casterman Archives)

selves upright again unaided if they were thrown down. When masons attempted to cut away the great stone slab of Peyrolebado, in Aveyron, they saw blood spurt out at each blow of the hammer, and stopped in fear. Workmen preparing to knock down the menhir at Saint-Quentin-la-Chabanne near Felletin were driven back when they saw threatening flames spring up from the earth. No doubt the Catholic Church was at various times a threat to the cult of the stones; several Councils condemned it, and individuals such as St Éloi inveighed fiercely against 'pagan' idols. Although there is no record whatsoever of a megalithic monument being destroyed by the Church, there are many examples of stones being gradually absorbed. Some megaliths were seen as the work of the Devil, the master of agitation: passers-by were advised to keep away from such unhealthy places and cross themselves for protection against evil influences. This was normal practice near a stone-polishing site at Nettonville, which was well-named the Devil's Water-Stoup. Elsewhere Christ, the Virgin, and certain saints – including St Cornelius, St Genevieve, and St Martin – contributed their miraculous powers to the building of

This 1900 postcard shows women dancing round a suggestive standing stone at the Pardon of Plonéour-Lanvern in Finistère. Prehistoric megaliths were a frequent part of popular tradition until modern times.

(Collection Abbaye de la Source. Photo ©J.-L. Charmet)

monuments or to ceremonies nearby. Priests in Charente-Maritime organized a procession near the Sainte-Madeleine dolmen before 1789.

Crosses have been carved on megaliths, or placed on them. There are many such Christianized menhirs in Brittany, particularly at Cap-Saint-Mathieu and at Plonéour-Lanvern, as well as at Champ-Dolent in Ille-et-Vilaine. Some dolmens were also crowned with a stone cross. Megaliths have had cemeteries built round them or even churches beside them, such as the church at Rudston in Yorkshire, and the cathedral at Le Mans in France. The druidic tradition frequently associated with megaliths is also often based on Christianity. At Locoal-Mendon in Morbihan, a rosary and pendant of translucent chalcedony strung on a blue and scarlet thread was found hanging by a box bed; the stone had been picked up inside a dolmen and was used for several generations to ease menstruation for the young girls of the house.

Beliefs and traditions like these were an integral part of peasant thinking down the ages. Such living stones, haunted by invisible and all-powerful beings, could not be seen as the work of human hands; hence the great respect they inspired, and sometimes too the consider-

Sacrificial Stones?

able anxiety. Was the stone satisfied or not, would prayers be granted? In this context it was not sufficient simply to refer to the stone, it was essential to use it according to custom. Because they were generally the focus of religious practice, megaliths sustained social cohesion and strengthened belief. In a world where the past is no more than legend, history loses all meaning: the very concept of the past may be entirely lost if a megalithic monument becomes a house or a stable.

From the eighteenth century onwards megaliths became the subject of a written tradition alongside the essentially oral popular beliefs: this may be considered genuine scholarship, and it drew extensively on references in ancient texts. Oral tradition then absorbed certain themes of this new learning, which was probably the origin of the suggestion that flourished in the nineteenth century associating megaliths, and dolmens in particular, with human sacrifice. Beyond these powerful suggestions appeared the first notion of classification: categories of megaliths were defined by 'Celtic' names, and so too were their supposed functions. Thus appeared the first theories on what are known as dolmens. The name corresponds closely to the general concept of a megalithic monument: some very large stones set up in table form.

Early in the eighteenth century the Marquis de Robien, President of the Parliament of Brittany and lord of the château of Plessi-Ker on the banks of the river Auray, shrewdly identified the dolmens round Carnac: 'The tombs consist of stones of immense size borne upon others raised upright to support them.' Some time later, in 1767, the Comte de Caylus' *Recueil d'Antiquités*, in a discussion of Caesar's *Commentaries*, sought in vain for an explanation for megaliths. He chose caution: 'In the end, since the singular form of this dolmen and others like it could not provide a dwelling, should it be considered a religious object? How far is it reasonable to guess at the reason for it? What possible solution could there be? There is no answer, and silence is best.'

An alternative view met with some success after 1796, the publication year of La Tour d'Auvergne's book on *Les Origines Gauloises*. In it he explained confidently that 'according to Diodorus of Sicily' dolmens were altars where the Gauls swore treaties or their priests, the druids, sacrificed their victims – generally human – to their gods. La Tour d'Auvergne's authority became unquestionable when, as France's leading grenadier, he was killed at Oberhausen and became a hero.

Although some scholars, such as Legrand d'Aussy, were disturbed by the new theory, all doubt was soon swept away. The creation in 1805, in France, of the Celtic Academy under the direction of its first president, Cambry, appeared as if in response to the romantic ideas which could easily envisage the possibility of human sacrifice on an altar. Those caught up in 'Celtomania' described the ceremonies with a somewhat morbid excess of detail: the druids plunged the knife in 'below the diaphragm', the victims staggered, and their entrails were examined while blood poured out, flooding the flat surface of the dolmen and streaming down the channels. This at least is the explanation given for the covering stone slab of a broken dolmen at Bougon. The slab had become a sacrificial stone, and the groove visible in its corner-stone was a gutter for the blood to flow away.

Such theories had to be justified by references in ancient texts. Father Mahé asserted in 1825: 'Dolmens are altars', and 'proved' his theory from the classics and the Bible. Lucain speaks of altars set up for the cult of Hésus, Teutatès, and Taranis. Tacitus, writing of the inhabitants of the island of Mona (Anglesey), described how 'steam rose from the blood of their captives on the altars erected for them'. Moses wished that altars set up for the Lord to be 'untouched by iron'. The discovery of the first human bones at the foot of upright dolmen stones appeared to confirm such massacres, while the polished axes and flint blades that were also discovered seemed certain to be instruments of sacrifice.

From Druids' Altar ...

The priests' reason for raising most of these 'sacred tables' was, it seemed, to enable all present to witness the ceremony, and some commentators also saw the dolmen as a pulpit for addressing the crowd. Michelet's 1833 *Histoire de France* asserted that the clan chief was elected by public acclamation at the stone which served both as altar and symbol of divinity. But when Mérimée, the second Inspector of Historic Monuments, wrote in 1836 after travelling through western France that none of the theories regarding dolmens was proven, his was one of the very few voices of caution in the first half of the nineteenth century.

After 1850, however, a new generation of scholars, including Émile Cartailhac in the Causses region of southern France and Paul du Châtellier in Brittany, abandoned textual explanations and studied the actual monuments instead. They excavated a considerable number, and their frequently very precise observations combined to prove that dolmens covered by an earth tumulus or a stone cairn could only have been used from the inside, as a setting for mass burial. The altar theory was therefore disproved and the theory regarding Gallic druids became equally untenable, for the funerary furnishings inside the monuments showed that they were constructed in Neolithic times, substantially predating the Iron Age in Gaul. They were, therefore, undoubtedly Prehistoric tombs.

The great stones were often invoked in prayers for a wife or a husband. This Kauffman and Pibaraud engraving shows the Pierre aux Maris at La Baroche, near Colmar in Alsace. While the women watch slyly, one man on the left questions the balanced stone, in the middle a future husband shows his delight, and two men on the right are downcast by the stone's reply.

(Photo © J.-L. Charmet)

... to Funeral Stele

As with dolmens, a variety of explanations has been offered for the origin of menhirs. In the early days of such research they were seen as the most rudimentary type of monument, simple standing stones. For Lepelletier de la Sarthe in 1853, they were 'peulvans' (upright long stones) set on high points to act as markers for travellers and sailors. There was nothing new in this suggestion. In 1803 Baudouin-Maison-Blanche had suggested that standing stones could have supported great torches, to be lit for occasional important ceremonies in honour of the Eternal Being. In 1789 Father Déric proposed the theory of the sacrificial stone, but without any detail on its use – a problematical point in view of the height of most such stones. Among the most keenly refuted interpretations is Paniagua's 1897 theory that 'the menhir is a phallic deity'. Those who, like Godard-Faultrier in 1862, saw the stone needle as 'the image of a ray of sunshine' came closer to the proponents of astronomical theories related to 'alignments' and cromlechs.

Other functions attributed to menhirs were more generally accepted in the nineteenth century. Scholars such as Cambry, Robiou and Le Gal saw them as markers indicating territorial boundaries. Those who disagreed pointed to the size of the stones, somewhat out of proportion with such a commonplace function.

The theory that menhirs were idols was better sustained, and Father Millon collected references tending to justify it. These were, essentially, ancient texts of Pausanias, Minutius Felix, Arnobius, St Clement of Alexandria, and Apuleius, which suggested to Don Clamet that 'the gods of the Ammonites and the Moabites, like those of the Teutons, the image of Bacchus at Thebes, or the god Elagabalus, were mere rough stones or simple columns.' Renan, in his *Poésie des Races Celtiques*, also stated that 'stone was the fetish of all peoples in their early development. It seems to be the symbol of the Celtic race: unchanging, like the race, it stands as everlasting evidence.' He too quotes the Bible, but above all he quotes the texts of the Councils of Carthage in 398, of Arles in 452, of Tours in 567, of Toledo in 681 and 692, Mainz in 743, Paris in 826 and 829, Valence in 1557, Cambrai in 1565 – all of which threatened stone-worshippers with excommunication. The efficacy of such threats is open to question: how is it that so many menhirs are still upright in some regions, such as Brittany?

Some authors cling to the theory that the menhirs were monuments erected in honour of important individuals or to commemorate notable events. They stress humanity's universal need to record the great days of the past, taking biblical texts as their support. For example, when Jacob heard God's promises he set up a stone on which he spread oil, saying 'This stone will be the house of God'. Another stone was erected to record the alliance between Jacob and Laban, while after the Israelites' victory over the Philistines Samuel set up the stone 'of help' at Mizpah, for this was where the Lord had sustained him. The theory has been attacked: there are thousands of known menhirs, and there could scarcely have been so many important events and individuals. Some see the menhir as a monument set up in honour of someone whose body has not been traced, that is, as a memorial stone. Monseigneur Laouënan emphasized that this is so in Indre, and Cartailhac also cites Madagascar where this type of menhir is known as *tsangambato*.

Other archeologists go further and consider that menhirs are simply funeral steles. Their arguments are based on nomenclature: in France, the Tréhorenteuc group of menhirs is called the Tomb Garden, for example, the Plouarzel menhir is in the Kerlaos field, the 'place of mourning', and the setting of the two at Plounévez-Lochrist is called Kervéret, which means 'the place of burial'. Archeological digs carried out round the base of these menhirs support this proposition. In 1825 Father Mahé announced the discovery of 'eleven skulls found in a large bowl' at the foot of a menhir pulled down near Quimper, and ten years later Fréminville claimed to have found vertebrae and human teeth near a menhir at Plouhinec. Father Collet, Aveneau de la Grancière, Fouquet, and du Châtellier described similar finds of shards of coarse pottery, trimmed flints, fragments of polished axe-heads, charcoal, and assorted pieces of quartz. All these were sooner or

'The human sacrifice of the Gauls', illustrated in this anonymous nineteenth-century engraving, includes all the romantic Celtomane's favourite themes: the megalith is a sacrificial altar; faithful to Caesar's description, the mistletoe-crowned druid officiates before an ancient oak tree. The morbid aspect is matched by the presumed savagery of the Gauls.

(Photo © J.-L. Charmet)

later found to resemble findings near dolmens, leading to the conclusion that they probably dated from the same period and were intended for similar funeral use. In reply to comments that there were insufficient human remains to confirm the burial theory, the authors pointed out that the soil in Brittany, where the digs took place, is so acid that most bones disappear.

Father Millon, after examining these suggestions, concluded in about 1910 that science could offer no definite conclusion as to the menhirs' function, that no one argument appeared more convincing than any other, and that the question therefore remained open.

The Mystery of the Alignments

Many of the theories put forward concerning menhirs were naturally also applied to alignments, which consist of rows of menhirs, and particularly the most impressive alignments, those at Carnac, which have attracted much comment. James Fergusson, for example, touched upon various theories relating to this Breton site before settling on a single possible explanation: people could not have expended so much time and so much trouble except for 'the erection of monuments commemorating some great battle, which took place on this plain at some time. Each menhir must represent one soldier.' It only remained to decide which battle!

Those same authors who saw the menhir as a funerary stele saw the Carnac alignments as a vast necropolis. Does not Kermario, the name of one such alignment, mean 'village of the dead'? Various pseudo-historical interpretations were attached to this simple theory,

EARLY EXCAVATIONS

In 1811 the 'Auray Society for Extracting Gold from Dolmens' marked the beginning of a steady interest in remains buried at the foot of the great stones when they investigated the Tables des Marchands and Pierres Plates monuments at Locmariaquer.

What are known as 'Chief's tombs' were excavated with the intention of discovering their hidden treasures: polished semi-precious stones, human bones, perhaps even gold objects. Contemporary accounts indicate feverish exploration as workmen were hired to dig out the mounds with pick and shovel, to reach the holy of holies. The prime objective was to uncover something really spectacular – an unbroken vessel, a jadeite axe, or a trepanned skull. The best finds were bought from the workmen, and went to make up scholarly collections or to form the basis of archeological museums such as at Carnac and Vannes. Such treasure hunts were very popular. In the middle of the nineteenth century, in Denmark, King Frederick VII himself was present to see a trench dug through to the tomb at the centre of a mound.

These early excavations were extremely destructive, although the accounts of these nineteenth-century scholars were often acutely observed. Simultaneously geologists, botanists, zoologists, historians and archeologists, they created the basis for scientific research.

Every region had its own pioneers in field research. In the eighteenth century John Aubrey realized the importance of examining the stones themselves at Avebury and Stonehenge, mapping and excavating round them. He discovered Stonehenge's famous 'Aubrey Holes', but the site was not fully explored until Gowland's work in 1901. At the end of the nineteenth century Paul du Châtellier realized that any fragment found in a grave or at the foot of a standing stone in Brittany might be important. He numbered each item and noted its position in the ground, and his collection is still of great interest. Early in the twentieth century, Zacharie Le Rouzic was active in excavating monuments in Morbihan, studying them and ensuring their restoration. It is to him that we owe the rescue of several groups of megalithic ruins.

of which the most imaginative must surely be that of Hirmenech in 1906:

> Neptune had ten sons, one of whom was called Mnese. This name, no doubt spelt incorrectly, is none other than that of Menes or Menevi, the first king of Egypt. The last of these ancient Atlantides, named according to region Celts, Pelasgians, Iberians, or Aryans, gathered round his throne and formed a nation called the Veneti. They took part in the siege of Troy, and then dispersed, each group returning home. On the way back from their distant expedition the Veneti of Great Britain reached Armorica with their fellow-soldiers from that region, bearing with them with great care the remains of those who had fallen in battle. Briefly, the famous alignments at Carnac make up a rebus based on the Trojan War.

Thus each menhir would indicate the tomb of a brave warrior or his companion, and the general layout of the steles would set out, in coded fashion, the great epic of this famous war. The religious function of the Carnac alignments is often mentioned but very rarely spelt out. Mérimée acknowledged in 1836 that 'only religious belief and practice could have produced such remarkable results in barbaric times', and du Châtellier agreed. For some the parallel rows of menhirs constituted a temple; for others they were no more than an outer temple court, or sacred avenues leading to temples represented by cromlechs. In 1796 La Tour d'Auvergne suggested that they were a centre for politico-religious gatherings at the orders of a druid, the grand master of Carnac.

The theory that the orientation of the alignments was intentional and designed to observe the course of the sun appeared quite early. In 1805 Cambry emphasized the 'celestial theme' of the Carnac lines, 'referring to the stars, the planets, the Zodiac, to the thirty-year cycle adopted by the druids'. This idea was subsequently revived and developed regularly: in 1897 Gaillard published his enormous *Astronomie Préhistorique* and 1926 saw the publication of Dr Baudouin's *La Préhistoire par les Étoiles, un Chronomètre Préhistorique*.

The circular or oval formations of standing stones associated with the Carnac alignments proved more of a puzzle than an inspiration to writers. Such layouts have been seen variously as temples, funerary steles, or perhaps courts of justice.

In Great Britain the variety, quantity, and above all the impressive appearance of these monuments fascinated both twelfth-century sorcerers and, subsequently, eighteenth-century astronomers. The latter turned to Caesar's text on Celtic druids' cosmology – those same druids who were credited with construction of the megaliths, a view supported by ancient Irish and Welsh texts. The Stonehenge architectural ensemble was first illustrated in a thirteenth-century manuscript, and its construction has successively been ascribed to Phoenicians, Romans, Danes, Saxons, Celtic druids, the original inhabitants of the British Isles, Brahmans, Egyptians, Chaldeans, American Indians, and even to giants, the builders of Atlantis, and extra-terrestrial beings! It has been seen as an observatory, a memorial, a parliament, a necropolis, a temple. In 1620 King James I instructed the architect Inigo Jones to make a plan of the monument. Impressed by Stonehenge's architectural perfection and its horseshoe-shaped entrance, Jones thought of the engineer Vitruvius and in particular of the Tuscan order, and deduced that building took place just after the Romans reached southern England. John Aubrey was the first to carry out field research at Stonehenge, and in about 1660 he discovered the cavities known as 'Aubrey Holes'. The druidic monument hypothesis was thus strongly reinforced.

One of the eighteenth century's most original characters was also fascinated by the circular monuments at Stonehenge and Avebury. Dr William Stukeley (1687–1765) was a member of the Society of Antiquaries in London; in 1725 he published his *Itinerarium Curiosum*, a collection of pictures of English megaliths drawn from life. At the age of forty he became a mystic, gave up his London activities to take holy orders, and dedicated himself to the service of 'druidic science'. He saw Stonehenge and Avebury as temples inspired by the religious philosophies of Moses, Plato, the Phoenicians, the druids, and the Christian Church. He recognized the importance of the solstice in the orientation of Stonehenge's axis, and in 1759 published an engraving illustrating a druid offering up his sacrifice in front of the monument, at the moment of the winter solstice, with the victim crucified in the same manner as Christ. He saw the menhirs at Avebury as an integral part of an enormous snake to which the druids offered sacrifices. This sacred serpent, symbol of the sun, was also invoked by Penhouët in 1826 with reference to the Carnac alignments, and the discovery in 1846 of an earth monument in the shape of a snake in Ordams County, Ohio, supported his theory. Each example was associated with a cromlech representing the serpent's head. In 1872 James Fergusson revived a very ancient tradition, recorded in the twelfth century by Geoffrey of Monmouth, that the monument of Stonehenge had been built by English nobles defeated by the Saxons in 462.

The druids have resurfaced from time to time ever since. Recently they have yielded to the astronomer–priests whose 'science' fascinated astrophysicists in the 1960s; their 'revelations' are studied later in this book.

In this late eighteenth-century gouache the Carnac alignments stand like a petrified army in a completely bare landscape, with the mound of Mont-Saint-Michel to the right. The diminutive human figures exaggerate the relative height of the standing stones.

(Bibliothèque des Arts Décoratifs, Paris. Photo © G. Dagli-Orti)

The megalith tradition thus consists of legends and myths, local customs, and festivals and fêtes held at certain precise times of year. It frequently inspired eighteenth- and nineteenth-century antiquaries to offer explanations, and the doubtless very diverse origins of this traditional knowledge were sometimes sought in very remote times. Plato knew the strength of sacred traditions, and recommended in his *Republic* that any religion supplanting an older one should build its new temple over the earlier structure and reconsecrate the same setting. Many megaliths were Christianized, both in Brittany and in Great Britain. A survey carried out in Britain in 1922 by Walter Johnson shows that a substantial number of old churches were built on sites already identified with megaliths, and this also applies to certain manor-houses. Such places may also coincide with geological and magnetic sites favoured for the practice of magic; these elements were sought out for the building of Roman temples or Shinto sanctuaries, and there is therefore no reason to question such theories concerning megalithic monuments. In his book published in 1978 Anthony Roberts gave a description of 'geomythical' entities, and there has been similar research in France, particularly in Brittany.

The landscape has thus been marked by the power of tradition associated with particular places ever since Neolithic times. Acknowledgement of this magical and sacred landscape must constitute an essential phase in humanity's evolution which is necessary to us today,

La Roche's late nineteenth-century druidess bears the classic symbols of the mistletoe and sickle. In association with the dolmen or megalithic burial chamber, she expresses the dark aspect of this closed architecture.

(Private collection. Photo © J.-L.Charmet)

and in which some authors would like to rediscover creative and spiritual vitality. It was this druidic phase which William Stukely sought to rediscover in the the eighteenth century, with the intention of reestablishing theocratic authority. His prediction, illustrated by William Blake's poem *Jerusalem*, implied that the nation must rediscover its historical identity and the essential truth of the land's esoteric traditions. It is the entire earth which must be resanctified and reconsecrated: all chauvinistic nationalism is thus transcended. Each nation must rediscover its true destiny by reconciling its own traditions and culture.

Stukely and Blake still have their followers today. In some eyes the twentieth-century acceleration of the rural exodus, the neglect of oral tradition, the destruction of the landscape – denounced by ecologists among others – and the development of rational thought make it more than ever necessary to return to the true nature of the cosmos, enlightened by ancient knowledge and monuments. Hence the great annual gatherings at Stonehenge for the summer solstice, with neo-druids in attendance. At the beginning of this century Welsh druids met round the Rocking Stone at Pontypridd in South Wales. In

In contrast to the picture opposite, the druidess, depicted by Leftwich-Dodge on the cover of the *Monde Illustré* in 1899, symbolizes nature's new beginning and the lightness of megalithic standing stone architecture.

(Bibliothèque des Arts Décoratifs, Paris. Photo ©J.-L. Charmet)

Cornwall bards have officiated at the centre of the circle of standing stones at Boscawen since the establishment of their group in 1928; they wear blue robes, while the druids wear white. The authorities may not always see such gatherings as being genuinely religious, since they may take on the atmosphere of a political rally. On 21 June 1914 the Chief Constable of Wiltshire prohibited the gathering arranged at Stonehenge by the Grand Druid, who was forced to leave. Since Stonehenge passed into state ownership measures have had to be taken to protect the monument, because of the large crowds wishing to take part in the solstice ceremonies. Megaliths have also been used for openly political assemblies, in 1910 the Labour party organized a rally at the Pontypridd Rocking Stone.

The late nineteenth-century academic world abandoned the whole-hearted positivism which had resisted the esoteric approach, and suddenly began to favour the study of megaliths. A new myth arose out of their amazement at the complexity of ancient society where semi-primitive civilization might have been expected. In the enthusiasm for exploring the past there was a suggestion at the time of the 1900 World Fair that the broken Great Menhir of Locmariaquer

Some of the 'Celtic temples' drawn and engraved to illustrate the *Itinerarium Curiosum* published by William Stukeley in 1725.

(Bibliothèque Nationale, Paris. Photo © B.N./Casterman)

should be reconstituted and set up in the Place de la Concorde to accompany the Luxor obelisk, as a monument to symbolize the technical skill and science of our prehistoric ancestors! Local opinion, voiced through hostile press articles and petitions, finally killed off the idea.

The many interpretations of these 'silent giants' formulated in pre-twentieth century days are astonishing. In his *Manuel* published in 1908 Déchelette offers a good resumé of the situation:

> Prehistoric archeology cannot disguise the uncertainties of its theories as to the purpose of these important monuments from primitive times. Neither the study of their architectural layout nor the critical analysis of popular traditions attached to them can offer a solution to the problem. Hypotheses abound. Some offer a fair degree of likelihood; others, the greater number, can be put aside with the jumble of works known as prehistoric novels.

Recent writing illustrates the overwhelming gulf between esoteric tradition and archeological knowledge, although several authors have stressed that the thinking of prehistoric peoples was doubtless closer to certain aspects of the former than to the analytical approach of the latter – a wise observation that, however, does not go far enough. What connection can be established, for example between the menhirs and an alleged fertility cult surviving today in some parts of Brittany? The examination of prehistoric offerings found at the foot of certain menhirs scarcely allows us to confirm their connection with fertility; nor does the type of iconography found on certain standing stones agree with modern popular interpretation. Here as in other cases, therefore, archeology appears to possess the advantage of introducing critical observation which, though often limited, nevertheless offers the detachment necessary for the discovery of a remote world very different from ours.

Megaliths have been measured in all sorts of ways since the middle of the nineteenth century. The spaces between standing stones, the angles formed by the various axes of alignment or by the passage-ways of megalithic tombs – all have been calibrated, producing sets of figures all the more dangerous in that they give an illusion of objectivity. This archeo-astronomy has in fact sometimes reached the ultimate in confusion, and indeed of fantasy – Dr Baudouin's manual published in 1926, *La Préhistoire par les Étoiles*, offers a perfect illustration of such excesses. Certain facts are essential for an understanding of megalith constructions, but they are little known because the frontiers between accurate observation and imaginative interpretations are blurred.

A Passion for Calculation

Some twenty years ago an American astrophysicist, Gerald Hawkins, followed by Alexander Thom, an English professor of engineering, caused a stir by publishing conclusions as dazzling as they were questionable. So far as Brittany is concerned, the most conclusive theory on this delicate question comes from Pierre Roland Giot, whose historical analysis of the problem was published in 1979, while in relation to the British Isles Douglas Heggie's conspectus *Megalithic Science* (1981) is reasonably comprehensive and offers various statistical arguments.

In 1740 it seemed agreed that Stonehenge was built on the axis of the solar solstice. In the late nineteenth century Henri du Cleuziou, followed by Beaupré, elaborated the solstice argument for the Carnac alignments, but their calculations could not be described as rigorous. Commander Devoir was more accurate: he indicated several axes corresponding to the sunrise on days of equinox and solstice, time markers which are important elements in the rhythm of the passing seasons. No monument was studied in depth, however, and the reasoning remained generalized.

From 1916 onwards the archivist René Merlet concentrated his observations on the stone circle at Kergonan on the Ile-aux-Moines, one of the islands in the Gulf of Morbihan. Using very accurate theodolite measurements, he proved that a solstice-based system linked the Kergonan group of stones with several others: with the Er-Lannic monument, the broken Great Menhir at Locmariaquer, the standing stone of Men Guen at Coporh-en-Sarzeau, the stone circle of Grand Rohu at Saint-Gildas-de-Rhuys, the Penhape monument on the Ile-aux-Moines, and the Graniol group at Arzon. These links were verified with great accuracy by taking a unit of length of 0.3175 metres. The most surprising aspect was the estimated age of the groups studied, which Merlet calculated according to the obliqueness of the ecliptic: the result obtained, between 3000 and 5000 B.C, corresponds with dates established only in the 1970s! Sir Norman Lockyer carried out a similar study at Stonehenge at approximately the same time.

Other observers, such as Admiral Somerville at the beginning of the century, remarked that certain groups of standing stones in Ireland and Scotland corresponded with lunar orientations. By applying his calculations to the groups in the Carnac area, Georges Charrière suggested in 1964 a classification of megalithic orientation which retained both solar and lunar axes, and at about the same time Dr Cariou affirmed that the solsticial angle of 53° 8', corresponding to the azimuths of sunrise and sunset at the summer solstice at the latitude of Carnac, was that of a Pythagorean right-angled triangle with sides in the ratio 3:4:5.

Accurate lunisolar observations and a mastery of relatively simple Pythagorean geometry are the pre-requisites for predicting eclipses. Thus it may be that some monuments were vast calculators used by priests to foretell an eclipse. Stonehenge was identified as an astronomical observatory in the eighteenth century, and the researches of Sir Norman Lockyer, followed by those of modern scientists such as Gerald Hawkins and Fred Hoyle, have led to the same conclusion: that this observatory indicated not only the positions of the sun, the moon, and probably some major stars, but was also conceived as an impressively accurate instrument for calculating the dates of future eclipses.

In his book *Stonehenge Decoded*, published in 1966, Gerald Hawkins points out that the two figures 30 and 56 were fundamental to the construction of Stonehenge. At the centre of the group the trilithons form a horseshoe orientated round sunrise at the summer solstice, and these are surrounded by 30 columns supporting lintels, the sarsen stones. Two rows of 30 ditches are set in two concentric circles parallel with the columns. Hawkins saw this 30-base system as corresponding to the lunar month, or lunation, during which the moon passes through all its phases. A marker post or stone served as an indicator within the cycle. The figure 56, the number of post-holes known as 'Aubrey holes' surrounding the group, corresponds to 56 years, the triple lunar cycle of 18.6 years, (223 lunations), at the end of which the moon returns to the precise point in the sky at which it stood when the cycle began. To achieve a virtually whole number meant multiplying 18.6 by 3. By moving the marker one hole each day on the 56 year system the prehistoric observer identified each day in the lunar month. As the total or near-total lunar and solar eclipses, of which there are four or five each year, occur on approximately the same date every nine years in different phases, and every eighteen years with matching phases, it was possible to predict the date of each eclipse after observing one complete cycle. Since these predictions could never be more than approximate they were cross-checked by examining the furthest position of certain stars, a procedure that offered a simple verification of the annual cycle on the day of the solstice. Hawkins identified numerous distinctive astral axes within the complex circle of Stonehenge, and was able to represent the site as a vast prehistoric observatory.

The boldness of argument and style in Hawkins' book created a stir among the general public and archeologists alike; its Appendix B, indeed, was entitled *Stonehenge, a Neolithic Computer*, which could hardly fail to be sensational at a time when the computer was hardly more than a dream. This stir was augmented by the personality of the author, professor of astronomy at the University of Boston and associate member of the Harvard Observatory. The *Daily Express* commented, 'If Hawkins is right, and most experts now concede that he is,

Stonehenge is the eighth wonder of the ancient world.' Enthusiasm is somewhat moderated nowadays: although some of Hawkins' points are virtually irrefutable, there is nevertheless considerable approximation in his calculations. And, although the different phases of construction of this monument were spread out over several centuries, and the date of the central 30-base system is also different from the outlying 56-base system, yet they are suggested as being complementary in the theory of eclipse prediction.

At the Callanish monument, however, Hawkins was able to confirm his ideas on prehistoric man's need for speculation based on the movement of the major stars.

In Search of the First Astronomers

Between 1970 and 1976 Alexander Thom, professor of engineering at Oxford, applied his experience gained at the megalithic circles of Wales and Scotland to the measuring of the Carnac alignments. This led him to several conclusions: that the unit of measurement known as the megalithic yard, 0.829 metres, was used in placing standing stones in relation to each other on both sides of the English Channel, and that the multiple of this unit is the megalithic toise, equivalent to 2.5 yards. This same attention to precision appears in geometrical constructions: Pythagoras' right-angled triangle appears to have been invented more than 2,000 years before Pythagoras! Thom also demonstrated the use of triangles with very similar ratios, such as 4:8:9 or 5:7.5:9. The oval areas of standing stones set at the edges of the Ménec alignment appear to be the result of correlation between such triangles. The theoretical speculation behind the stones is intended to aid the participant-spectator's astronomical observation of the astral cycle at times of eclipse.

Finally, Alexander Thom returned to Hawkins' theories on Stonehenge, and attempted to identify a similar plan at Carnac. He suggested that the broken Great Menhir at Locmariaquer was the centre of a vast observatory designed to predict eclipses, a pointer 20 metres high for observing the moon; the reference-sights would have been other single menhirs, some of them very distant, which would make it possible to establish the extreme positions of the lunar declination. He published a map, with text by Pierre Roland Giot, indicating eight sites near the Locmariaquer menhir from which it was possible to observe the eight extreme lunar positions. These points are dependent on the lunar cycle of '18.6 years, which modulates the monthly variations between the points of rising and setting.' The alignments at Saint-Pierre-Quiberon and the Petit-Ménec at Carnac were seen as solar calculators designed to correct for the small errors in the daily observations which arise because the moon does not progress through

PREHISTORIC SCIENCE

The Carnac alignments in Morbihan consist of 2,671 stones in three large groups. This view of the Kermario alignments shows clearly the standing stones' varied shapes and sizes, particularly the slightly wavering line of the alignment. Alexander Thom's survey of the Ménec stones shows the degree of interpretation of his theory of the unit of length, the megalithic yard.

(Photo © R. Estall)

By definition, a megalith is not a chance phenomenon but was erected through deliberate human effort. Why? How? Moving such massive objects obviously required a sound understanding of traction, elevation, material resistance, in short an extensive fount of knowledge. The problem lies in assessing how far prehistoric 'engineers' and 'worshippers' progressed in theoretical understanding. In the sixteenth century, Olaus Magnus considered that prehistoric peoples were great geometricians; more recently scientists have explored this area – not always restraining their own enthusiasm!

What unit of measurement?

After careful measurement of distances between the Carnac alignments, the British astronomer Alexander Thom deduced a unit of 0.829 metres, which he called the 'megalithic yard'. Another fairly common unit was the 'megalithic toise' of 2.5 yards. The stones had been set up more than once, however, and their original setting could not always be established with the degree of precision implied by Thom. Further, these were three-dimensional objects and it was impossible to define their exact position, even taking a point half-way between the edges of the block. Thom replied

that his unit of length was a statistical conclusion verified many times over, expressing a genuine mathematical concern by indicating regular spacing with stone markers.

Two Thousand Years Before Pythagoras

It is not difficult to apply a unit of measurement to two-dimensional plans. Alexander Thom demonstrated at Ménec how the group of alignments and the oval forms at each end were erected on a basis of Pythagorean right-angled triangles, with sides of ratio 4: 8: 9. Here too it is difficult to analyze mistaken observations and interpretations. There are two fine examples in Olaus Magnus's pyramidion-form steles and the principles on which Stonehenge was built, based on circles and isosceles triangles. In each case the reference to geometry appears to be guaranteed but is also an attempt at a universal explanation. It is impossible to

disregard the rectilinear, circular, or oval designs of megalithic constructions; no doubt there are constants, even if they are based on simple aids such as cords and markers.

Celestial Reference Points

The orientation of certain monuments (Stonehenge, Newgrange, Gavrinis) on the unique axis of the rising sun on the day of the summer solstice, has long attracted the attention

of researchers. The American astrophysicist Gerard Hawkins made a thorough investigation of Stonehenge, which he saw as an enormous celestial calculator – a theory confirmed by Alexander Thom, who applied it to the Callanish monument and the Carnac alignments. Without denying the importance of orientation in megalithic construction, the limitations of current knowledge of this subject must impose caution.

In 1555, Olaus Magnus saw Swedish megaliths as geometrical forms indicating 'warriors' tombs'. Schematization made it possible to classify and define the stones as 'steles', and this interpretation was the determining factor in representing the monuments.

(Photo © B.N./Casterman)

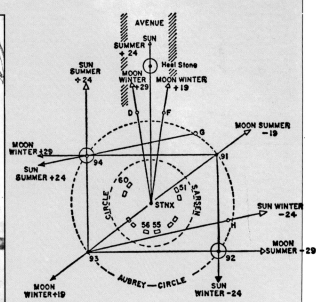

Plans of Stonehenge reflect the author's vision of the monument: in 1723 William Stukely prepared a plan (left) of an ancient temple based on Greek geometry. In 1965, the astrophysicist Gerald Hawkins demonstrated (right) that the distinctive positions of the sun and the moon could be observed from different places of the monument.

(Photo © B.N./Casterman and Photo © G. S. Hawkins and J. B. White)

Breton landscape two kilometres north of Huelgoat, with a prehistoric menhir – a mere curiosity in today's world.

(Photo © Drillaud-A.P.I.)

the sky at a constant speed. The large Manio standing stone at Carnac would have been a similar observatory.

The astronomical considerations of the megalith builders are very plausible, and are even indeed confirmed to some extent at Stonehenge. Archeologists hesitate to go along with Thom in the detail of his proof, however. His arguments stand on a very simple theoretical base and are reinforced by minute empirical observation; they are persuasive, but there is reluctance to accept totally the construction of a system which depends too much on contingency. The path is clear, however, and the problems reasonably well set out. More recently, in 1981, Aubrey Burl published the results of his survey of Scottish stone circles; he showed that in forty-two cases out of fifty, the horizontal stone flanked by by two standing stones – which is characteristic of such monuments – is orientated with reference to the path of the moon across the sky, not with the axes of its rising and setting. To an observer standing at the centre of the circle the moon took almost an hour to pass from one standing stone to the other, over the horizon-

A World
to be
Rediscovered

tal slab between them; this simple observation was required for certain ceremonies. One of the most promising avenues for the advancement of archeo-astronomical knowledge is now the careful examination of the vestiges of this ritual setting.

No scientific analysis carried out by specialists, particularly by astrophysicists, can have meaning unless it fits into a global study of the monuments, including examination of their ecological environment and their historical, social, and religious context. Archeological digs are a rich source of architectural information, but this is still insufficient, not to say derisory. Expertise such as that of the archeologist Roger Joussaume, who discovered not only the megaliths of Madagascar but also, thanks to oral tradition, their precise function in Madagascan eighteenth-century society, stresses the depth of our ignorance regarding prehistoric monuments, their rituals, and their adherents.

Deprived of such oral or written tradition, archeologists are hampered, although they have managed to discover some of the pictures in the book of the past whose lost text still fascinates us. Several complementary steps are needed in order to recover modest traces of its message. They include gaining an understanding through popular tradition of the importance of activities focussed on the megaliths, a proper assessment of their historical scale, and finally an analysis of their cosmic setting as offered by those skilled in esoteric interpretation and by astrophysicists. This comparative study, combined with strictly archeological analyses, will make it possible to reconstruct some aspects of prehistoric megalithic civilization in western Europe.

The Universality of Megaliths

Apart from the magnificent painted caves dating from about 15,000 B.C., the most remarkable traces of prehistoric Europe still remaining must be the megalithic monuments built between 5000 and 3000 B.C., which are very numerous and cover a wide area, from Scandinavia to Spain and Portugal. The remaining alignments in the Carnac area of southern Brittany still consist of more than 3,000 of the original 10,000 monoliths, covering some six kilometres. The Great Menhir of Locmariaquer nearby, now broken in four and lying on the ground, was once 20 metres high. What we gaze at in admiration today is frequently nothing more than the ruined remains or the skeleton of a monument which was originally much more complex and imposing, as recent research has shown.

The megalithic tombs of the San Agustin region in the Magdalena valley in Colombia form a unique ensemble. Grouped in several burial centres, they were built from the sixth century B.C. onwards, on terraces cut out of the mountainside at an altitude of about 2,000 metres. The statue-menhirs associated with them evoke the iconography of Central American pre-Colombian civilizations.

(Photo © Serge Cassen)

The word 'megalith' (from the Greek *mega*, great, and *lithos*, stone) was apparently used for the first time in 1849 by Algernon Herbert of the University of Oxford, in his book *Cyclops Christianus*. The Morbihan Société Polymathique adopted the name in its reports, and it was officially accepted by French prehistorians at the Paris Congress of 1867. In England it appeared some years later in James Fergusson's book *Rude Stone Monuments in All Countries*. Megaliths aroused considerable curiosity and interest, whether they were standing stones or 'menhirs', either isolated or ranged in circles or lines, or 'dolmens' – funerary chambers, the most common category in western Europe – or 'temples' such as those in Malta and at Stonehenge.

The monument of Stonehenge on the Wiltshire plain in southern

England is, after the Tower of London, visited by more sightseers than anywhere else in the British Isles and it has inspired more writers than any other archeological site in the world, even taking into account the abundant literature devoted to the Egyptian Pyramids or the great statues on Easter Island. The Irish tumulus of Newgrange, 93 metres in diameter and containing an impressive megalithic tomb, has effectively become a national monument since Michael J. O'Kelly's excavations.

There is something ambiguous about such fascination. Visiting the megalithic ruins of Malta or the monuments at Antequera in Spain, discovering the art of Gavrinis in the Morbihan area of Brittany, walking among the rows of stones at Ménec or Kermario at Carnac, seeing the sun rise at Stonehenge or Newgrange at the summer solstice, travelling to Quanterness in Orkney: all these arouse not only respect but also imagination – sometimes to excess. The powerful architectural presence of these monuments has attracted human fixations and fantasies down the ages; their construction has been attributed in turn to fairies, giants, and extra-terrestrial beings; they have been enveloped in ceremony, impregnated with religious faith. More recently they have been presented as the remains of a sort of lost paradise inspired by the wisdom of pre-dynastic Egypt and of Sumer, in Mesopotamia (Euan MacKie, 1977), and even famous astrophysicists have been tempted into speculation.

Meanwhile, the archeologists labour on with patience and a certain obstinacy. For about a century now they have been excavating, listing and classifying these monuments with increasing rigour and caution. They see them as a source of knowledge about the past, and have come to define more and more precisely the double problem posed by the megalith phenomenon: the problem of the true original aspect of the monuments and that of the level of technical and social sophistication necessary for their construction.

The universality of megaliths was revealed by James Fergusson in 1872. A great traveller, he had seen 'rude stone monuments' not only in European countries, but also in Algeria, the Sudan, Ethiopia, Palestine, the Caucasus, Persia, Baluchistan, Kashmir and India. Further reports followed from archeologists and explorers from almost all over the world. Roger Joussaume's survey, published in 1985, extended the domain of megaliths to South Africa and Madagascar, and revealed their extraordinary diversity.

The architectural and chronological range which is evident from recent work shows that the phenomenon lies outside any single historical circumstance, and that from Neolithic times onwards it occurred in widely different periods and in different regions.

43

What was the Origin of Megalithism?

Most nineteenth-century archeologists thought that architects from Greece or the Near East were responsible for the 'great stone' monuments of western Europe, and this view prevailed until about 1950. Few traces of the diffusionist theory of this phenomenon remain, however, and it is uncertain whether in this context any link between western Europe and the eastern Mediterranean can be identified.

Megaliths are still not widely known in the Aegean world. The work of Olivier Pelon and René Treuil is helpful in defining the question of funerary monuments in an area which, according to supporters of the 'diffusionist' theory, played an important role in the development of megalithic Europe. Mass tombs appeared from early Neolithic times; for example, three superimposed layers of human remains found beneath the floor of a house at Prodomos in Greece contained eleven skulls. At Kephala, in the Boeotian region of Greece, chests dated from the late Neolithic period (from the fifth to the early fourth millennium) lie beside trench tombs most of which contain individual burials, but which also include five tombs with two skeletons each and five more containing the remains of between four and thirteen bodies. The following era, the First Early Bronze Age lasting from 3200 to 2700 B.C., saw the development of the type of beehive-shaped, corbel-vaulted tomb known as a *tholos*, found in Crete and most notably in the Mesara plain. The lower part was built of dry stone, which still remains, and some may have been vaulted in brick.

The earliest Cretan tholos tombs contained dozens, and in some cases hundreds, of skeletons. By the middle of the third millennium, in the Second Early Bronze Age, there were many more such tombs, showing certain similarities to some Iberian megalithic tombs. The corbelled tombs on the island of Syros contain rectangular or hexagonal chambers with narrow access passages, while on mainland Greece the tumulus at Thebes, made of unbaked brick, is 20 metres in diameter and covers a small funerary coffer or cist. The tumuli at Steno, near Ithaca, are smaller, between 3 and 10 metres across, and are made of earth and gravel flanked by a kerb; they contain between one and five tombs of varying kinds – simple trench tombs, stone-faced tombs, cists, or coffers. Similar tombs without a tumulus are also found in western Anatolia and generally throughout the Aegean area. They were used as much for individual internment as for mass burial. This raises the question of certain semi-subterranean monuments in the Peloponnese, such as the megalithic hypogea (underground chambers) at Kato Bourlajoï, which consist of a trench 12 metres long, covered by large blocks of stone. Many similar monuments exist in central and western Mediterranean areas, but unfortunately such Greek chambers cannot be precisely dated and their furnishings in ancient times are unknown. The famous Mycenean tholos tombs, no-

For many years the tomb of the Atridae at Mycenae was thought to have inspired the megalith builders. In fact, it represents an individual and fairly late style dating from the fourteenth century B.C.

(Photo © Dagli-Orti)

tably those of the Atrides at Mycenae itself, were not constructed until the middle of the second millennium.

Bulgaria's monuments are grouped in south-eastern Thrace, on the shores of the Black Sea. The tumuli are laid out in a semicircle with block ends, covering small square or rectangular megalithic chambers. There may be one or several antechambers, and sometimes a very short passage-way. Access from one chamber to the next is often via a rectangular port-hole slab with grooves for a stone or wooden door to close it off. There may be large blocks overhead, and some tombs even have roofs made up in sections. Other monuments with a similar layout are carved out of the rock.

Bulgarian archeologists have discovered objects dating from the beginning of the Iron Age inside these tombs, which therefore places their construction towards the end of the second millennium at the earliest. They were abandoned in the sixth century B.C., the time of the construction of the Gärlo 'fountain-temple' in south-west Thrace; its appearance recalls both the rock-cut and the tholos tombs.

There are similarities between the groups in Thrace and those on the north-east shores of the Black Sea; however, from their funerary fittings it would seem that the Caucasian monuments were in use more than a thousand years before those in Thrace. In the late nineteenth century Ernest Chantre drew attention to the megalithic tombs of

45

Abkhazia in the northern Caucasus; in 1973 Vladimir Markovin identified three categories there. The first category of tombs were made of large stone slabs, with rectangular or trapezoid chambers often approached through an antechamber which might be open or covered, the second and larger category were made of smaller slabs, and the third consisted of enormous hollow parallelepipedal blocks, like coffers, with a doorway and a covering slab of stone; this type of tomb might also be cut out of a cliff. Megalithic tombs with a closed antechamber, the best known, are associated with a Chalcolithic culture (the Copper Age) in the middle of the third millennium. This Novosvobodnajan culture followed the Maïkop culture which was already famous for its princely tumulus.

Like the *kurgans* of Maïkop, the megalithic tombs of the Caucasus do not appear to have been used for mass burials. They do contain characteristic princely offerings, however, as in the Kurgan I at Novosvobodnaja with its mass of copper objects – daggers, lance-heads, axes, awls, pins, meat-hooks, perfume burners, rings, large flint blades delicately finished, and fine pottery. Similar objects were found in a tomb studied in 1979 and 1980 at Ourotchicha Kladi. The megalithic chamber, reached through a port-hole slab, contained exceptional furnishings: amongst the fifty copper and silver artefacts were seven vases, two meat-hooks, a solar wheel, twelve daggers, a sword

This group of megalithic monuments in the northern Caucasus is characterized by rectangular chambers with porthole-slabs; a stone plug was sometimes used to block the opening. The stones of the antechamber (foreground) have collapsed.

(Private collection. Photo © D.R.)

63.5 centimetres long, chisels and five axes, the handle of one decorated with a band of silver. There were two hundred necklaces and other pieces of jewellery made of gold, silver, rock crystal and sardonyx. Some of these resemble objects found in Anatolia and the Near East, in megalithic tombs which are also very like the Caucasian tombs: there are tombs at Ala-Safat, in Jordan, containing rectangular chambers hollowed out of parallelepipedal monoliths, with access through a covered antechamber and a port-hole slab.

In the Near East, megalithic culture is found on a coastal strip running from Syria to Israel. The oldest monuments in the area date back to the fourth millennium, but most belong to the Ghassulian culture of the third millennium. There are also standing stones as enigmatic as in most other countries, although they bring to mind Jacob's consecration of a monolith as a 'house of God' by pouring oil on it (Genesis XXVIII, 16–22).

Megalithism seems to have been developed in the Near East within fairly narrow geographical and chronological limits. It was preceded by the appearance of monumental brick architecture. Jericho, some 8,000 years before Christ, had solid ramparts and an imposing tower ten metres in diameter and 9 metres high, indications of a sophisticated combined effort which would also have been essential for megalithism. Funerary ritual objects discovered at Jericho have also been found in megalithic tombs – model skulls no doubt intended to assure the dead person of eternal life, and manipulated human bones. The local way of life was agricultural, as for the builders of western megaliths; the difference lies in the urban phenomenon of Jericho, since some two or three thousand people lived within the four hectares covered by today's ruins. Three thousand years later the existence of the city of Çatal Hüyük in Anatolia also showed that at least part of the population was settled and included artisan workers.

Megalithism seems to have been unknown at this period in the Near East; it was not until the fourth millennium that megalithic monuments grouped together as a necropolis appeared on the plains and valley sides. A secondary consequence of taking possession of the land, they constituted very characteristic groupings at a fairly late stage in relation to the earliest eastern forms of architecture; for in western Europe, tombs in the Iberian peninsula and in France were first constructed around 4500 B.C., while in Great Britain and Ireland they did not appear until after 3700 B.C. The earliest temples in Malta date from about 3500 B.C.

African countries bordering the Mediterranean equally lack centres sufficiently ancient and dynamic to have been the originators of western European megaliths. This was also, and above all, true of Egypt: the prototype for megalithic burial was thought to have been

Megalith construction in North Africa is characterized by chamber tombs often forming impressive necropolises. That of Bou Nouara in Algeria dominates the vast landscape for miles around. The Berbers erected the first megalithic chambers during the second millennium B.C. It is not known whether this simple style of building was inspired by monuments in south-west Europe, or whether the concept was a purely local one.

(Collection Camps. Photo © M. Bouis-D.R.)

the *mastaba* (the square Egyptian tomb) and – reasonably – the Pyramids. The chronological discrepancy disproves this theory, since the first Pyramids were built in about 2700 B.C., some two thousand years too late! Gilbert Camps has described two groups in North Africa, one in northern Morocco and the other in northern Algeria and Tunisia. These funerary monuments are modest in scale: the quadrangular chamber with its large stone covering is rarely more than 3 metres long; it is surrounded by a circular structure which forms the boundary of a tumulus. They are of fairly recent date: the Iron Age Algerian necropolises of Roknia and Gastel were built during the first millennium B.C. while others, dating back to the previous millennium, were probably inspired by Spanish, French, or Italian monuments with diffusion around 2000 B.C. There are several longer tombs in Great Kabylia similar to the late monuments of the western Mediterranean islands. Many megalithic tombs, such as those in southern Spain or Sardinia, have small steles near them. North Africa has many other stone constructions of widely varying form, but these have only the most distant connections with megalithic monuments and generally date from historic times, such as the *bazinas* (architecturally spectacular tumuli).

The Tall Stones of Africa

It was thought briefly that black Africa possessed a type of very ancient megalith culture. At Bouar in the west of the Central African Republic, coffers surmounted with steles were found near hearths where the charcoal has been dated by carbon-14 studies at between 5490 and 4750 B.C. Such dates caused a sensation, but in fact they related to the hearth and not to the neighbouring megaliths, which have been dated by further charcoal at around 500 B.C. This brings the Bouar monuments closer in date to other megalithic groupings in the region, all established between the second century B.C. and the fifteenth century A.D.

Further to the east, in Ethiopia, thousands of monoliths were erected in more recent times. Some are sculpted steles. Cists made of large flat stones covered by blocks forming a tumulus were explored by Roger Joussaume; the oldest may date from the second millennium. In the centre of a group of cists at Tchelenko, three monuments with a circular chamber and cella hollowed out of the ground form mass tombs. The human remains laid there with their ornaments and weapons made it possible to date the tombs from between the eighth and twelfth centuries A.D.

Ethiopia has hundreds of standing stones, of which one, in the north of the country, is the tallest of the ancient monoliths still remaining upright; set up around the third century B.C., it stands 33 metres high. In the south there are phalloid steles beside plain standing stones; others are anthropomorphic, sometimes carrying an impres-

The Beforo megalithic monument near Bouar in the Central African Republic represents the type known as *Tajunu*, meaning 'group of standing stones'. These stones indicate a coffer burial beneath a small tumulus. The tallest stone measures 3.70 metres. Discovered in 1969, the site was explored by Pierre Vidal in 1975.

(Photo © R. de Bayle des Hermens)

Three steles from the Soddo Tiya site, in southern Ethiopia. The swords and other symbolic designs with which they are decorated, and the offerings found at the foot of some of the stones, make it possible to date their construction to the tenth century A.D.

(Photo © R. Joussaume)

sion of a sword, and stand on top of individual tombs dating from the tenth to the fifteenth century A.D.

The rich and varied megaliths of the Arabian peninsula are still not very well known. Towards the middle of the third millennium the inhabitants of the Bahrein Islands began to build tumuli and join them together to form a necropolis. Burial took place in chests. One type of tomb to be found in these islands is known as 'royal', 12 metres high with internal kerbs and a complex network of chambers.

In the Yemen, Roger de Bayle des Hermens discovered stone platforms near the village of Al-Khurays, with a long megalithic chamber at the top, and there are also parallel lines of standing stones extending for 50 metres, increasing in height and leading to a circular area surrounded by stone blocks – somewhat reminiscent of Carnac. They also bring to mind a similar group in central Tibet: high in the mountains near the Pang-gong lake at Do-ring, eighteen parallel rows of standing stones connect two enclosures, each bordered by monoliths

Groups of dolmen cists, like these at Ganda-Midjou, have been excavated near Harar in eastern Ethiopia. They were probably designed for the burial of one person. A characteristic feature of these monuments is the walling of small stone slabs fitted together and sealing the tomb hermetically. This feature is clearly visible on the plan and elevation shown below.

(Photo © R. Joussaume)

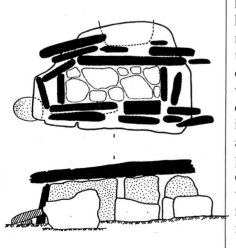

and containing an altar made up of three stone blocks.

In northern India, according to James Fergusson, the megalithic tradition was still active in the nineteenth century. He recorded in 1872 that the Khassia peoples placed the ashes of their dead outside their villages, in chests that were used as seats at public gatherings. Standing stones were set up to express a wish or to obtain the assent of an ancestor spirit who would come to live in the stone.

Megalithic monuments in the Deccan are much older but, as in the Near East, should be dissociated from agricultural civilization, which developed in the Indus region after the sixth millennium and led to the urban development of Mohenjo Daro and Harappa. Following the abandonment of these cities in the middle of the second millennium megalithic tombs multiplied in number, until there were thousands in the peninsula. In these necropolises, square or cruciform chambers made of flat stones held the stripped bones of several individuals. A passage with a port-hole slab led to the edge of a circular or quadrangular tumulus. The rich grave goods included pottery and iron objects – weapons and tools – placing the use of these monuments at the end of the second millennium and into the first. During the same period, but in the west Deccan, enormous stone blocks were used to construct buildings to protect a cave or trench tomb, and hypogea were also dug out of laterite. Chambers with port-hole slabs have been found in Pakistan, while in the east the dead were enclosed in terracotta sarcophaguses before being laid in megalithic tombs.

From Korea to Japan

The Far East also has megaliths of very simple form, and the vocabulary to describe them may be compared to Breton names: *che-pin* indicates in Chinese a 'stone table', the exact equivalent of a dolmen, and the Korean word *Ko-in-dol* means 'supported stone', expressing the same concept slightly differently. Large rectangular megalithic chambers are visible in Manchuria and southern China, and also in northern Korea; the covering stone of one of these Manchurian chambers, known as Che-pin-shan, weighs 70 tonnes. At Gwanson-ni in North Korea a chamber made of large flat stones is covered by a monolith measuring 8.70 by 4.50 metres. Such tombs, constructed in the first millennium B.C., and no doubt surmounted by a tumulus, appear to have held only one body, as did the slab-covered tombs, almost certainly contemporary, found in the south of the country.

It was probably through Korea that megalithism reached the Japanese island of Kyushu; slab-covered tombs in fact began to appear on the west side of the island towards the middle of the third century B.C. A little later megalithic pillar tombs spread through the north of Kyushu, accompanying the use of metal and the cultivation of rice in flooded fields – three cultural aspects influenced by Korea and characteristic of the Yayoi culture. Recent research published by archeologist Tsuboi Kiyotari indicates that the original megalithic or monumental shapes spread at the same time across other parts of Japan. Funerary barrows, surrounded by a rectangular trench, were built for the burials of privileged families in both the Okayama and

Megalithic coffers built in Korea in the first millennium B.C. were covered with enormous blocks. Sangapp-Ni Kochang is particularly spectacular.

(Photo © J. Briard)

Standing stones at Banam-Ni Kochang, dating from the same period as the Korean coffers.

(Photo © J. Briard)

Chusenji regions. Between 1976 and 1979 Japanese archeologists explored an enormous circular tumulus at Tatetskui near Okayama, 43 metres in diameter by 5 metres high, crowned with two concentric rows of standing stones a metre or two high to consecrate the edifice. The offerings they found within the tumulus included two female statuettes, cylindrical beads, a large stone decorated with a curvilinear design, and a quantity of pottery. The rites that these suggest were performed in honour of the two individuals lying in the stony mass of the tumulus, but above all in honour of the man stretched out on a layer of ochre in the wooden central tomb. An iron sword and hundreds of tiny jasper and glass beads lay by his side; he wore a necklace formed of a jade pendant, seventeen jasper beads, and one agate bead. This was a princely form of megalithism, a fore-runner of the imperial monuments or *misasagi*, of the following period.

This period, known as Kofun (from the third to the seventh centuries A.D.), saw the building of thousands of tumuli. Some were modest while others, known as 'keyholes', were colossal – the largest, for the fifth-century emperor Nintoku, measured 486 metres long and 36 metres high. Many such monuments contained a stone chamber with a long access corridor. They generally held one or two bodies, but one at Shimosuke contained fourteen. The most surprising discovery was made in 1972 at Takamatsuzuka, near Nara: for the first time a seventh-century tumulus, a stone tomb, revealed cave paintings inspired by Chinese Tang art, including the dragon and the snake,

Megaliths in Modern Times

and a scene with four women. There was at that moment a hiatus in the construction of large megalithic monuments, According to tradition, in 646 the Emperor Kotoku issued a decree regulating funerary custom according to the dead man's rank. He restricted the size of the tomb and laid down that dry stones should be used rather than large flagstones, to prevent unnecessary waste of manpower: his controls are reflected in the design of the Ishinokarato tumulus near Nara which, notably, returns to the rectangular layout. At the end of the seventh century the Japanese adopted the practice of cremation, and megalithic practices came to an end.

Even more recent monuments, both memorials and tombs, can be found among the Kelabites in northern Borneo. Tom Harrisson records how in 1959 an old man without heirs had a tumulus built 'taller than the height of the long-house above the ground and twice as wide as the distance which can be covered in one leap'. In order to achieve this he summoned together his friends and relations, several hundred people, for a great feast lasting several days. On the last day he announced the construction of his monument. Putting all his non-perishable possessions together on the ground he had them covered by a pile of stones brought up from the river bed by a long line of men: small stones first, followed by large blocks covering the possessions and protecting them so that the old man would not be forgotten.

Two concentric circles of standing stones on the summit of the enormous Tatetsuki tumulus at Okayama in Japan; 5 metres high and 43 metres across, it contained two bodies with their offerings. Monoliths were often associated with a monument constructed in honour of a prince.

(Photo © Yoshiro Kondo)

The megalithic tomb of Takchara in the Fukuoka district of Japan, decorated with paintings inspired by Chinese Tang art of the late sixth century A.D. The dragon motif is recognizable.

(Photo © Shogakukan/Artephot)

The custom of another Borneo tribe was to set up a large stone in honour of a rich or powerful man, or in memory of someone who had died or of an act of courage. Stones were from a distance of three or four days' journey. The operation was carried out by a large crowd, and its ceremonial provided a rhythm for their activities. If the stone was to commemorate an act of courage, one buffalo would be sacrificed each day; a buffalo and a pig were killed to enhance the social standing of the benefactor, or if he wished for a child. Sacrifices and feasts could be repeated each year to reinforce the memorial ritual. Such occasions were written into the calendar of ceremonies offered to neighbouring tribes, so as to maintain good relations with them and sustain the ecological balance of the land.

In Madagascar, the first megaliths are thought to have been constructed as a consequence of Indonesian influences. Since these monuments are recent, or even still being built today, their role in society can be studied in detail.

Megalithism in the Imerina region in central Madagascar is particularly interesting because some of the motives for it, and certain aspects of its rituals, are known. The monuments are no more than 300 years old. In 1985 Roger Joussaume and Victor Raharijaona carried out a survey in the village of Iravoandriana, one of the king's ancient fiefs, which is governed by a member of his family and which provides a good illustration of the Madagascar megalithic world. Four stones stand at the four cardinal points, on the extreme edges of the village territory. The village itself is oval, 130 metres long by 110 metres, and surrounded by ditches. Access is through two megalithic gates, one to the north and the other to the south, each closed by a great stone, which is rolled away in the morning and back at night. A monolith 3 metres high stands just outside the northern gate, and a series of tombs borders an avenue to the west which connects the two entrances. To the east the separate tomb of the founder of the village lies beside the public place where the inhabitants would listen to their overlord's speeches, which is marked by another standing stone. The free men's houses lay to the north and those of the slaves to the south; the orientation of each house and each tomb was decided by an astrologer before construction began. The inside of the house also required orientation: the head of the family had the place of honour on the north side, while the east, the side of the rising sun, was for praying to ancestors. The west, the profane side, was for the openings, making it the point of contact with the outside world, and on the south side were kept material possessions – stores of rice and agricultural tools.

Megalithic tombs within the village belonged only to noble families, and each family had its own mass tomb. Originally this was simply a stone chest enclosing a single burial; the mass element came later, resulting in ever-larger megalithic tombs. The ceremonial changing of shrouds seems to have been a regular part of ancestor worship.

According to Father Callet, it was King Andrianampoinimerina at the beginning of the nineteenth century who, wishing to improve the cohesion of his kingdom, instructed important families to build megalithic tombs: 'Work together to quarry the stone; this will be proof of your mutual friendship; work together to transport the stone – this will contribute to your happiness.'

The enormous barrow known as the 'Mausoleum of the Emperor Nintoku' in the Osaka district in Japan is the largest of these burial monuments. Its plan is the shape of a key-hole.

(Photo © WPE/Artephot)

This Madagascar monument, the burial chamber for one of the most important families in Imerina in the nineteenth century, was photographed just before it was destroyed at the beginning of this century. The plan of the tomb (below) was drawn by Roger Joussaume.

(Collection R. Joussaume.
Photo © Tananarive Archives)

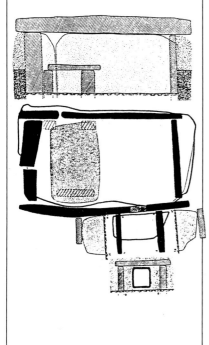

Such tombs then became more numerous, and held up to 300 skeletons. The boulders of which they were built might weigh 30 tonnes. One of these constructions, for instance, required eleven stones for the chamber and for the beds where the corpses were temporarily laid. First the stones were carefully selected in the quarry; then, as the block was cut away, a cock or a sheep must be sacrificed. Under the direction of the 'stone master' the whole population co-operated in hauling the stone on a sledge-type litter from the quarry. Once all the stones were assembled at the building-site, three oxen were killed: the fat from their bodies was used to grease the blocks, and everyone had some of the meat. The astrologer indicated where to dig holes to set up the columns, and the stones were finally put in place and then covered with a tumulus. The remains of ancestors laid in a temporary tomb were then transferred to their new resting place, and the occasion was marked by wrapping them in fresh shrouds – twenty for a particularly important person. Then followed more sacrifices.

When the tomb was opened for a new burial, or to celebrate some feast, each ancestor was wrapped in a fresh shroud. A nobleman who died while on a voyage or away at war, so that his body could not be brought back home, was commemorated by a standing stone set up beside the tumulus. The tomb was also used to store family treasures; money hoarded here could be retrieved in case of need. A small cell was erected over the tombs of the noblest families, to receive offerings of honey and rum.

At sites that were to some degree sacred, stones were erected to commemorate great occasions: departure to war, reconciliation between tribes, the passage or arrival of a king. When King Ambohimanga married his cousin in 1797 he ordered the quarrying of a monolith 5 metres long, 80 centimetres wide and 20 centimetres thick.

It took two months to cut the stone to size and transport it to where it was set up some thirty kilometres from the quarry west of Tananarive, and a hundred oxen were sacrificed to mark the occasion.

Memorial stones were often personalized: they held the spirit of an ancestor who could grant a wish or aid the birth of a child. More simply, the stone might also symbolize the law establishing the boundary of a village or a field.

'Dolmens' in Colombia

On the other side of the world, the megalithic tombs of the San Agustin region in the valley of the river Magdalena in Colombia form an interesting and very isolated group, which has been studied by Serge Casen. They are grouped together into several funerary and probably religious clusters, constructed on terraces cut out of the mountain side at an altitude of nearly 2,000 metres. Around the sixth century B.C. the inhabitants who had settled in the San Agustin area buried their dead in cists and coffers made of slabs of stone. The bones are in a poor state of preservation, but individual and mass burials seem to have taken place together. Statue-menhirs were set up near-by. In the next stage, known as the 'classical' era, the tombs became vast, and their megalithic chambers were accessible through a passage, the whole being covered by a tumulus edged with flagstones which were sometimes carved. The more numerous statue-menhirs indicated a connection with the iconography of Central American civilizations: apart from anthropomorphic representations there were images of jaguars, monkeys, and reptiles. Funerary pits and hypogea were also created, bringing the San Agustin group still closer to great civilizations such as that of the Olmecs.

Nevertheless, the Colombian megalithic culture developed independently. The resemblance of its monuments to those of Europe or Asia provide a good illustration of the phenomenon of convergence – the way in which architecture develops in a similar fashion over great distances and different epochs without any direct connection between the regions concerned.

Writers on megalithic monuments often refer to other types of remains, more elaborate and with their own names, such as the Cyclopean *nuraghe* constructions in Sardinia, the ramparts of Mycenae and Tiryns in Greece, or the pre-Colombian fortresses of Peru. In some of these enormous blocks of stone appear to have been trimmed and fitted together, and monoliths of considerable size have also been used in their construction, such as the parallelepipedic blocks used as foundations for the temple of Jupiter Heliopolitan at Baalbek in the Lebanon. Some steles and sculpted human-form statue-menhirs are connected with megalithic monuments, for example in Brittany, Switzerland, southern France, and Sardinia; others are isolated.

Several types of megalithic construction have been found near these statues at San Agustin, which have long been the focus of intense archeological interest. There are rough stone coffers and passage graves which are startlingly like those in western Europe, and also various styles of small tomb: small stone coffers set in red clay, slab-roofed trenches, and pits – some intended for vertical burial and some ending in a lateral vaulted chamber.

(Photo © Serge Cassen)

There are similar forms with equivalent proportions in Egypt – the colossi and obelisks so often evoked in connection with megaliths, the quarries of their origin, and the transport techniques.

Another inevitable comparison is with the great statues on Easter Island in the Pacific Ocean. Known as *moai*, these creations carved out of *tufa*, without legs, measure between 2 and 11.5 metres high. Three hundred remain unfinished in the quarry from which they were cut. Only seventy are standing, alone or in groups near the platform of a ceremonial rallying-point (*ahu*). The island population shaped a hundred of these sacred monuments between the tenth and seventeenth centuries; they are related to a Polynesian tradition also found in seventeenth-century Tahiti, belonging to the first inhabitants of the island in about A.D. 500. Each platform shows the ancestor worship of one of the ten tribes.

The chief tribe, the Miru, claimed direct descent from the founder of the island community. They held a great annual feast for the

other tribes, providing an opportunity to distribute their main supplies according to the system of gifts that operated in the Polynesian hierarchy. Ancestors were of great importance in these ceremonies; they descended among the *moai* and stayed with them briefly, before becoming true gods. Prayers were offered to them at the death of a member of the tribe. In 1919, Mrs Scoresby Routledge reported a funeral ceremony:

> While the corpse remained on the *ahu* the district was marked off by the *péra*, or taboo, for the dead; no fishing was allowed near, and fires cooking were forbidden within certain marks – the smoke, at any rate, must be hidden or smothered with grass. Watch was kept by four relatives, and anyone breaking the regulations was liable to be brained. The mourning might last one, two, or even three years, by which time the whole thing had, of course, fallen to pieces. The bones were either left on the ahu, or collected and put into vaults of oblong shape, which were kept for the family, or they might be buried elsewhere. The end of the mourning was celebrated by a great feast, after which ceremony, as one recorder cheerfully concluded, "Pappa was finished."

Ceremonial life was integrated into the pyramidal structure of the chieftaincy. The principal tribe at the top of the pyramid controlled competition between the other tribes through feasts. Subsequently the situation degenerated, and for its own protection each tribe had to offer more feasts and construct ever greater monuments. These efforts demanded by their ancestors thus outran, very substantially, the material scope of the tribes. The *moai's* evolution towards gigantism – the largest, 20 metres tall, remained unfinished in the quarry – was also due to the isolation of this population, the density of which (three to four thousand inhabitants in 160 square kilometres when the Europeans arrived in 1722) caused considerable social tension. In the seventeenth century this led to such disorder that the monuments were destroyed one after another. When Cook called there in 1774 Forster, the expedition's naturalist, thought that the destruction was the result of a natural disaster, an earthquake due to volcanic activity on the island, which at that time had no trees on it.

Explorers at the beginning of this century also envisaged some sort of devastating activity on the part of Chinese or Peruvian invaders, to explain the presence of the stone colossi and the final cataclysm. The anthropologist Thor Heyerdahl crossed with his raft Kon-Tiki from Peru to Easter Island in 1947, to prove the possibility of such an invasion. We know now that this theory is partly redundant, and that the statues and their history reveal the island's internal con-

The famous Easter Island figures, the *moai*, were placed on a ceremonial platform known as an *ahu*. Each platform illustrates the ancestor-worship of one of the island's ten tribes. The setting up of these monoliths, weighing up to 80 tonnes, between the seventh and the eighteenth centuries A.D. must have presented immense problems.

(Photo © H. Gruyaert/Magnum)

ditions; the only damaging raid was that of the Peruvians, who in 1862 wiped out its indigenous population.

This population had certainly come from somewhere: several cultural traits suggested an ancient landfall from the west. Explorers of Polynesia in the eighteenth century discovered large funerary platforms on Tahiti, with steps 80 metres long, on which the dead were exposed for several months: these platforms were thus the equivalent of the *ahu*. The social context of these monuments is that of the Polynesian chieftain hierarchy, rediscovered on Easter Island.

The functions of many other monuments remain a mystery. We do not know the motives of the builders of the great rectilinear patterns of the Nazca desert in Peru, nor of those who set up lines of monoliths to mark out an immense rectangular enclosure at Calasasaya near Tiahuanaco, in Bolivia. Nor do we know why Serpent Mound (the earthworks of which stretch for almost 500 metres across the hills of Ohio) was constructed by the Adena Hopewell people 2,000 years ago. This vast gigantic zoomorphic form – carrying a white design 110 metres long – which is best seen from a great height above the ground, recalls the White Horse of Uffington in England. The ditches outlining this extraordinary design were cut out of the chalk hillside at about the time of Christ, and the relative proportions of their curves are similar to those of the horses seen on Celtic coins. It hardly seems necessary, however, to invoke representatives of other worlds to explain these vast collective works: for example, the importance of the horse associated with the Celtic goddesss Epona is well known.

It is inescapable: the word 'megalith' indicates monuments throughout the world whose geographical, historical and cultural contexts vary widely. Some writers, particularly at the beginning of the century, have been more aware of characteristics common to all these architectural structures than of the differences in their settings. They have built up an improbable theory, suggesting that some sort of genetic link connected all the monuments: their builders must be a 'people' or a 'megalithic race' invented out of thin air. This theory has been abandoned, and it is accepted that, if the monuments look the same across the world, it is entirely because they were all constructed in the simplest way possible! The alignment of standing stones and stone 'tables' – exactly the same principle as an architectural span – are the most elementary methods of building possible: two standing megaliths used as columns to support a third stone placed horizontally across them. It is thus scarcely surprising that a megalithic chamber constructed some three thousand years B.C. in Ireland resembles another built in southern India at the time of Christ's birth, or one erected by Madagascans in the eighteenth century A.D.

In their enthusiasm for comparisons, the early twentieth-century researchers fairly successfully ignored the study of contextual circumstances. Although comparisons remain fruitful in certain areas – as, for example, those concerning construction techniques – they must be treated with infinite caution when it comes to funeral rites. Similarities in the appearance of monuments or in the arrangement of their objects may in two different places have differing, or even opposing, meanings: here the disordered bones in a tomb reveal secondary rites, evidence of particular attention paid to the dead man, while elsewhere they indicate disregard of an older skeleton at the time of a later burial. In such circumstances, meticulous examination of the arrangement of the bones and their setting is essential to an accurate interpretation. The passage-ways of megalithic chambers are likewise very varied: one a sacred and swiftly sealed passage, another used for longer periods, a sort of antechamber-ossuary, an annexe to the chamber itself, an area for offerings. Such differences encourage archeologists to improve their observations for a better understanding of the monument, rather than seeking elements elsewhere for an interpretation disastrously remote from the case in hand.

Taking the context of these structures into account implies an entirely different approach, in which the comparative method comes into its own: an examination of the actual process. It hardly matters if we are ignorant as to which deity or ancestor was being honoured. It is much better to know how many people were involved in building the monument, how many could be supported by the land owned by the group who built the tomb, what sort of economy or society linked this group with its neighbours. We need to consider what rites brought this parcel of long bones or that trepanned skull to the megalithic chamber where it was discovered in modern times. Such questions prompted the labours of historians and ethnologists, whose precise observations have led to a degree of understanding of various aspects of western Europe's megalithic civilization. This civilization, more than any other, justifies detailed examination for its monuments are particularly numerous, and in addition make up homogeneous groups in relation one to another. Its study therefore offers a further interest in that it offers an understanding of the megalithic phenomenon in general terms, and more precisely of its beginnings.

The increasingly systematic use of carbon-14 dating since the 1950s has made it possible to place the megalithic monuments of western Europe within a limited and very ancient chronological time span, between the fifth and the second millennium B.C. These constructions are thus among the very first known stone edifices. This fact effectively demolishes Gordon Childe's theory that the missionaries from the Near East, land of the builders of the great civilizations, arrived in western Europe at the end of the third millennium and extended the megalithic religion there. The discovery of this early time scale poses in new terms the question of the genesis of these monuments: we must envisage a local origin for each of the main groups – Iberian, Breton, Irish, and Scandinavian. Moreover, since the custom of building these monuments persisted over long periods, connections appear between the different cultural groups and the diverse forms of their building styles. Interest now turns to the nature of megalith-building societies: one of the first rural cultures to become settled in the west.

The collective nature of the tombs tends to suggest a form of primitive communism; yet there is still a need to discover more precisely which social organizations corresponded with these great workshops, and what significance was accorded to them by the peoples of those times. Most of the monuments have been visited over very long periods, far outlasting their initial function. In stressing this, archaeologists indicate how essential was the role of these sites in the cohesion of human society.

Renewed study of these questions has been accompanied by further excavations and some spectacular discoveries: the great Breton cairns at Barnenez and Gavrinis, and those at Bougon in central western France and at Newgrange and Knowth in Ireland, have revealed the elaborate ornamentation and complexity of these great tombs. At Stonehenge and in Orkney, or in the Iberian peninsula, open monuments made up of circular trenches or rings of standing stones form ritual groups, which are probably complementary to the covered tomb construction. Such observations further enrich our conception of megaliths: they are more than simply tombs, even if many contain human bones.

Apart from such traces, we must also seek out the presence of the ancestor-builders, in some ways the soul of the group. In the simultaneously rigid and subtle setting of this architecture, the many ritual aspects of death and offerings wait to be rediscovered; beyond the paintings, engravings, and carvings of megalithic art, the import and the probable origins of the forces engaged for these constructions remain to be understood. The effort entailed will be worthwhile for, clearly, the observation of celestial axes by means of the monuments suggests a concept of the universe worthy of any great civilization.

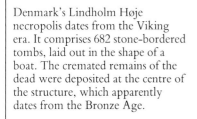

Denmark's Lindholm Høje necropolis dates from the Viking era. It comprises 682 stone-bordered tombs, laid out in the shape of a boat. The cremated remains of the dead were deposited at the centre of the structure, which apparently dates from the Bronze Age.

(Photo © Dagli-Orti)

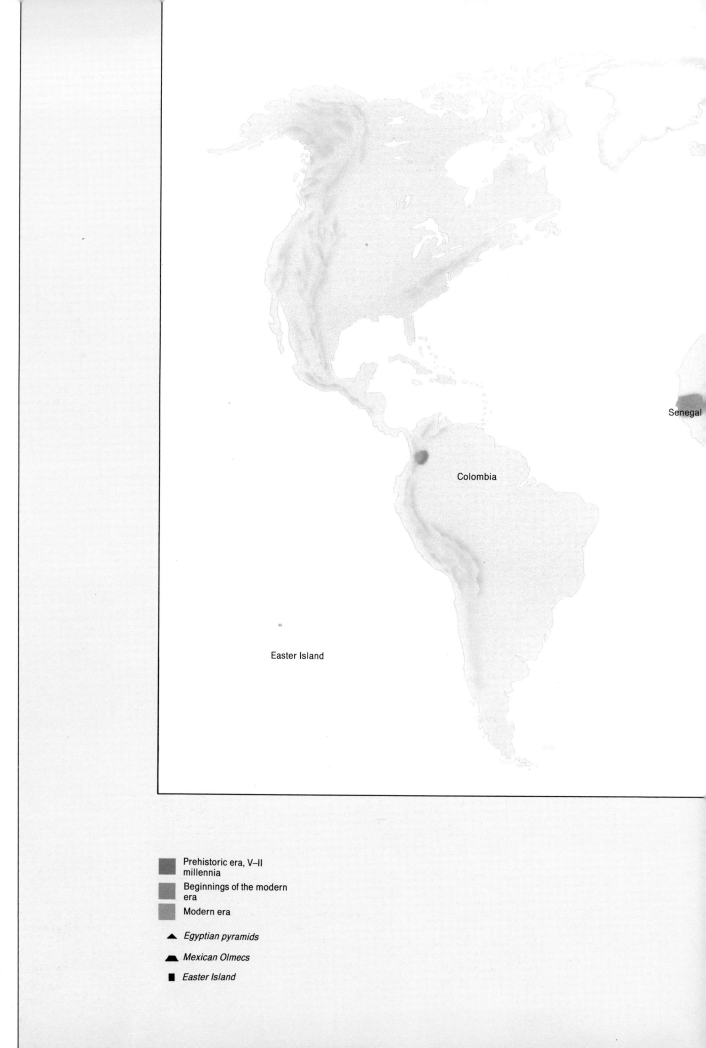

Senegal

Colombia

Easter Island

Prehistoric era, V–II
millennia

Beginnings of the modern
era

Modern era

▲ *Egyptian pyramids*

◣ *Mexican Olmecs*

■ *Easter Island*

MEGALITHS THROUGHOUT
THE WORLD

Megalithic monuments are widely dispersed throughout the world. Each mark on the map indicates a centre which was generally independent, with its own historical and cultural context. Western Europe probably has the oldest and most varied forms of megalithism, now being rediscovered by archeologists after some five thousand years of oblivion, and their studies help to explain the challenges of the use and worship of the great stones. Three sites are indicated which are always referred to with their megaliths: the pyramids of Egypt, the monuments of Mexico, and Easter Island with its statues.

THREE THOUSAND

YEARS OF

BUILDING

In Search of the
First Architects

There may perhaps be constructions older than those which are now described as the world's earliest buildings; it is likely that many ancient styles of megalith remain to be discovered. This is a reasonably well-founded supposition, for the earliest known monuments, built over the period of a few centuries, show a surprising diversity that suggests a variety of origins. There are certainly some extremely ancient groups in the Iberian peninsula, in western France, northern Germany and Denmark, and perhaps also in the British Isles and other sites such as Malta. This recognition of sites showing very early and widely varying forms of megalithic construction inevitably leads to reflections on the 'birth' of megalithism; there must have been a close relationship between the earliest architects and the local setting.

The Iberian peninsula's oldest megalithic tombs are in southern Portugal, where the Monument I of Poço de Gateira in Upper Alentejo dates from the fifth millennium. It was explored in 1948 and 1949 by Georg and Vera Leisner; inside the tumulus, 12 metres in diameter, a small east-facing passage-way of two low stone slabs was roofed over with a large stone. This led into a polygonal megalithic chamber measuring 3 metres by 2, with inward-sloping walls of large slabs that originally supported a covering stone. The chamber contained polished stone axe-heads, trimmed flints, and twelve globular vessels which in the searchers' opinion probably corresponded to twelve skeletons whose bones had dissolved in the acid soil. A shard dated by thermoluminescence gives a date of 4510 B.C. ± 360 years. A similar result (4440 B.C. ± 360) was given for another megalithic monument in the same region.

Buried stone cists have been found in the same province. Rectangular tombs – which were probably individual – contain artefacts that recall ancient megalithic burials: polished stone axe-heads, triangular and trapezoidal flint microliths, a few scattered undecorated round-based pottery. Similar cists, with similar contents, have been excavated a little further south, in the Algarve; the Palmeira 4 chest found at Monchique is an example of this simple form of sepulchre. Another buried monument, Palmeira 3, is effectively a small oblong chamber, measuring 1 metre by 6, lined with small flat stones and orientated east–west: this is a place of collective burial. In the same community a chamber of very similar layout but complete with a short corridor facing south-east is part of the tumulus 7 at Buço Preto. The three Monchique tombs may represent three stages in the development of Portuguese megalithic tombs, or at least some part of it.

Another type of monument common in Portugal is the corbelled tomb. These circular or oval chambers do not appear to have developed out of the tradition of polygonal megalithic chambers, even though the latter may be older; they are more likely to have developed from domed rock-cut tombs. One such, Carenque 2, near Sintra to the north of Lisbon, has been dated by thermoluminescence at between 3390 and 3400 B.C.

There is still, however, the problem of judging whether development was local or inspired by external influence. Some examples from south-eastern Iberia would appear to indicate local inspiration. In Andalusia there are circular collective trench tombs, some of which have dry-stone sides, while others are lined with flat stones. Some have a very short passage-way, but most have none; it is not known how they were covered. Their grave-goods have made dating possible: polished stone axes, triangular, diamond-shaped or short-stemmed flint arrow-heads, highly stylized stone idols, terracotta plaques, and containers, some with shoulders – all of which, taken together, indicate the middle phase of Almerian culture. These tombs may therefore date from about the middle of the fourth millennium. They may be seen as prototypes of corbelled passage graves, as constructed at the large later site of Los Millares.

It may be possible to reach further back in time in seeking the first megalithic tombs in this region. Small circular trench tombs, built around 4000 B.C., also had dry-stone or slab-lined walls. Built first for one or two bodies, they later became used for collective burial. Grave

Aerial view of the Barnenez megalithic monument (late fifth millennium B.C.) at Plouézoc'h in Finistère, showing the scale of the double mass of rubble held within a series of walls or kerbs. On the south face can be seen the entrance passages to the tombs.

(Photo © Ed. Jos.)

Offerings placed in the Barnenez monument included several vessels: the round-based pots were in chamber A, and the hollow-footed vase (bottom) was found in front of the entrances to graves C and D.

(Photo B. Acloque © CNMHS/SPADEM)

goods found there include triangular or trapezoid microliths, flint blades, polished axes, bracelets carved out of shells, and rare round-based urns. Such objects indicate the earlier phase of Almerian culture as seen in taller dwellings at El Garcel and Tres Cabezos – dwellings which may have been the prototypes for fortified sites such as Los Millares.

These ancient collective sepulchres were sometimes the forerunners of polygonal stone-built coffers, such as those found in Granada, which contained similar carved bracelets; the megalithic Granada group, with rectangular chambers, no doubt derived from them.

When André Malraux, the French man of letters and statesman, visited the Barnenez monument at Plouézoc'h just after its rescue from destruction, he declared in his speech to the assembled public: 'This is our Parthenon!' Barnenez is indeed a marvel in more than one way: in its setting, facing the sea, in the scale and extent of its construction, in its extreme antiquity, and in the deeply spiritual atmosphere which surrounds it. It stands amongst the finest buildings in western France; and it poses forcefully the question of its origins: what can have preceded it?

Some of the mounds near Carnac, in Morbihan, are extremely old, certainly dating from the fifth millennium. The stone coffers inside them recall the very earliest collective tombs, covered by a small tumulus, discovered at the Téviec site (also in Morbihan). Téviec dates from the same period as the neighbouring site of Hoëdic, 5800 B.C., and similarly predates agriculture: these two Mesolithic sites (not Neolithic like the other sites) indicate that the extremely ancient roots of this type of burial may lie here. This does not exclude an element of variety. Although some ancient coffers, at Bougon or at La Goumoisière in Vienne, also indicate the concept of megalithic collective burial, two important characteristics of megalithism – method of access and style of construction – are not yet in evidence. The group of tombs discovered in the north of Loiret offers a good illustration of this diversity; they are small sunken chambers, dry-stone lined and covered by a single block, containing one or two skeletons lying in a crouched position, and a few trimmed flints. Some have a standing stone nearby. This small and very distinctive group appears to be very old: although the date of 5210 B.C., obtained from a specimen from the La Chaise tomb near Malesherbes, seems too remote, the connection of these monuments with the pottery items decorated in the Cerny style – the cultural grouping of the Paris basin – is a sound argument for placing the use of such tombs as far back as the end of the fifth millennium. Like the earlier coffers, this 'protomegalithic' architectural style indicates the emergence of megalithism.

The necropolis of Pontcharaud 2 near Clermont-Ferrand in the

Parts of the Barnenez monument
are entirely megalithic in style, such
as this passage with its massive side
columns supporting thick roofing
slabs.

(Photo B. Acloque © CNMHS/SPADEM)

Puy-de-Dôme, a fine example of collective underground burial, confirms the diversity of megalithic styles from the earliest days. This site
was excavated in 1986 by Gilles Loison and his team; several burials of
the late fifth millennium were found, with some stone elements; two
double tombs were confirmed, as well as some fifty individual burials
with the skeleton lying crouched on its side. The most spectacular
discovery was a mass tomb containing the skeletons of two children
and five adults, lying prone; the tangle of bones proves that all the
bodies were laid there at the same time, most with their hands and feet
cut off. The tomb was covered with blocks and slabs of stone, and has
several of the characteristics of megalithic tombs, quite apart from
architectural style. The fairly numerous grave-goods include tools
made of dressed flint, polished axes, bone awls and polishing sticks,
containers showing certain southern influences, and others showing
the northern influence of the Cerny style.

Monumental scale is certainly apparent in the Paris basin at the
Yonne necropolis of Passy, where Pascal Duhamel and Michel Pre-
steau have identified some thirty funerary monuments between 20
and 300 metres in length, grouped round an area of about 20 hectares.
Bounded by one or more ditches, they must have been seen as earth
mounds surrounded by a fence. A 'façade' or 'gate' structure appears
several times along the broader of the two short sides: this part of the
monument held a wooden coffer containing a single body lying

73

supine, with its head to the east. In some of the monuments several construction phases are often clearly distinguishable: for example, traces of fire may suggest that a part of the structure was destroyed during one such phase. Some tombs have very few grave-goods, others are richly supplied. So far this site is unique in France, and appears to resemble similar necropolises surveyed in northern Germany and in Poland.

The long trapezoidal style of monument is clear at Maisse in Essonne, south of Paris. This 45-metre mound discovered in 1986 is made of gravel and is orientated north–south. The wider southern end contained a funerary coffer and two large blocks of sandstone forming the frontage; the coffer held four adult skeletons, a bone awl and five flint blades, and is made of flat stone slabs of which one is decorated. Traces of three houses of the late fourth millennium, 75 metres to the north-west of the tumulus, may have some connection with this earliest true megalithic monument in the Paris basin.

These still poorly dated examples give us a glimpse of the development of the earliest large-scale building styles in western France. They appeared in the middle, and perhaps at the beginning, of the fifth millennium, and have in common their oblong shape and frequently

The Breton Parthenon

Three polished stone axes have been carved on one of the uprights of chamber H at Barnenez. Dating from the late fifth millennium, they represent ancestral male power-symbols.

74

The great Barnenez tumulus was
built in two stages at the end of the
fifth millennium. In the 1950s the
removal of stones from the
monument had begun to destroy it,
when chambers in the rubble
mound, roofed with stone slabs or
dry-stone vaulting, were uncovered.
Excavation revealed the full extent
and exact layout of the tombs, as
well as offerings, vessels, and shaped
and polished stones, making it
possible to reconstruct the history of
2,000 years of worship at the
sanctuary.

(2 Photos © Ed. Jos.)

First phase of construction:
around 4700 B.C.

Second phase of construction:
around 4300 B.C.

0   100 m

their imposing dimensions. The best known style has a more or less circular chamber with corbelled roof and passage approach, but there are other forms – rectangular megalithic chambers, coffers, cists, even wooden constructions. The simplest structures (fewer posts, small coffers, and so on) are difficult to find and to interpret. It is first necessary to examine the overall grouping of the monument to which they belong, which is only rarely possible because of the size and internal complexity of the mounds.

For instance, the Barnenez tumulus in the Finistère is made of two juxtaposed sections. The first, to the east, measures from 32 to 35 metres. It is made up of five chambers, with a passage orientated towards the south-east: the roughly rectangular central chamber has megalithic sides, while the other four are circular, of dry-stone construction. All are covered by corbelling. A further block was subsequently added to the west of this first monument, measuring 39 metres and containing six further chambers, approximately circular, built of dry stone with with or without added slabs.

The entrance to the most westerly chamber is closed by a flat stone preceded by a kind of hatchway; several of the monoliths in this chamber display carved and and picked-out motifs, representing what is known as the 'shield idol', axes, and a bow. Radiocarbon dating places the construction of the first monument at about 4700 B.C., and that of the second some 400 years later. There are few remains inside: most of the bones have dissolved in the acid soil – a considerable problem for archeologists in the Armorican massif – but the paucity of fragments found indicate that the tombs never contained more than a small number of bodies. Some shards from round-based pots define the period of building ('old Carn style'), but others are more recent, indicating later intrusion: in the passage-way of two adjoining chambers in the most recent mound were found fragments of a pot-stand dating from the fourth-millennium Chassean culture, and other bell-beaker shards were left there much later, towards the year 2000 B.C. Excavations have even uncovered traces of the somewhat later Early Bronze Age.

The Carn Island monument at Ploudalmézeau in Finistère looks today like a hemispherical tumulus; this shape corresponds to what remains of an earlier and probably oblong mound. Excavation has uncovered the dressed stones of a flat façade from which three short passages lead to dry-stone chambers. Two of these are approximately circular, and the third, to the east, is almost rectangular and divided in two by a thick wall, creating effectively a double chamber approached along a single passage. The central tomb, unlike the others, appears to be surrounded by a curved boulder kerb which disappears behind the straight façade. Was this tomb with its circular mound the first to be

The Carn Island tumulus or cairn, at Ploudalmézeau in Finistère, has dominated the landscape for more than 6,000 years. Its worn appearance today should not diminish its claim to be the oldest known stone building.

(Photo © Ed. Jos.)

used, before the construction of the two lateral tombs and the long façaded tumulus? Is the curved ornamentation simply a buttress in this unique three-chamber monument? Dating has not provided the solution: the central chamber offers two dates, 4095 and 4160 B.C., and the oval south chamber two others which pre- and post-date them, 4205 and 3625 B.C.. Their contents include round-based vessels – some decorated with a smooth narrow band, either curved or straight – a few trimmed flints, and some schist beads.

One of the three tumuli dominating the island of Guennoc, off Landéda in Finistère, is associated with a very remote date: 4720 B.C. The sample dated was taken from one of the four chambers with passage-ways inside the oldest part of the third tumulus – for this monument was also built in two phases. The square older part was enlarged by adding a cairn containing two circular passage graves. The entrances to these two chambers balance each other, one facing south-west and the other facing north-east.

The oldest anthropomorphic steles were found in the circular chambers of these great Breton monuments of the fifth millennium. They show no decoration now, but they may originally have carried painted motifs.

Mounds for Burying the Dead

Normandy also has extremely ancient constructions, with monuments characterized by chambers radiating out within the body of the tumulus. These are circular passage graves. The monument of La Hoguette at Fontenay-le-Marmion, in the Calvados, contains seven or eight chambers 4 or 5 metres in diameter within its 30 metres of length; each chamber held the remains of from four to fourteen individuals, in a crouching position. A few modest offerings have been found in the tombs, particularly in front of the outer kerb – flint blades and knives, and shards of round-based pots; the collection corresponds to dates between 4400 and 3500 B.C. At ground level beneath the mound outside excavators found fragments of two decorated vessels belonging to the Cerny group of the fifth millennium; it is difficult to understand the connection between this Paris basin group and the builders of the monument. Similar shards have been uncovered in Jersey, also in connection with a megalithic monument, Les Fouillages. They appear to show that local original ceramic ware, influenced by the Paris basin culture, was contemporaneous with these first constructions which were closer to the Atlantic tradition. Does such an encounter reflect the assimilation of one culture by another ('acculturation'), or the presence of two different communities?

Six hundred metres from La Hoguette lies the La Hogue tumulus

The Saint-Michel tumulus at Carnac, in Morbihan, is an artificial mound surmounted by a modern chapel. It is one of the most impressive of all long barrows. The tombs inside date from the late fifth millennium.

(Photo © Ed. Jos.)

– larger, as its name implies: 43 metres long, with twelve chambers. Although excavation began as early as 1829, one chamber remained intact until recently, when it was found to contain the bones of six individuals – but without skulls! Another Calvados site, at Colombiers-sur-Seulles, illustrates how widely these great monuments can vary within a single region: it is a trapezoidal tumulus 65 metres long, containing only two small circular chambers with corridor access, one at the western end and the other in the central section.

Central western France also has oblong monuments with circular chambers, with their corridors facing east. The tumulus E at Bougon in Deux-Sèvres, 22 metres long and 10 metres wide, displays a double kerb. One of its chambers is surrounded by flat stones; its corbelled covering fell in on its dozen skeletons and their homogeneous grave-goods, dated by radiocarbon studies at 4720 B.C.: blades and small arrow-heads with transverse cutting edges, perforated teeth, variscite beads, and shards of round-bottomed pots not unlike those from Carn Island, but undecorated.

A bone uncovered in the circular chamber of another tumulus of the same necropolis has been similarly dated. This tomb with its corbelled covering and short entrance passage was also intact beneath the collapsed vault. The remains of a dozen skeletons have been identified within it, some lying together in a crouched position, the others scattered. Blades and arrow-heads with transverse cutting edges, polished bone pins, and two pots had been laid on a stone slab, and the remains of an old man were huddled among the blocking stones in the corridor.

These monuments may be described as classic, but the first thousand years of megalithism also saw the construction of others equally spectacular: the giant tumuli. The best known are the Carnac mounds on the shores of the Gulf of Morbihan. The Saint-Michel tumulus dominating Carnac is 125 metres long, 60 wide, and 10 high. Explored at the end of the last century, this immense artificial mound encloses stone coffers and chests. A megalithic chamber tomb lying at the edge must have been constructed later. Similar monuments have been recorded at Carnac itself, and at Le Moustoir, Locmariaquer, and Le Mané-Lud. The Arzon tumulus at Tumiac is circular. These mounds are famous for their enormous size, and for the wealth of grave-goods found inside their coffers, which distinguishes them from, say, Barnenez: there are, for example, large state axes of black and green stone, variscite beads and pendants, and disc-rings made of serpentine. Archeologists working in the long barrow of Mané-er-Hroeck found fragments of a decorated stele among the blocking stones of the tomb. These strange tombs are thought to date from the end of the fifth millennium, but all bones have dissolved in the acid soil and recent excavations have added nothing to our understanding of them.

The tumulus E at Bougon, in Deux-Sèvres, is surrounded by a double kerb of dry stones, and contains two passage graves at its centre. The covering of the chambers and passages, fallen in and now disintegrated, has not been reconstructed.

(Photo © J.-P. Mohen)

Sometimes a long tumulus lies beside a classic monument. The circular Fo Bougon tumulus, for example, provides the starting point for a 70-metre long trapezoidal construction extending towards the north. This extension, most of which has been excavated, contains only three individual burials spread through the body of the mound along an inner kerb. At the northern end a large megalithic tomb, built in about 3500 B.C., occupies a secondary position; the effect is thus of a mound of a single necropolis. The C2 mound, 40 metres long and 20 metres wide, lies next to the circular C1 mound; dating from 4000 B.C., it contains a small rectangular megalithic chamber which was not a tomb – as in the preceding case, this addition was not built for burial purposes – but three burials, one of a single skeleton and the others of two each (one adult and one child) have been found in front of its dry stone kerb.

What then can have been the purpose of these imposing mounds of stone which were so little used for burials? They appear to have been created more for prestige than for practical use. The Demoiselle monument at Le Thou in Charente-Maritime is over 100 metres long and 9 metres wide; constructed of earth, it covered a stone chest containing a single fragment of a human skull! The Bernet barrow at Saint-Sauveur in Gironde, made of sand held within a dry-stone kerb, was 26 metres long and 14 wide, with, at the centre, a stone box enclosing a single skeleton and two fourth-millennium pots. A little to the north, post-holes found in the ground have been interpreted as the remains of a funerary building, while to the south a megalithic tomb may have been constructed at a later period. Post-holes have also been recorded beneath the long Grosse Motte barrow at Bouhet, in Charente-Maritime. The group of monuments at Tusson, in Charente, is spectacular: three giant tumuli were surrounded by some twenty smaller ones, which were destroyed recently: the largest, the Gros Dognon, measures 150 metres long, 45 wide, and 10 high, but it is not known what lies inside. The Motte-des-Justices at Thouars in Deux-Sèvres was longer still, at 174 metres, although its width and height were less. Rescue excavations carried out there before its destruction have revealed very few funerary traces. It is not clear whether these monuments should be associated with certain long barrows discovered in the Lot and Aveyron *départements*, some of which have a megalithic tomb at one end. The tradition of the long barrow must have been long-lived, and this no doubt explains their wide distribution.

Regions bordering on the North Sea and the Baltic also have considerable numbers of long barrows. They conceal wooden structures, known as 'houses of the dead', and megalithic constructions – two systems of ritual which sometimes appear complementary.

The two developmental characteristics typical of all megalithic groups in western Europe – their nature as monuments, and collective burial – coincide here in a variety of constructions.

Long barrows without a megalithic tomb include monuments of varying styles, but all appear as a long mound of earth. The group of mounds at Kujavia in Poland was the first to be recognized, by Konrad Jazdzewski in 1969. These are large barrows, between 15 and 150 metres long, shaped like a tapering trapezium, almost triangular. Orientated east–west, the highest point of the façade is to the east, and is between 3 and 4 metres high, the same as the longer of its short sides. At Wietrzychowice, in the province of Wloklavek, the mound is surrounded by a row of blocks, giving it a megalithic appearance. Two quarry-trenches run along the longer sides. These long barrows were most frequently built for a single person, who was buried in a ditch hollowed out near the front, but other human remains have sometimes been discovered among the stones covering the skeleton; the Wietrzychowice tumulus V contained two men with trepanned skulls. Sometimes several individual burials are found superimposed on each other. Grave-goods are rare, and consist of pots, bottles, cups, flint tools and weapons, boars' tusks, and amber beads, dating from the first half of the fourth millennium, and characteristic of the funnel-

The Long Barrows of Northern Europe

beaker culture. A long barrow at Gaj I, near Kolo, covers remains, possibly burnt, of a rectangular wooden structure measuring 4 metres by 4.50 metres, with a trench at its centre. Was it, as in Denmark, an ordinary dwelling, a sanctuary, or a 'mortuary house', where corpses were laid? Several individual burials were certainly found nearby.

The Kujavia mounds may also be associated with single, flat graves, some of them older, grouped together to form a cemetery. Eight mounds are grouped together at Sarnovo; some contain megalithic chambers built earlier, others simple tombs. Did all these tombs belong to a single community developing over nearly a thousand years? Do their different designs reflect differences of social standing? And what became of earlier social connotations when fresh burials were made in the same monument? Such questions remain as yet unanswered.

Denmark and northern Germany have long barrows without megalithic tombs, rectangular or trapezoidal in shape like those of western France or southern England. Most are between 20 and 100 metres long; Stralendorf in east Germany has one of the longest, at 125 metres. There are some similarities between British and Danish monuments: the surrounds of the barrow consist of alternating stone blocks and dry-stone walls, with posts set into the façade. Such shared characteristics imply some connection between the two countries, without any indication as to which was influenced by the other. In Denmark a connection between long barrows with and without a megalithic tomb seems increasingly probable; the fundamental difference between the two categories appears to lie in the nature of the burials, individual in the first case and collective in the second. Observations in Jutland seem to indicate that, in tumuli without a megalithic tomb, successive burials can simulate collective graves.

Funeral rites for the two types of tumulus would thus appear more closely allied than first supposed: it has even been questioned whether the absence of a tomb was not simply due to its having been made of wood and therefore disappearing in time. If such be the case, did one form precede the other? It seems that mounds without megalithic tombs are concentrated in Jutland while those with ancient megalithic tombs are more common in Zealand. The latter may be older. They appeared first in the middle of the Early Neolithic age and subsequently spread to southern Sweden, the east and south of Denmark, and northern Germany. The two types of tumulus are therefore contemporaneous, and it may well be that they represent two closely allied aspects of the same phenomenon: the consecration of a spectacular funerary monument for the use of a precise caste of limited numbers.

A late fifth millennium collective passage grave lies within the southern end of the long barrow F at Bougon. The dry-stone vault of the chamber, found collapsed in 1979, has been restored.

(Photo © J.-P. Mohen)

Long barrows with ancient megalithic tombs are one of Denmark's oldest monument forms, indeed perhaps the oldest of all; they appeared in the middle of the fourth millennium. These mounds, with their stone surrounds, are very similar to others elsewhere. The tomb itself consists of a rectangular or polygonal coffer made of flat stone slabs set on edge, with a large block forming the cover, and no visible means of entry. In the case of a single tomb, it is placed centrally within the tumulus, as with the polygonal coffer found in the long rectangular mound at Sonderholm. At Gunderslevholm, however, three coffers are spaced out at regular intervals within a single square mound, beneath the mass of earth contained within a row of blocks.

Such ancient monuments also exist in northern Germany – for example, at Barkvieren in Mecklenburg, near Rostock, at Frauenmark, near Parchim, and at Mankmoos, near Sternberg. C. J. Becker has debated whether the coffers beneath long barrows might not have originated from the cists found half-buried at the beginning of the fourth millennium funnel-beaker culture. Some coffers, like those at Barkvieren and Frauenmark, were effectively half-buried before being covered by the mound. There are two major differences, however: firstly, the cists each contained a single skeleton while the coffer always contained several bodies; secondly, the coffers were always associated with a tumulus, which was never so for the chests.

The map of mounds with coffers in Denmark indicates that the rectangular coffers were always found in the south and polygonal coffers in the north, with an overlap zone in Zealand. There were thus two contemporary regional styles. Did the polygonal design derive from the rectangular design? Did it first appear in Zealand, where

The megalithic monument at Rostrup in Denmark consists of a plain stone chamber surrounded by wooden structures which have been reconstructed from the traces of post-holes. Wood and stone were often used together in this region.

(Photo © Dagli-Orti)

both forms have been discovered? Or perhaps should we recognize, yet again, two similar but original aspects of the same megalithic phenomenon?

The tradition of long barrows with trench tombs continued without alteration at least until the end of the fourth millennium. Some writers, such as Jurgen Jensen in 1982, have sought to prove a connection between the wooden 'houses of the dead' found inside some barrows, and other original constructions found recently on the outside.

This was the case at Tustrup, north of Aarhus, where Poul Kjaerum discovered three mounds. The first concealed a polygonal megalithic coffer; the second, to the south, contained two megalithic passage graves; one 10 metres long and the other smaller; the third, bounded by large blocks, contained a polygonal chamber with a passage. The remains of a small structure (5 metres square), open on one side, were uncovered near these monuments. A trench held posts and wall-planks, reinforced by small stone slabs set in the earth, and a central post helped to hold up the roof. This building had been destroyed by fire, as were some of the 'houses of the dead' discovered under the mounds. Twenty-eight pots and some spoons belonging to the early phase of the same funnel-beaker culture (the middle of the fourth millennium) were placed around the central post. As similar beakers had been placed as offerings in neighbouring megalithic tombs, the archeologist assumed that the dead were laid in this resting-

Mortuary Houses

house before being moved into their place of burial. Other archeologists consider that the small square Tustrup building, certainly connected to neighbouring tombs, was more likely to have been a sanctuary where the faithful could gather. The two theories are probably complementary.

Another construction uncovered soon after at Ferslev measured 5 metres by 6. Inside, a rectangular space was surrounded by stones: seven pots had been placed on the stones, and twenty-eight others were found elsewhere in the structure. These pots belong to an advanced phase of the same culture, and date from approximately 3000 B.C. Other, older, jars were gathered together in front of the west end of the house. This sanctuary thus appears to have been in use over a long period.

Evidence of funerary use was also not very apparent at Herrup, where in 1967 C. J. Becker discovered first two and then four more of these constructions. The largest, 6 metres square, had two lateral wings, each 3 metres long. The forecourt thus defined contained twenty-seven pots and spoons dating from the early phase of the culture. The absence of hearth and kitchen remains in these buildings made it clear that they were not dwellings; the religious function therefore became more likely and the identification of these 'houses' as burial places was confirmed in each case. Apart from the Tustrup study quoted above, the theory was fully confirmed when an account of the discovery of the Vrone Hede site in Jutland was published in 1977. Here a circular tumulus contained a square megalithic passage grave built beside a row of seven small 'houses of the dead', each related to two parallel burial trenches piled over with stones. Although it is still difficult to establish the precise chronological relationship between these different structures, there is nonetheless a general connection between a megalithic tomb and a wooden 'mortuary house'.

Other mounds without any megalithic chamber are to be found in the south and east of England, and in eastern Scotland; various radiocarbon dating results suggest that they were constructed between the end of the fifth millennium and the end of the fourth. Most are long trapezoidal monuments facing east–west, between 18 and 120 metres long, with an average length of 70 metres; the tumulus of Maiden Castle, 550 metres long, is exceptional. Some are rectangular, others oval or even circular, but all conceal a wide variety of structures of which frequently only meagre traces remain (hence the difficulties of exploring them). There is not the slightest trace of funerary use in the Beckhampton Road and South Street mounds near Avebury; only the rows of post-holes indicate the internal layout. Two pits have been identified beneath the Alfriston mound, one containing

THE BIRTH OF MEGALITHISM

Megalithism's three fundamental ingredients are collective burial, the use of very large stones, and monumentality. Some sites may reflect one aspect or another but not all three together, and can be seen as prototypes, or parallel forms illustrating the development of megalithic monuments.

Collective funeral rites are still little understood, but several recently discovered examples show that the practice was already widespread in the fifth millennium. In Denmark, eight people were buried in the Stroby Egede pit of the Ertebølle culture, probably all at the same

The large pit of the collective Pontcharaud 2 grave, near Clermont-Ferrand, contained seven skeletons lying prone, covered by large stones. The lack of any raised edifice marking the burial means that the grave cannot be regarded as a megalithic monument.

(Photo © G. Loison)

A large stone covered the chamber hollowed out in the ground in the Marsaules grave at Malesherbes. Constricted within the dry-stone walls, the skeleton was laid there in a crouching position. This site resembles Pontcharaud in having no monument.

(Photo © G. Richard)

time. Another Early Neolithic mass pit burial, probably of similar date, was found at Baden-Wurtemberg, and in 1986 the astonishing mass grave at Pontcharaud, near Clermont-Ferrand, was discovered at the centre of a necropolis of 1500 square metres containing the bodies of 70 people, buried separately in accordance with a wide variety of rites. The collective grave held seven bodies – two children and five adults – stretched out face down, most without their feet or hands, and covered by large stone blocks. There was evidence of complex funeral rites and also, possibly, an early example of manipulation of bodies and bones.

The large stone blocks at Pontcharaud represent another factor which was to become an essential part of megalithism. Blocks were thrown onto bodies without yet constituting a building; although in Loiret the use of slabs was closer to megalithic ideas. The two graves excavated in the Malesherbes region both reveal a chamber dug into the ground, with dry-stone walls and covered with a slab. Both had grooves and burnishing hollows, showing that the covering slab was used for sharpening or polishing: did this function determine the choice of slab for burial purposes? Was it used for this purpose after being placed on the grave? One of the graves (Les Marsaules) held one body, the other (La Chaise) two. The latter was unusual in being marked with a standing stone, indicating the need to mark the burial site which would soon become sacred. Neither collective burial nor monumentalism are fully developed at Malesherbes, although both are hinted at; the use of the covering slab, on the other hand, is entirely megalithic.

The elevation of the monument indicated the burial site, acquired commemorative value, and became in time a ceremonial site. Monuments varied in appearance from region to region. We have already seen the example of a standing stone that was purely abstract from the beginning: the standing stone as symbol. The monumental aspect may also be seen in the construction of a large enclosure surrounded by a palisade, sometimes with the addition of a bank and ditch, with a simple pit inside containing a single body. Monuments in the Passy area illustrate this style. The wooden mortuary houses in Danish mounds may have been buried under the mass of earth. The monument, which might be enormous, was more than a funeral marker, for it developed a clear ceremonial function: the façade became individualized, orientation seems to have been very important, and offerings were placed in front of its stones. The monumental aspect was thus not always associated either with collective burial or with the use of megaliths.

Europe's western and coastal regions were unique in their development of the architectural style known as the megalithic monument. This was probably the result of social structures: settlement linked with agriculture and stock-rearing, population growth, the need to organize social relationships according to specialized sectors of activity – everything favoured these great constructions. The importance of ancestor-worship must have been decisive in the successful achievement of the great sites. Megaliths are only found in areas with a plentiful supply of stone, the perfect material for ensuring eternal ancestral survival. Wood was kept for temporary funerary buildings, or houses for the living. Western European culture, therefore, contained everything it needed to develop from the small Portuguese or Breton megalithic coffers to the enormous Barnenez tumulus – and rapidly, as with any successful synthesis in which the composite elements became barely distinguishable.

The La Chaise grave at Malesherbes (Loiret) is marked by a standing stone; a large flat slab, used for polishing, shielded two crouched skeletons inside a small hollowed-out chamber.

(Photo © G. Richard)

Stone . . . and Wood

the remains of a single isolated burial. On the other hand the Fussel's Lodge monument in Wiltshire contained the bones of fifty people, placed at the broadest end of the mound, the east. These remains were gathered inside an area defined by post-holes – the remains of another mortuary house; this in turn was contained within a fenced trapezoidal enclosure. Other post-holes also indicated an individual design of the east façade. The archeologist Paul Ashbee suggests that the bodies remained in the enclosure for a long period, sometimes stripped of their flesh.

In the final phase, perhaps some decades after the placing of the first wooden posts, two long ditches were dug out parallel to the enclosure, and the whole covered by a mound. This would correspond to a final sealing of the designated funeral place, as confirmed by other similar monuments in southern England. There were frequently very few bodies (six burials on average) and also traces of incineration. At Hambledon Hill, Roger Mercer discovered a long barrow erected close to a causewayed-camp with discontinuous ditches, typical of southern England. This discovery indicates that there was a close relationship between the camp and the barrow, and suggests that both may have had funerary connections.

Such unchambered tombs are also linked to other barrows which do have such chambers. Wayland's Smithy near Ashbury, in the south of England, has two enclosed mounds; one, an oval tumulus with concave façade conceals not a megalithic chamber but traces of a wooden house containing the remains of fourteen people. The tumulus was covered by a trapezoidal mound containing a megalithic tomb.

Long suspected, the wooden construction of long barrows was spectacularly confirmed in 1987 at Haddenham, near Cambridge in eastern England. Ian Hodder's team of excavators uncovered a funerary chamber at the end of a long barrow, approached through an antechamber made entirely of granite and broad chestnut planks. The chamber and the antechamber were of equal length – about 2 metres – and of similar construction: one 1.20 metre plank for the floor, another for the roof, and one for each side, with a height of 1.50 metres. Two axial posts strengthened the chamber, which held human bones. Two pots, dating from the middle Neolithic period, were found in front of the antechamber entrance, level with the façade.

The Haddenham discovery revived the debate on the relationship between wooden and stone construction. Several authorities consider that the first British megalithic tombs were effectively copies: they were constructed of stone imitating the wooden funerary structures of long barrows. Lionel Masters compared two Scottish monu-

Excavations at Haddenham, near Cambridge in England, have revealed the remains of a wooden 'megalith' with a chamber and antechamber made of thick oak planks. The use of wood in monumental earth constructions was probably more widespread than present-day remains might suggest.

(Photo © Dr I. Hodder/British Museum)

ments, Lochhill and Slewcairn. The building at Lochhill began with a low dry-stone wall, dominating a funerary structure some 10 metres long round three trenches. At ground level a layer of remains contained fragments of burned human bones. The first phase involved a row of stakes, with a kind of porch built of four granite blocks placed at its centre. The second phase was the covering of the funerary structure with a subtrapezoidal long barrow, faced with upright stone slabs covering the wooden façade. The second monument, Slewcairn, also showed a secondary phase of building at the tumulus, with a façade of upright stone slabs. Lionel Masters considers that these two sites show the development of the tumulus from an unchambered construction to a mound covering a megalithic tomb.

A similar development might also explain the origins of Irish megalithism. It is an attractive theory, but still awaits chronological detail. The two types of mound appear to have existed contemporaneously for at least several centuries of the fourth millennium. Mixed forms are known, but this does not necessarily indicate a developmental link; it may be that the two categories reflect two traditions of differing origins.

Sanctuaries for Eternity

The traditional mound with a wooden funerary construction is thought to have been the origin of a series of megalithic monuments – the mounds with tomb and court, sometimes classed among the oldest example of island megalithism. There are 350 in the Carlingford group in Northern Ireland, and 80 in Scotland (the Clyde group).

The courtyard may lie inside the tumulus, reached through an axial passage-way as at Creevykeel, or a lateral one, as at Ballyglass in Northern Ireland. From one to four tombs open into it, and there is often an antechamber as large as the chamber itself, which in turn may be either plain or long and compartmentalized. The courtyard is not always internal. Many monuments, particularly in Scotland, possess what is really a forecourt or square, within the space defined by the concave façade of the monument. Usually found at the broader end of the mound, this forecourt was edged with stone slabs driven into the ground and set up on each side of the entrance. The opposite end would sometimes have a second façade and a second tomb, as at Ballymarlagh or Cohaw, in Ireland. Large flat slabs were cantilevered out from the the side walls to provide covering. Cremation was a frequent rite in these monuments: the remains of five incinerated bodies were found in the principal tomb at Creevykeel. The number of dead whose ashes were placed in the sepulchre was never very large; the figure of thirty, suggested for the Andleystown monument, appears to be an exception.

It seems virtually impossible to identify with certainty the earliest megalith of western Europe. Several parallel patterns of evolution, from Poland to western France, demonstrate the same tendency to build monuments of increasingly megalithic style. The only connecting factors that can be claimed with certainty for megalithism are the funerary aspect, the collective or mass part of this activity, and the desire for expression in monument form. Several human cultures from Scandinavia to Portugal via western France adopted this striking method of indicating their identity. Episodic relationships, and above all similar ecological and social circumstances, may explain such closely similar responses, which do not however conceal substantial regional originality. The image of the wandering architect, Gordon Childe's 'missionary', has thus been dispelled. The builders of megalithic monuments seem to have been rather the product of settled cultures that sustained vigorous traditions of architecture, ritual, and ideology.

The role of the architect must have come into being at a very early stage, judging by the scale of the monuments and the coherence of their design. The architect, the individual who conceives a plan and brings it to fruition, was known in Madagascar as 'the stone master'. His function was an innovation of the fifth millennium, appearing at the time of the development of a settled society and the construction of dwellings, such as the Danubian houses which might have been up to 40 metres in length. In western Europe dwellings were certainly more modest, and it was above all the funerary monuments which demanded architectural expertise. The tombs of preceding Paleolithic

Monument with tomb and court at Creevykeel in County Sligo, Ireland. Inside a large rubble mound, the tomb consists of a chamber and antechamber (foreground) opening into an internal court. The tomb was originally covered in stone slabs.

(Photo © Commissioners of Public Works, Ireland)

epochs might be established, according to region, in caves (such as the Grimaldi near Menton), in shelters beneath rocks (Cro-Magnon in the Dordogne), or in simple pits (Verberie in the Oise). The arrangement was generally limited to a few stones round the corpse, sometimes sprinkled with ochre. Such forms of burial continued to be used throughout the Neolithic age, and some were even imitated: the rock-cut tomb, the hypogeum, seems very similar to a natural cave although its symmetrical layout is closer to those of above-ground structures. The tumulus may also have been simply an artificial hill, created in naturally flat regions, in which the funerary chamber was nothing more than a burial cave. Even regarding the tumulus as the simple technical and spiritual shelter of a tomb, the cavern within it was much like any natural hollow in the earth's surface in which human remains were laid.

Megalithic building methods brought two innovations, however. Firstly, they established a fixed settlement in bare landscapes and people began to abandon their old protection of caves and shelters. Secondly, the construction of artificial places was lasting proof of such settlement: the village, built of perishable materials, might last for a single generation, but the megalithic monument, with its immense stones and its relics, assured the spiritual survival of the group. The architect was, thus, entrusted with the new responsibility of building the sanctuary.

What particular circumstance provoked this 'birth' of megalithism in the regions of western Europe? The answer is uncertain. Indeed there was probably more than one. We have seen the extent to which a megalithic monument was the cultural synthesis of several original and often varying elements. The meeting together in this 'far west' of cultural elements of central Europe, the Mediterranean, and the Atlantic zone must have encouraged the growth of original formulae in response to new requirements: hence the multiple centres of innovation that have been discovered. The need for such innovation arose, according to Colin Renfrew, from the density of a population avid for new lands to colonize but restricted by the sea. The energy expressed in megalithic monuments to some extent legitimizes ownership of the soil in a world where competition was becoming fiercer. To such arguments may be added the intoxicating excitement of challenging the massive intractability of the rocks, an impulse of mystical fervour which is encountered in the greatest monuments at the peak of this civilization.

1 Barnenez
2 Guennoc Island
3 Carn Island
4 Carnac
5 Arzon
6 Téviec
7 Hoëdic
8 Les Fouillages, Guernsey
9 Vierville
10 Fontenay-le-Marmion, La Hogue and La Hoguette
11 Colombier
12 Bougon
13 Le Montiou, Sainte-Soline
14 Saint-Martin-la-Rivière
15 Malesherbes
16 Pontcharaud 2
17 Passy
18 Thouars
19 Saint-Sauveur
20 Avebury
21 Maiden Castle
22 Alfriston
23 Fussel's Lodge
24 Nutbane
25 Aldwincle
26 Kilham
27 Haddenham
28 Hambledon Hill
29 Lochill
30 Slewcairn
31 Clyde
32 Creevykeel
33 Ballyglass
34 Serra de Aboboreira
35 Poço de Gateira
36 Anta dos Jorginos
37 Carenque
38 Palmeira 4, Monchique
39 Granada
40 Los Millares
41 Serra d'Alto
42 San Andrea Priu
43 Wietrzychowice
44 Sarnavo
45 Gaj
46 Stralendorf
47 Barkvieren
48 Frauenmark
49 Mankmoos
50 Tustrup
51 Bygholm Norremark
52 Bildsø

▢ Hypogea

● Megalithic tomb

▬ Long or giant barrow

○ Paramegalithic tomb

⊙ Western great tombs

▮ Standing stone

△ 'Mortuary Houses'

THE EARLIEST BUILDINGS

Western Europe's earliest megalithic construction took place during the fifth millennium and the beginning of the fourth millennium B.C. The great tombs of western France were the most spectacular and the most 'megalithic' of the many different styles. The coastal distribution shows up clearly: these were the most dynamic regions, open to influences from both land and sea. Each marker indicates a focal centre of megalithism.

93

Monumental Daring

The imposing bulk of the tumulus, the use of more and more massive blocks, and their deft, even scientific deployment, together convey an impression of real architectural daring: the builders seem to have been seeking an indestructibility, both material and spiritual. This daring is apparent in these composite monuments, enlarged by new tombs, and in the use of ever heavier stones. In several regions the second half of the fourth millennium witnessed the peak of megalithism's achievements: the building of the famous monuments at Newgrange in Ireland, at Gavrinis and Bagneux in France, and at Antequera in Spain, for example. Subsequently boldness took a different form, that of great numbers – hundreds of tombs, temples and standing stones were erected.

From the earliest days of megalithism the coffers assembled in a single necropolis or in funerary chambers constructed under a single long tumulus might show considerable diversity, at least in certain progressive regions. Such diversity reveals a concern for assimilation of funerary or cultural forms. The problem thus arises: was there continuity of ritual, or competition? There are three possibilities: firstly, that either the burial chambers multiplied in number within a single tumulus or the chamber was enlarged and divided into cells or compartments; secondly, that structures were superimposed within a single composite monument; thirdly, that different constructions were placed next to each other to form a necropolis.

Architectural styles in various regions showed differing aspects of this continuity, indicative of the monuments' extended use – sometimes for as long as 2,000 years.

The Increasing Size of Graves

In their division of burial chambers and their development of the square-based modular plan, the great monuments of western France dating from the end of the fifth millennium onwards show evidence of advances in design. The Larcuste site at Colpo, in Morbihan, has two mounds surrounded by a kerb of dry stones. The first contains two small round chambers with short passage-ways; the slabs that form the walls support the covering blocks in an entirely megalithic style. The construction of two chambers within a single mound follows a fairly widespread pattern, seen for example in northern Germany, England (the Carlingford group), Ireland (Knowth), even Brittany which has some fifteen examples, and in central western France (Bougon E). The second Colpo monument, dated at 4250 B.C. from a sample taken from its passage, is an oval mound containing six slab-roofed chambers laid out on each side of a long passage; the division of the chamber, as in the tumulus III on Carn Island mentioned above, is thus systemized, to such an extent that the Colpo monument may be considered the prototype of the divided megalithic chamber (the transepted chamber

The interior of the chamber of the great Newgrange monument, in Ireland, clearly illustrates how the ambitious megalith-builders piled up their blocks to create a vast enclosed space. On one of the columns a triple spiral motif is the supreme sign of the site's spirituality.

(Photo © Commissioners of Public Works, Ireland)

tomb). Two magnificent chambers of this type can be found together in the Mousseaux tumulus at Pornic in Loire-Atlantique.

For burial places were growing, not only by increasing numbers of circular chambers around a single axis, but also by dividing up quadrangular chambers. One end of the quadrangular mound of Kerleven at La Forêt-Fouesnant, in South Finistère, contains two fairly broad rectangular chambers divided into compartments by large stone slabs. This construction device allowed the use of larger and heavier roofing stones, and also separation into individual burial compartments. The same system can be seen in the fourth millennium, in the very large megalithic chambers of Angoulême style at Bougon, and of the Anjou style at Bagneux. The design also developed from a more or less circular chamber to a rectangular layout, which was easier to modify. The Montiou tumulus at Sainte-Soline in Deux-Sèvres is a large quadrangular mound, now partly demolished. It contained four chambers with long passages, two of which have been excavated in recent years. One of these fourth-millennium tombs is hexagonal and the other quadrangular; their sides are made of rough-hewn stone slabs and dry-stone panels, and they are roofed with stone blocks. An ogival door-post of carved stone separates the first chamber from its passage.

Ian Kinnes' recent excavation of the complex Les Fouillages monument in Guernsey, has uncovered, lying inside a triangular mound surrounded by blocks, (the covering mass of earth has been removed), a series of burial sites used in succession, indicating the continuity of worship at the site.

(Photo © W. F. Tipping/British Museum)

Houses, Graves, and Large Stones

According to Ian Kinnes the square or short rectangle layout is the initial form of a fairly widespread three-way development, giving rise to dispersal, aggregated, or linear patterns. In a dispersal system the units have multiplied in number without inter-connection, forming a necropolis of small monuments; an aggregated system is made up of accumulating units with passages linking one to another; and a linear system consists of a row of units, as seen in the extremely long chambers of the third millennium.

Many of the giant mounds are the composite result of several building phases. The complex interior of the great monument of Bygholm Nor-remark in Jutland, excavated in 1979 by P. Roenne, combines the region's different types of funerary structure. It consists of a tumulus 60 metres long and its construction began in the middle of the fourth millennium, during the early development of agriculture, which first appeared around 4200 B.C. Within a fairly broad trapezoidal enclosure inside a palisade, Neolithic people built a wooden dwelling over a shaft tomb. Then they added two more houses, one at each end of the enclosure. One protected the grave of a thirteen-year-old youth buried in a wooden coffin, killed perhaps by the arrow found at chest-level. An amber bead hung round his waist. The other house was empty, and might have been connected with another trench at the centre of the enclosure containing the skeletons of four adults. An earth tumulus covered the whole after the collapse of the thatched wooden houses. The mound was later lengthened by 20 metres and its limits marked by a row of stones round the outside. A square megalithic chamber with a fairly short passage was constructed laterally within the mound.

This monument thus combines several types of construction: wood (the houses and palisades), earth (the trenches and slopes), and

RADIOGRAPHY OF A SITE

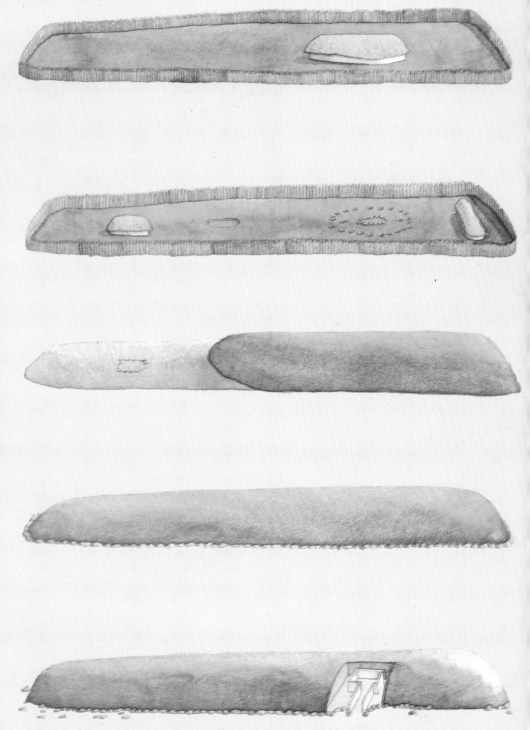

Detailed excavation of the fourth-millennium Bygholm Norremark site helped to explain how a limited space surrounding a burial site was sanctified, followed by its gradual transformation into a megalithic monument.

1. First, a long trapezoidal enclosure surrounded by a palisade (possibly reflecting the layout of contemporary long houses) contained a 'house of the dead' built over a grave hollowed out of the ground.
2. The house collapsed. Two more buildings were constructed at either end of the sacred space, with a fresh burial pit at the centre.
3. The new buildings and the palisade vanished in their turn, either naturally or deliberately. The memory of the sacred site was confirmed by covering it with an earthen mound covering more than half the original area.
4. The outline of this space were not forgotten because the completed mound exactly covered the area of the first enclosure. The palisade was replaced by a stone border.
5. Inside the resulting long mound, prehistoric people constructed a megalithic tomb on the same level as the first grave, with an access passage opening on the long side of the mound.

This illustrates the permanence of worship within varied forms of architectural expression, including megalithism.

megalithic (the lateral tomb and the external row of stones). These
three frequently complementary building styles are characteristic of
northern Europe. The monumental aspect is equally characteristic: its
aim is to seal one or more funerary and religious events in perpetuity,
and sustain their memory by means of an impressive earthwork. This
particular monument indicates that the large stones were used at a
late phase of construction. It can be seen as a fine example of the
meeting point between two distinctive traditions, those of the tumulus
with and without an internal megalithic tomb.

Other great mounds also have a long architectural history. Three
phases of monument construction have been discovered in the two
Mid Gleniron mounds in Scotland. In both, a circular tumulus containing a plain rectangular megalithic tomb preceded a trapezoidal
tumulus with a concave façade. The few radiocarbon dates so far
established in the British Isles are less remote than those observed on
the Continent: two samples from the chamber III at Ballymacdermot
in Ireland have provided dates of about 3500 and 3000 B.C. Traces of
the house discovered under the Ballyglass mound, which predate its
megalithic construction, have been dated at the late fourth millennium.

Many of the British monuments classified under the Severn-
Cotswold heading are similarly composite, a trapezoidal mound
having been added at the final phase of construction. The Ty Isaf
tumulus in Powys is characteristic of these: the original double-faced
oval mound containing a transepted megalithic gallery grave was
later covered by a trapezoidal mound surrounded by a kerb of dry

The plan of the Petit-Mont monument at Arzon reveals four successive phases of construction. An oval earth mound came first, in the centre; part of this was then covered by a large rectangular cairn, slightly to the left. A further section was added to the right, containing a megalithic chamber. The monument was then heightened and enlarged with two further megalithic tombs.

-------- First phase
           Second phase
           Third phase
           Fourth phase

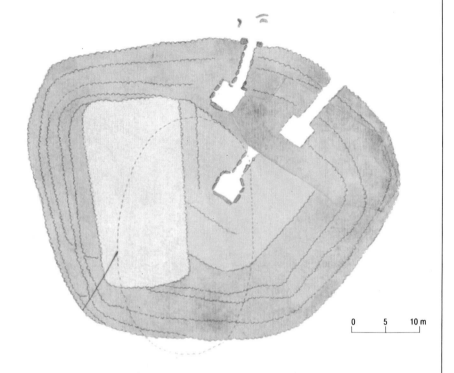

0   5   10 m

Centuries of Continual Adaptation

stones. The broad face to the north was cut away to form a forecourt, which appeared to lead to a passage-entrance at its deepest point – two lateral slabs set on edge evoked passage walls and framed a third stone that apparently blocked all access. At the centre of the smaller southern façade lay the opening to a rectangular chamber with a passage which was virtually part of the chamber itself. Two matching dry-stone passages opened out on the two long sides, and led into two long rectangular megalithic chambers. The two recently excavated long barrows with megalithic chambers at Gwernvale and Peny-wyrlod, in the west of England, show that some of these complex monuments were built in a single phase of construction – just as at Barnenez in France.

The triangular mound at Les Fouillages in Guernsey is another fine example of a composite monument: 20 metres long and 10 wide, it is bounded by stone blocks. Behind the façade lie on the west side a coffer covered with three stones, then a double megalithic chamber without covering, related to an anthropomorphic stele, then a cist enclosed within a pile of stones, and finally a circular paved area 1.60 metres in diameter. Seven vessels were placed in the paved circle and the chamber; in shape and decoration, they belong to the large group of ribbon-decorated pottery which appeared in Guernsey towards the end of the fifth millennium, on the dwelling sites of Le Pinacle and Mont Orgueil. They appear contemporaneous with the earliest peasants of the Channel Islands, and are of the same type of pottery as the shards found around and beneath the great monument at La Hoguette in Calvados, Normandy.

The Petit Mont megalithic group at Arzon is another remarkable example of the composite monument. The excavator Joël Lecornec began work here in 1979 by continuing earlier but limited excavations; eight years later this trapezoidal mound, 55 metres along its large side, had been fully surveyed. Several phases of construction were noted. According to current knowledge, the oldest monument was an elliptical central mound, over 30 metres long, now badly eroded. Pieces of charcoal from this structure, a kind of modified platform, have been dated at 4685 and 4405 B.C., but its exact nature remains obscure. The earliest stone tumulus (cairn), bounded by a roughly trapezoidal kerb 28 metres long, covered the north-east section of the original mound: no burial chamber has been found there, but a collapse observed within the south-west section may perhaps indicate the presence of a hollow, wooden structure now fallen in and vanished. The body of the barrow then appears to have been extended towards the south-east where a pentagonal megalithic chamber and its passage were uncovered from 1984 onwards. This tomb was notable for the inclusion of a large number of re-used decorated blocks: the head-stone was the base of a large anthropomorphic stele erected here, of which the fallen upper part formed the floor of the chamber. The pentagonal form of this large fragment dictated the shape of the sepulchre. The stele originally stood 5.60 metres high, and it is not known whether it had been erected in conjunction with the earliest mound or with the first cairn. Two further enormous segments of an anthropomorphic stele with shoulder-piece covered a section of the passage. Like some of the wall slabs, they displayed several motifs of megalithic art on either a hidden or an exposed surface – further proof of their re-use: the axe, with or without a handle, the cross, the long-haired idol, and a set of parallel curves that recall the Gavrinis decoration, though in shallower relief. Shards recovered show affinity with certain features of Morbihan, and possibly with Cerny in the Paris basin. This tomb has been dated at between 3930 and 3170 B.C.

There are thus three monuments. Many more or less concentric kerbs were built later to surround and seal existing structures. Two chambers with passage-ways were constructed to the east of the added mass of rough stone. One was destroyed during construction of a German bunker in the the Second World War, and only the recently recognized extreme end of the passage remains. The other has been known since the nineteenth century, and was restored by Zacharie Le Rouzic between 1905 and 1936. It too suffered damage during the war: the flat stone slab covering the chamber has disappeared, likewise four columns which bore an engraving of feet, in false relief. Excavating the façade of the monument in the final phase, Joël Lecornec discovered the remains of a carved stone door frame like those found in some tombs of western France (Angoulême style sepulchres). There too the embankments seem to indicate that the passage entrances were sealed up in prehistoric times, probably soon after the chambers were constructed and used.

Some vaulted dry-stone circular chambers are of a later date than the polygonal megalithic chambers, as proved by two Portuguese monuments, Herdade da Farisoa and La Comenda at Reguengos de Monsaraz not far from Lisbon. At its centre the round Farisoa tumulus contains a polygonal chamber 3 metres across, classicly lined by seven large flat stones; a fairly short megalithic passage leads into a dry-stone section into which another passage opens, giving access to an oval

The vitality of the megalith phenomenon is sometimes apparent in the existence of several large monuments within a limited area. At Loughcrew, County Meath, Ireland, a stone circle (foreground) lies next to a mound (background).

(Photo © P. Caponigro)

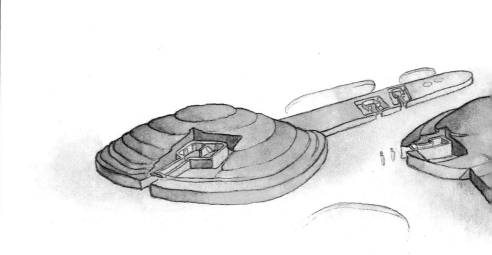

slab-lined chamber which is corbel-roofed. The grave-goods of the first, older, chamber, correspond closely to the advanced phase of megalithic long-corridor tombs: trapezoidal microliths, concave-based arrow-heads, flint blades, polished stone axes, small plaques of engraved schist, and shards of round-based vessels. The later tomb contained no microliths, but the other elements were all present. Among the vessels, the more varied and decorated cup shapes and those carrying a few lines incised parallel to the edges confirm the date obtained by thermoluminescence of 2675 B.C.

The other monument, La Comenda, is a circular tumulus also containing two chambers. The older is placed centrally; polygonal and with megalithic covering, it has a short low passage. A second chamber to the south, which is oval, is walled with close-linked slabs and covered by corbelling. The passage of this chamber, which is also short, runs beside that of the first tomb.

In another composite monument in the Lisbon region, Praïa das Maças, a corbelled tomb seals an artificial cave. A small domed circular chamber was cut into the rock, with a passage-way and two small lateral cells; the grave-goods included triangular arrow-heads and large flint blades, plaques of carved schist, bone pins, both plain and carved, necklace beads, and some undecorated vessels. Two samples from this first tomb have been dated at about 2800 B.C. Later, another tomb was constructed in the extension of the first, after the passage had been seated by a large stone. The circular base of this second chamber was carved out of the rock, and its dry-stone walls lean

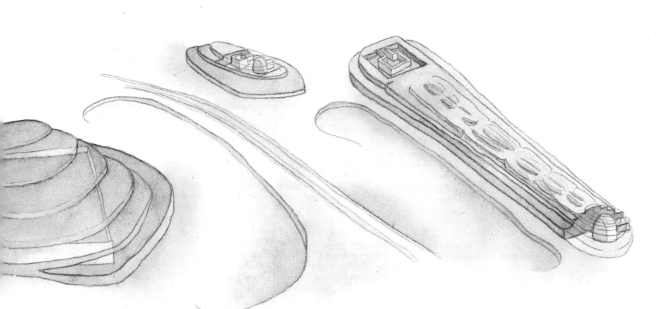

together to form a corbelled roof supported in the centre by a post, of which the foundation hole has been discovered. The funerary offerings were flint arrow-heads and undecorated vessels; a considerable quantity of jumbled Chalcolithic material included some copper items – pins and a tanged dagger. Carbon 14 analysis of two samples produced a date close to 2000 B.C. These dates have provoked much debate: do they relate to the latest active use of the sepulchres, or should they be associated with their construction? In any case, this is a fresh example of the perpetuity of a burial place, since the renovation-phase respected the tomb's earlier status.

Necropolis Structure

The Petit Mont mound at Arzon provided an example of a large anthropomorphic stele, erected and later broken and re-used for the construction of a megalithic chamber. The same region of Morbihan offers many other standing stones of considerable size, sometimes decorated, which were broken and re-used in megalithic tombs at the end of the fourth millennium. They were used in particular to cover passages and chambers; the best known is the covering stone at Gavrinis which, together with what are now the slabs of the Table des Marchands and of Er-Vinglé at Locmariaquer, formed an enormous standing stone 14 metres high.

The connection between the open construction of standing stones and a closed construction of megalithic tomb barrows is as well recognized in the British Isles as in Brittany. At several British sites one construction is superimposed on another, raising the question: was

The coastal Scania region of southern Sweden is rich in megalithic monuments. This is the stone framework of grave 5 at Tagarp, in the Ö. Tommarp region, as it was when excavated.

(Photo © Märta Strömberg)

there continuity of the same ideology, or competition between two ideologies?

The Bryn Celli Ddu monument on the North Wales island of Anglesey displays this type of superimposition. At an early stage a ditch 30 metres in diameter was dug out with, possibly, a break on the eastern side. A circle of fourteen standing stones was set up round the inner edge of the ditch. At the centre of the ring a small pit contained a tiny human bone, from the inner ear, and showed traces of fire. Carbonized bones were found at the foot of some stones – those of a girl aged between eight and ten, and of another of fifteen. Later, the standing stones were pulled down: eight were broken, five were removed, and one was burned. The pit itself was stopped up by a decorated block, and a megalithic tomb was built on the site with a polygonal chamber approached through a corridor. A mound of the same diameter as the original ditch, ringed by stone slabs standing on edge, covered everything during the third millennium. What was the implication of these changes?

The long duration of the megalithic tradition is also apparent where separate monuments are built next to each other, forming a necropolis. At Téviec, for instance, the chambers were grouped together within a restricted area from the very beginning. The great Barnenez monument was not originally isolated: another mound, parallel to the first and apparently similar to it, was destroyed before it could be excavated. It has already been mentioned that at the highest

point of the island of Guennoc there are three separate barrows, covering a dozen passage tombs. Three neighbouring mounds appear to
have been built successively at Colpo, in Morbihan, developing from
the circular to the transepted gallery. Elsewhere, long barrows too
were grouped together to form a necropolis, as with the eight Sarnovo
monuments in Poland. In 1829 the eastern and southern area of the
small north German island of Rügen still had 229 megalithic monuments within a strip of land some 40 kilometres long (most have now
been destroyed); the island was certainly a vast necropolis. In Ireland
the more substantial central tumulus might be surrounded by small
satellite mounds, as at the two necropolises of Loughcrew in County
Meath. The large Knocknarea tumulus at the top of a hill in County
Sligo is surrounded by four small mounds, two to the north and two to
the south, and at Carrowmore in the same county a large cairn dominates fifty-five small tumuli. The Knowth necropolis near the Newgrange complex in County Meath was excavated over a period of
more than ten years. Lying on the high banks of the river Boyne, it
consists of an enormous central tumulus containing two passage tombs
of transept design. It is rich in carved and decorated stones, both on
the surround of the great mound and inside the funerary chambers.
The central mound covers a small tumulus, which is thus of earlier
date; the others were built after the construction of the central monument, and the whole group dates from the end of the fourth millennium.

This large tumulus at the centre of the Newgrange complex in Ireland was restored at the end of the 1970s, following excavations by Michael J. O'Kelly. The large external retaining wall consists of white quartz stones interspersed at regular intervals with dark granite pebbles. At the base there are large decorated blocks, and imposing stones arranged in front of the monument.

(Photo © Commissioners of Public Works, Ireland)

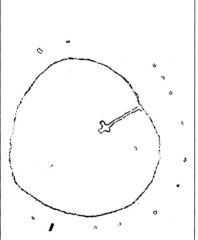

The heart-shaped Newgrange mound is 85 metres across, and bordered with blocks and surrounded by a circle of standing stones. The passage opening on the south-east façade leads to the burial chamber.

Central western France undoubtedly had many necropolises, but many have been destroyed and very few properly explored. At Vervant-la Boixe in Charente, ten round barrows covered circular or rectangular chambers, and at Taizé in Deux-Sèvres each of a dozen round barrows contain a circular or quadrangular chamber at its centre. Saint-Martin-la-Rivière-Maupas, in Vienne, has another group of fifteen mounds. The best known necropolis is Bougon, in the Deux-Sèvres, where over a period of fourteen years five mounds were surveyed, covering eight collective tombs and some individual burials. The monuments were built between the second half of the fifth millennium and the end of the fourth, and were in use until the end of the third. This site is a fine example of the respect held for ancient barrows and the continuity of the tradition throughout the whole Neolithic period.

There are many third millennium mounds with megalithic chambers on the Causses, and some appear to have been grouped together deliberately, sometimes close to a larger or more carefully finished monument – as, for example, at the five Carennac-Noutari mounds and those at Gralou-Pech-Laglaire in the Lot. Slightly further south, in the Aude, the most fully surveyed necropolis is La Clape at Laroque-de-Fa, with its eight megalithic tombs.

Some of the necropolises of southern Iberia are spectacular, and also date from the third millennium. Those of La Salvina, Los Castellones, and La Gabiarra on the rio de Gor consist of several dozen barrows, while there are twelve monuments grouped together at Cruz del rio Cogollero near Fonelas. At Laborcillas, the necropolises of Los Eriales (with sixteen mounds) and El Espartal (with seventeen), are only a little over one kilometre apart, while at Purenque Larraez at Cadiz there are no fewer than fifteen monuments, and the Mairena del Alcor and the Gandul sets make up a single vast group. Finally, at Los Millares at least seventy-five tombs are related to a third-millennium fortified dwelling, as recent excavations have confirmed.

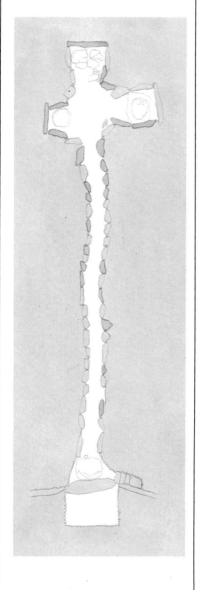

A long passage, lined with stone slabs, leads more than 20 metres into the great Newgrange tumulus to a chamber opening into three small cells. The orientation of the passage allows the sun's rays to shine through to the back of the chamber on the day of the summer solstice. A decorated slab stands in front of the passage entrance.

Hypogea were often grouped together to form a necropolis during the same period, as in Sardinia, in Portugal – at Palmella – and in the Marne, where the Razet group at Coizard consists of thirty-seven tombs hollowed out round a central ancient sepulchre.

As with the birth of megalithism, the enlargement of mounds and necropolises indicates both a single overall tendency and varying local expressions within this tendency. This development appeared at a very early stage, as shown by the two phases of construction of the Barnenez monument. As a general rule, the earlier monument was respected: later builders added another mound beside the first tumulus, or superimposed another on it, without destroying the chambers. In some cases the architectural style remains the same from one phase to another, while in others it alters. Such transformation seems to suggest a reaffirmation of the cult rather than a ritual competition.

In Morbihan there are examples of an alternative practice: the re-use of monoliths from monuments pulled down and broken up. Some walling stones at Gavrinis and Arzon are decorated on their hidden surfaces, a feature that suggests that they were re-used. This hypothesis is supported by other undoubted examples of re-use; large sections of anthropomorphic steles (at Arzon) and decorated standing stones (at Gavrinis, the Table des Marchands, Er-Vinglé, and Mané Rutual) have been recycled as covering stones. The destruction of the earlier monument might suggest rivalry between cults, all the more probable since this has been observed more than once. The most significant point, however, is that when the blocks were integrated into a new monument, they acquired a fresh use; this too would indicate a strengthening of the cult following renewed architectural expression.

Stonehenge is clearly the finest example of this continuity of a cult that grew stronger with the monument's growing complexity and impressiveness. The first construction phase dates from the Neolithic period, towards the middle of the third milllenium: a circular ditch 100 metres in diameter was enclosed by a bank 2 metres high. Three stones stand to the north east, including the famous Heel Stone, which for an observer standing at the centre of the circle is the sighting point for the rising sun at the summer solstice. The purpose of this stone seems to have remained unchanged throughout the whole active period of this ritual site. Later a double ring of blue stones was set up within the boundary; during a third phase of construction this double circle was destroyed and replaced by a large circle of sandstone blocks, linked across their tops by lintels, the 'stone-henges' (suspended stones). Within this new structure were built the five trilithons of the 'horseshoe', each consisting of two stone pillars supporting a lintel. The axis of the horseshoe is aligned so that the midsummer sunrise can be seen along it. In the final phase in the middle of the second millen-

107

nium, rows of blue stones were added, matching the layout of the sandstone blocks.

There was a genuine golden age of megalithism, marked by the use of the largest and heaviest stone blocks, and by the greatest constructions. These massive monuments appeared at various places in western Europe towards the middle of the fourth millennium, at a time when neolithization seemed complete, and it had assimilated all its new ideas. Stonehenge was one of the brilliant exceptions constructed after the beginning of the following millennium.

In northern Europe the tradition of a mound complete with a megalithic tomb continued at least throughout the fourth millennium. The ancient rectangular coffers were lengthened, resulting in passageless megalithic chambers more than 2 metres long.

The portal megalithic chamber consists of two uprights supporting an enormous covering block, with a third column, usually shorter, as the head-stone. These 'dolmens', which are typical of north-west Ireland, are only the remains of much larger monuments. This is the Groleck 'dolmen'.

(Photo © Commissioners of Public Works, Ireland)

The impressive group of barrows at Visbeck, fifty kilometres south-west of Bremen, offers some fine examples. The tumulus known as the Bridegroom (der Braütigam) is 108 metres long and 10 metres wide; orientated east-west, it is surrounded by blocks reaching 2.40 metres high to the east and 1.40 metres to the west, with a chamber at its centre covered by five large blocks. Beside it lies another mound, the Bride (die Braut); 80 metres long and 7 metres wide, it too is surrounded by an alignment of large blocks. Within its western section is a megalithic chamber, without any passage, measuring 6 metres by 1.60 metres. This type of construction was widespread, and has been recorded as far away as Bronneger in the Netherlands. Some monuments also show evidence of a prototype corridor. Megalithic chamber tombs might also be complemented by two small exterior slabs. The two small quadrangular tombs in the Noblin barrow on the island of Rügen display this rudimentary corridor which, opening to the outside world through a break in the row of blocks, is thus definitely a passage giving access to the chamber. The idea of constructing an entrance to the megalithic chamber then spread rapidly throughout northern Europe.

The polygonal chambers at Trollasten in southern Sweden and at Mols in Denmark are thus preceded by a very short passage. These are both original monuments, their circular rather than trapezoidal mounds reminiscent of certain tumuli in western France or in Great Britain. Could this resemblance indicate a connection? For some archeologists, Breton or British influence would explain the development of the access corridor in the Nordic megalithic chambers at this fairly late period of the fourth millennium.

Silbury Hill, in Wiltshire, lies near the West Kennet long barrow, and must date from the same period; it is the highest known artificial Neolithic hill. It remains an enigma, for it appears to lack any of the usual signs of burial use.

(Photo © J. Foley)

Adaptation to Strengthen Worship

Another facet of evolution was that these same chambers tended to become larger and larger – up to 8.50 metres long and 1.50 metres wide. It was probably for technical reasons of the covering that the circular plan was progressively abandoned, with the development of a rectangular layout either in line with the corridor or at right angles to it. The Mecklenburg monuments in northern Germany display fine large oblong chambers built on the same axis as the fairly short passage-way; their mounds may be circular (as at Schwasdorf, near Teterow) or trapezoidal (Poggendorfer Forst, near Grimmen, and Kruckow, near Demmin, in both of which the barrows are surrounded by blocks and the short corridor has its exit on one of the long sides).

Large chambers are found throughout western Europe, from Sweden to the Netherlands, always quadrangular but with a lateral passage. There are two magnificent monuments at Carlshögen and Ramshög in the Hagestad area of Sweden, while Emmenschimmeres in the Netherlands has a long barrow edged with blocks and containing two chambers. Some of the passages are short, while some are up to 6 metres long, and the chambers vary considerably too. This is the period, around 3000 B.C., when Nordic megalithism demonstrated its greatest dynamism. Strenstrup in Denmark has two interconnected chambers, and Alsbersg three that are juxtaposed. The builders took great care over architectural details: they wedged the megaliths carefully, filled the gaps between blocks with dry stones, placed a threshold stone at the entrance to the chamber, and sometimes developed a façade round the passage entrance; above all, they paid great attention to interior layout, laying paving stones and dividing chambers into compartments with small stones placed on edge. These little niches, about a metre across, contained selected human bones, and must have had fairly precise reliquary functions. In this way the interior space of the chambers became regulated. This tendency developed in the Nordic world at the end of the fourth millennium as soon as the interior measurements grew larger, and remained a constant concern for users of the tombs throughout the third millennium.

A mound, a passage, a tomb: there are more than 300 monuments of this type in Ireland, where they represent the peak of megalithism, and include the famous monuments of Newgrange, Knowth, Carrowkeel, Fourknocks, amd Loughcrew. Some were built on the western coasts of Britain and, particularly, in the isle of Anglesey, where the decorated monument of Barclodiad-y-Gavres is well known. Some of the barrows are immense – that at Knowth is 90 metres across, and that at Newgrange is nearly as large – and beneath each lies a chamber made up of several cells, one axial and two or four lateral, approached through a long passage – over 20 metres long at Newgrange, over 30 metres at Knowth. In layout these burial places resemble the transept tombs at the mouth of the Loire. But the Irish monuments are clearly characterized by their corbelled covering, the abundance of decorated blocks that surround them, and the practice of cremation.

The notion of a largely local process of evolution must therefore be accepted; it explains the original features of this group. The polygonal burial chamber at Bryn Celli Ddu, in Anglesey, is often quoted

'The Bridegroom' tumulus in the Visbeck region of northern Germany has been levelled. The only remains are the blocks that bordered the long rectangular mound and the central stones that covered the burial chamber.

(Photo © T. Schneiders/Artephot)

as proof of Armorican influence, but it offers no pertinent conclusions for Ireland itself; indeed the local birth of the transept design as a development from rectangular chambers may be apparent in the Knowth necropolis. George Eogan's excavations have revealed the antiquity of small circular barrows, in which the chamber may be rectangular or transepted. Could the circular chambers, resembling certain chambers inside long barrows with forecourts, be the prototypes for rectangular designs? The great central cairn of the Knowth necropolis reveals both types, apparently dating from the same period. Could they belong to two different but contemporaneous communities? Did one influence the other? Radiocarbon dating for the transept tomb at Newgrange indicates a phase of construction at the end of the fourth millennium, and two Knowth dates tend to confirm an approximately similar age; these monuments would then be contemporary with certain court cairns (tombs with an unroofed semicircular forecourt). The Behy monument in Northern Ireland, with its deeply concave façade, resembles these mounds: but the design of its megalithic chamber is not rectangular but transepted. There is here a probable example a link between court cairns and gallery graves.

One of the most impressive megalithic monuments in the whole of the British Isles is West Kennet, in Wiltshire. Enormous blocks of stone form the side walls of the passage to the burial chamber and the bases of the roof corbelling.

(Photo © R. Estall)

The entrance to the megalithic grave at Wayland's Smithy in England was sealed. Enormous slabs emphasize the breadth of the façade, which marks the barrier between the worlds of the living and the dead.

(Photo © Fay Godwin's Photo Files)

At its peak, Irish megalithism would therefore also have included various types of tomb, and certain forms must have developed earlier than has been thought. Two tombs in the Carrowmore necropolis in north-west Ireland pose the same problem in relation to an earlier period. The first lies inside a small circular mound; simple and rectangular, it is approached through a short passage which is almost part of the chamber itself. It dates back to 4100 B.C. The second has a similar circular mound but the chamber is transepted and has virtually no corridor; dating here indicates 3900 B.C. The two forms of megalithic chamber therefore appear to have been from the same period; we know of no explanation for the difference between them. Analogous to transepted chambers, composite chambers with subsidiary cells exist in the northern British Isles, in Scotland and in Orkney, where Colin Renfrew has surveyed the two famous monuments at Quanterness and at Maes Howe. These vaulted dry-stone constructions, still intact, have an air of perfection due no doubt to the systematic use of small stone slabs. The circular Quanterness mound is about 30 metres in diameter, and the mass of stones is contained within three or four concentric kerbs. A long passage gives access to a principal rectangular chamber, out of which lead six small corridors to rectangular lateral cells. The remains of 157 bodies were discovered here, as

The particularly imposing façade of the West Kennet long barrow. A row of immense stones stands in front of the passage entrance, which was once hidden. The symbolic role of the mound's façade in separating the worlds of the dead and the living is particularly clear here.

(Photo © M. Sharp)

well as the bones of animals consumed. Dating suggests that the tomb was built in the second half of the fourth millennium, and indicates a long period of use – between 3400 and 2400 B.C. The Maes Howe monument, is more recent, however, and dates from around 2800 B.C. The tomb also includes a passage 24 metres long, leading into a square burial chamber giving access to three low and similarly square cells. These two barrows form part of a whole complex of other barrows, two large circles of standing stones, Stenness and Brogar, and the village of Skara Brae, which is also built entirely of small stone slabs.

There are other tombs within round barrows in the Orkneys – at Vinquoy Hill and Wideford Hill, for example – with layouts very similar to those of Quanterness and Maes Howe. These monuments and those of the Boyne valley date from the same period; they share the principle of a funerary chamber with lateral cells and corridor. In their detail, however, there are as many differences between the Orkney and the Boyne tombs as between the latter and those at the mouth of the Loire.

The problem of their origin also arises for another type of mega-lithic chamber tomb: the portal dolmen, so called because its covering stone is held up by two side-wall stones. This type is found in north-west Ireland, where 165 have been found, and also in Anglesey, Wales and Cornwall. This type of chamber is quite small; it is made of two fairly tall lateral columns and a lower head-stone supporting a large leaning stone; the granite slab topping the tomb at Brownshill, in Ireland, weighs 100 tonnes. Where today the monumental structure of these megalithic chambers dominates an eroded mound their appear-ance is spectacular, and some of them are very well known. That of Pentre Ifan, near Clydach in Wales, has columns 2.50 metres high supporting a slab 5 metres long; the chamber lies at the end of a 40 metre mound behind a concave façade that recalls the court cairns of Ireland and Scotland.

There are similarities between the two types of monument, which have stimulated attempts to explain the evolution of portal dolmens (a chamber approached through two portal slabs forming a porch) from the chamber tombs within long mounds with forecourt. If there are obvious links between the two types, it is once again impossible to indicate which came first. The barrows of these portal tombs may be round or long. The example of Dyffryn Ardudwy in Wales indicates the earlier date of one of the two forms, since here a long barrow with a concave façade overlays a circular mound. Both have a portal chamber.

Recent investigations of the Gavrinis mound, which now lies isolated on a small island in the Gulf of Morbihan, revealed a broad dry-stone façade, in front of which quantities of offerings had been laid. Some modifications, in the form of post-holes, have been recorded; they confirm the concentration of activity and continuous use of the area beside the mound, which formed a kind of forecourt.

(Photo © Ed. Jos.)

Layouts of Increasing Complexity

The 180 monuments grouped together under the Severn–Cotswold classification in southern England are very varied. Their sole common characteristic is that they take the form of a long barrow covering a megalithic tomb (sometimes several), which may lie axially or laterally. They are of either a simple rectangular or transepted shape. Some writers see in these monuments the megalithic continuation of the long barrows without megalithic tombs, which they hold to be older. The differences between the two types would depend on their particular functions.

One of the finest megalithic monuments in the south of England is at West Kennet, in Wiltshire. It was built not far from the circular groups of Avebury and Windmill Hill, and no doubt at about the same time. The mound, surrounded by blocks, is 101 metres long. Behind the highest point (2.50 metres), on the east side, lies the megalithic tomb to which access is gained from a small forecourt. The chamber itself, preceded by a short passage, consists of an axial cell and four lateral cells forming a double transept, the whole covered by flat stones forming a vault. The bones of at least forty-six people have been discovered inside the tomb, which had been sealed up after a period of use: a large slab (3.70 metres high) was set up just in front of the entrance passage, while further blocking slabs filled out the curved forecourt, producing an uninterrupted façade.

In France, the fourth and third millennia saw a great increase in the number of modest monuments with a single chamber, corresponding to partitioning of places of burial, although this did not stop burial megalithism reaching its peak during the fourth millennium. In the third millennium the chambers lengthened enormously, although in some regions they remained small but multiplied in number. Many more skeletons were found inside.

In monuments with a single tomb the circular chamber, so com-

The Gavrinis mound contains a central chamber with passage access. Most of the side stones are decorated in a florid style that is impressive in its vigour and originality. Substantial research has gone into the reading and understanding of these motifs.

(Photo © M. Sharp)

monplace earlier, became increasingly rare and finally disappeared altogether towards the middle of the fourth millennium. The Cous monument at Bazoges-en-Pareds in Vendée contains a chamber 4.50 metres across. Such width considerably weakened the corbelled vault, however, and this type of roofing was gradually abandoned and replaced by increasingly large stone slabs for the broader chambers. The two dates established for this tomb fall close to 3450 B.C., and must reflect the more recent use of an earlier construction. There are also circular chambers beneath round barrows in the necropolis in the forest of La Boixe in Charente; here the sepulchres are no longer grouped together beneath a single tumulus, but inside several mounds at the heart of the burial site. At Bougon, we can see the same care to

117

Covering 85 square metres, the 'great' Bagneux dolmen near Saumur is the largest-known megalithic chamber in France. It was originally buried beneath an enormous mound, of which traces still remained in the nineteenth century.

(Photo © Dagli-Orti)

group the monuments together while at the same time varying their design. At both Bougon and La Boixe, barrows with a single rectangular chamber and those with a circular chamber were built in close proximity to each other. The rectangular design of chambers, linked to the use of megalithic stone slabs, began to appear from the end of the fifth millennium onwards, the date obtained for one of the rectangular tombs of the Chenon necropolis in Charente. At one tumulus at Benon, in Charente-Maritime, the sequence of two quadrangular passage-chambers is visible: the older lies at the centre of a circular mound with double concentric facings; the second was built later, to the east of the first, and a trapeze-shaped barrow covered the whole. In both cases the passage was little more than 3 metres long. As the passage-way increased in length, it tended to become more than a simple means of access and developed into a full-scale burial site, occasionally decorated. The finest example of a square megalithic chamber with a long passage can be seen at Gavrinis: the chamber is 2.60 metres square, while the south-east-facing passage is 14 metres long. Of the twenty-nine slabs which line the tomb, twenty-three are fully decorated, while the block covering the chamber is itself a fragment of an enormous stele decorated in the same manner as the broken Grand Menhir at Locmariaquer. The mound was excavated between 1979 and 1984 by Charles-Tanguy Le Roux; it still possessed, beneath the mass of stone rubble that sealed it, a large façade wall which is now exposed.

Originally modest in size, some of the quadrangular chambers were enlarged in the early fourth millennium to impressive dimensions. The tumulus A at Bougon is 42 metres in diameter. It is made of rubble retained by concentric facings and contains a 10-metre passage leading to a large rectangular chamber, 7.80 metres long, 5 metres wide, and 2.25 metres high; a central column divides the chamber into two compartments, and provides further support for the enormous 90-tonne monolith that covers the whole space. Moreover, the slab-columns of the sides, which alternate with dry-stone panels, have been rough-hewn and their edges straightened; they are set obliquely like buttresses, to resist the thrust of the covering stone. The end of the monument F in the same necropolis was flanked by a semicircular tumulus with a similar tomb, slightly smaller. This type of tomb, best known in the Angoulême region, is known as 'Angoumoisin' ('Angoulême style'). 'Angevin' tombs are found in the Anjou regions of Angers and Saumur; here the long rectangular chamber, entirely megalithic in construction, has a short portico-passage on the same axis. France's largest megalithic chamber tomb is of this style: the Grand Dolmen at Bagneux, near Saumur, lies in a café courtyard. This chamber is 17.30 metres long by 4.25–5.40 metres wide, but it was partially excavated in 1775, and is now no more than a noble remnant. The monument to which it belonged looked like a structured tumulus, and traces were still visible in 1847. Equally imposing is the famous megalithic chamber of La Roche aux Fées at Essé, south-east of Rennes. The La Bajoulière monument at Saint-Rémy-la-

The Roche aux Fées at Essé, near Rennes, is one of the most beautiful and impressive megalithic burial chambers in western France. The chamber itself is rectangular and very long; it is approached via a short, low passage or portico, visible to the left of the photograph. These stones were originally covered by the mass of the tumulus.

(Photo © Dagli-Orti)

Varenne in Maine-et-Loire consists of a trapezoidal tumulus within a dry-stoned kerb, with a fine megalithic chamber 7 metres square, covered by a single slab. These enormous chambers were often divided up. Elsewhere, such Angevin-style monuments lie isolated on high ground. At Bougon, a tomb of this type at Les Sept Chemins is one kilometre from the necropolis.

Certain designs lie between the Angoumoisin and Angevin types; for example, the Pierre Levée monument at Nieul-sur-l'Autize in Vendée, inside its trapezoidal tumulus, combines the rectangular Angoulême design with the frequent compartmentalization of the Anjou dolmens.

In western France there are a great many standing stones which are generally known as menhirs. They may constitute genuine 'open' constructions which in some cases contrast with the closed construction of tombs and in others complements it. The most famous groups are in Brittany, but they also exist in many other areas. Areas of concentration of these monuments do not always coincide with areas rich in megalithic tombs: although there may have been links between

The broken Great Menhir at Locmariaquer, beside the Gulf of Morbihan, is perhaps the most impressive of prehistoric monoliths. It weighs 350 tonnes and is 20.30 metres long. Now broken into four pieces, it appears to have been pulled down in Neolithic times for religious reasons. It is decorated with a large axe and must have been much admired, whatever its purpose – perhaps a sighting point, or a commemorative feature.

(Photo © R. Estall)

the two categories of construction, they were clearly different in their nature. It is of course difficult to be sure whether the isolated standing stones of today stood equally solitary in Neolithic times or whether they constituted part of a complex group. The greatest monolith ever set up is the broken Grand Menhir at Locmariaquer, which stood 20 metres high before it fell. The tallest stone still upright today is the 10-metre Kerloas stone at Plouarzel in Finistère. All these stones were perfectly integrated into their surroundings, positioned either high up on a hillside or near water in a valley, and always in an open space and visible from far away.

Several standing stones may constitute an alignment, which may be a single straight line of stones continuing for some dozens of metres. Several alignments may make up complex groups, of which the three best known are at Carnac in Morbihan. There are others which have gradually been destroyed: the group in the Penmarch area of Finistère was once substantial, as was the Langon group in Ille-et-Vilaine, of which only thirty-four stones remain. Despite continual weathering, the great Ménec alignment at Carnac still consists of eleven more or less parallel rows and extends over a kilometre in length – 1,165 metres, to be precise. It links two large oval areas of standing stones. The progressively increasing height of the stones combines with the upward-sloping terrain to give this open-air monument an exceptionally impressive effect in this broad coastal landscape.

The Kerlescan alignment, also at Carnac, preserves traces of thirteen rows converging towards a large quadrangular area of stones grouped tightly together. Carnac has a similar area, called Manio, and there is one at Erdeven, known as Crucuno. Within the quadrangular grouping of the Jardin aux Moines at Néant-sur-Yvel in the Brocéliande Forest in Morbihan, excavated in 1983 by Jacques

121

The Cojoux standing stones at Saint-Just in Ille-et-Vilaine form an integral part of a ceremonial and funerary complex. The site's various phases of modification have been identified as a result of recent excavations.

(Photo © C.-T. Le Roux)

Briard, there are late Neolithic internal structures. Could this have been a funerary monument without a chamber? Its standing stones would seem to indicate an unusual type of sacred enclosure, still little understood. Another style can be seen on the little island of Er-Lannic, in the Gulf of Morbihan, where two semicircular groups are juxtaposed.

When Charles-Tanguy Le Roux excavated the Cojou alignment at Saint-Just in Ille-et-Vilaine, he identified several successive phases of construction in this strange monument, which dates from the same period as megalithic tombs. After the first use of the site, dated from the remains of hearths to the middle of the fifth millennium, quartz blocks were set in place; then large schist slabs were added, and probably wooden posts as well. A low mound was constructed next, with a coffer dating from the middle of the third millennium, and finally a circular tomb surmounted by a small earth mound, containing two cists laid against a horizontal stone from one of the alignments. Such a complex is difficult to survey, but the Saint-Just example demonstrates that it represents a genuine building style with successive relatively elaborate constructions. Much still undoubtedly remains to be learnt from such excavations.

Among Brittany's standing stones, many are undressed blocks simply placed on end, such as most of the Carnac stones: others have had their lines rough-hewn, or were carefully shaped, such as the stones at western Léon, in Finistère. Decorated stones, such as those at Locmariaquer, are rarer. The finest example is the La Tremblais stone at Saint-Samson-sur-Rance in the Côtes-du-Nord, with its design of axes with handles, goddesses, and cattle; it must have been set up before 3000 B.C. There is also the Kermarquer standing stone at Moustoirac, in the Morbihan, with crosses sculpted in relief.

Standing stones are not confined to Brittany, however; there are hundreds in regions such as the Gâtinais area of the Paris basin, and Vendée. There too, although many now appear isolated, others form part of a straight or circular alignment. Unfortunately nothing is known about whether they served as markers, or were for commemorative, funerary, or religious purposes.

The monuments of the Iberian peninsula, the fourth great region of west European megalithism, also have a wide variety of forms – oblong and polygonal chambers, with and without a passage, trapezoidal and rectangular – and some are no less spectacular than those in France or Ireland.

The tradition of the oblong chamber, very ancient in Portugal – Monchique dates back to the fifth millennium – does not appear to have developed to any great extent in the west of the peninsula. Two monuments with short passages, Poço da Gateria I and Anta dos

Gorginos II, have provided the most remote dates of the peninsula (4510 and 4440 B.C.); these belong to another typically Portuguese tradition. Some non-corridor tombs may also be very ancient, contemporaneous with passage tombs. Thus the Châ de Santinhos I tumulus, on the Aboboreira plateau in northern Portugal, contains a small polygonal passageless chamber, dated at about 3900 B.C. Another monument of the same group, containing a small polygonal chamber, dates from the same period, as does a similar monument in the Upper Beira province of Portugal, at Orca de Seixas.

The same remote era used large polygonal chambers, often defined by seven flat stones which might be substantial – over 3 metres high, and up to 4.50 metres in the Aldeia da Marta tomb at Grato in the Alentejo. They support a small covering slab. The passages to these tombs were fairly low, but tended to be built longer as time progressed; some exceeded 10 metres in length. Often dilapidated, the round or oval mound appears to have been bordered with slabs set in the earth, which can still be seen at the Prado Lacara monument at Caceres. Two of these chambers (Orca dos Castenairos and Carapito

Two contiguous circles of standing stones were set up at Er-Lannic, which became a small island when the sea level rose in the Gulf of Morbihan. Neolithic remains have been discovered all over the islet.

(Photo © Ed. Jos)

La Tremblais, the standing stone at Saint-Samson-sur-Rance in the Côtes-du-Nord, is carved and decorated all over. Unfortunately the designs are heavily eroded and can only be seen under very strong light. The best-lit surface is divided into rectangular panels, decorated with outlines of oxen.

(Photo © Ed. Jos)

I) in Upper Beira, have been dated at between 4000 and 3500 B.C. Carapito I contained a wide range of artefacts: microliths, flint blades, polished stone axe-heads, and callaïs and amphibolite beads.

Most of these large Portuguese monuments contain a wealth of grave-goods, but analysis reveals the presence of several different cultural phases: the site was colonized and recolonized repeatedly over a fairly lengthy period. Unfortunately many of these tombs have been disturbed since prehistoric times, and clear stratigraphy is lacking; it is therefore difficult to be confident of the sequence of cultures. Although somewhat intermingled, the objects found in the classic chamber of Anta Grande da Comenda da Igreja, near Evora in the Alentejo, are characteristic of this group. Triangular and trapeze-shaped microliths and polished axes of archaic design are jumbled up with artefacts considered specific to the middle Neolithic period in the Alentejo – flint arrow heads with bifacial retouch, a pendant in the shape of a rabbit, small carved schist plaques known as 'idols', polished and carved crosses made of the same material, and round-based vessels that recall Almerian ceramic products. On the other hand, very open plate-like forms, large flint dagger blades, and a copper awl are nearer to the late Neolithic period and the introduction of metal. Similar objects were found in the Olival da Pega monument at Reguengos de Monsaraz. This monument with its circular corbelled chamber is walled with dry stones dressed with stone slabs at the base.

The offerings in the Montefrio sepulchres near Granada are equally varied. The chambers are either trapezoidal or rectangular and measure about 3 by 2 metres; they are divided from the corridor

The Cueva del Romeral near Antequera, in southern Spain, represents a peak of megalithic architecture in south-western Europe. The photograph shows clearly the complementary roles of the stone slabs, some of them immensely thick, and the more fragile dry-stone walls, many of which have disappeared.

(Photo © Oroñoz/Artephot)

(which is always short) by a porthole-slab or by two notched slabs. These megalithic chambers are contemporaneous with the corbelled circular chambers. Surveys round the large fortified Los Millares site in 1981 revealed at least seventy rectangular megalithic tombs belonging to the Granada group; until then it was thought that the region was characterized exclusively by circular tombs. The Los Millares archeologists then debated whether perhaps each group of tombs belonged to a different community, the circular tombs to the coastal 'citizens' of Los Millares, and the rectangular tombs to the pastoral inhabitants of the Granada region.

Some of these rectangular passage tombs are of considerable size. They are unfortunately not accurately dated: imposing monuments have always attracted attention, and these were plundered long ago. The impressive megalithic group at Antequera, lying west of Granada

In the Viseu region of Portugal this 'classic dolmen', consisting of a chamber and passage, is only the ruined megalithic core of a tumulus monument which was very much larger and carefully constructed.

(Photo © J.P. Mohen)

Megaliths and the Sea

and forty kilometres north of Malaga, is made of up three monuments. The Cueva de Menga tumulus is 50 metres in diameter and contains a trapezoidal chamber 6.50 metres long with access through a 25-metre passage, and the Cueva de Viera mound is 60 metres long, with a square chamber and cell beyond, a long passage, and porthole-slabs. Finally, at the Cueva de Romeral monument a 90-metre tumulus covers two circular chambers; one, the smaller, opens through a passage into a larger chamber (4.50 metres across), which is in turn approached through a long passage; the two vaults and the passages are covered by stone slabs.

More vast megalithic tombs can be seen further west; the Soto sepulchre near Huelva is 21 metres long and consists of a corridor opening out into a chamber, a type that is also found among the large Gandul sepulchres near Seville. The many megalithic necropolises of southern Spain thus include tombs of widely varying forms, some of which are original, as in the cruciform tomb VII of El Pozuelo near Huelva. The precise chronology of their phases of construction and use has still to be established.

The peak of megalithism in western Europe, reached between 3500 and 3000 B.C., was characterized by the use of increasingly massive blocks, the daring of the architectural concept and in some cases a profuse graphic expression. All these features can be traced in monuments built in widely varying styles. These monuments, however, were all built on or near the coast; megalithism scarcely spread inland at all. This factor appears doubly significant.

Firstly, regions bounded on the west by the sea appear as an outer wall of continental Europe: here, therefore, Neolithic civilization was particularly dense, and cultural intermingling occurred easily and in new ways. Secondly, the sea undoubtedly facilitated contact between groups that had maintained a certain cultural autonomy within a shared civilizing influence that reached from Scandinavia to the southern tip of the Iberian peninsula. This has been established where building is concerned and will now be examined in relation to religious expression.

1 Maes Howe
2 Quanterness
3 Mid Gleniron
4 Behij
5 Knocknarea – Carrowmore
6 Carrowkeel
7 Loughcrew
8 Knowth
9 Dowth
10 Newgrange
11 Fourknocks
12 Dyffryn Ardudwy
13 Pentre Ifan
14 Ty Isaf
15 West Kennet
16 Avebury
17 Stonehenge
18 Emmen
19 Visbeck
20 Schwasdorf
21 Kruckow
22 Noblin, Rügen Island
23 Carlshögen, Hagestad
24 Trollasten
25 Onskulle
26 Stenstrup
27 Bygholm Norremark
28 Groenhoej
29 Maintenon, Saint-Piat
30 Barclodiad-y-Gavres, Anglesey
31 Guernsey
32 Carn Island
33 Plouhinec, Le Souc'h
34 Kerugou, Ploemeur
35 Penmarch
36 Kerleven, La Forêt-Fouesnant
37 La Tremblais, Saint-Samson-sur-Rance
38 Carnac
39 Locmariaquer
40 Gavrinis
41 Arzon, Le Petit Mont
42 Colpo, Larcuste
43 Brocéliande
44 Saint-Just
45 Langon
46 Essé
47 Dissignac
48 Pornic, Les Mousseaux
49 La Bajoulière, Saint-Rémy-la-Varenne
50 Bagneux
51 Les Cous
52 Nieul-sur-l'Autize
53 Benon
54 Bougon
55 Saint-Martin-la-Rivière-Maupas
56 Chenon
57 Le Montiou, Sainte-Soline
58 La Boixe
59 Carennac
60 La Clape
61 Châ de Santinhos, Aboboreira
62 Carapito 1
63 Orca dos Castenairos
64 Orca de Seixas
65 Praïa das Macas
66 Comenda da Igreja
67 La Comenda, Reguengos de Mousaraz
68 Herdade da Farisos
69 Soto
70 Monchique
71 Gandul
72 Antequera
73 Gorafe – Rio de Gor
74 Los Millares
75 El Barrenquete
76 Almizaraque
78 Ggantija, Gozo, Malta
79 Hal Safliéni, Malta

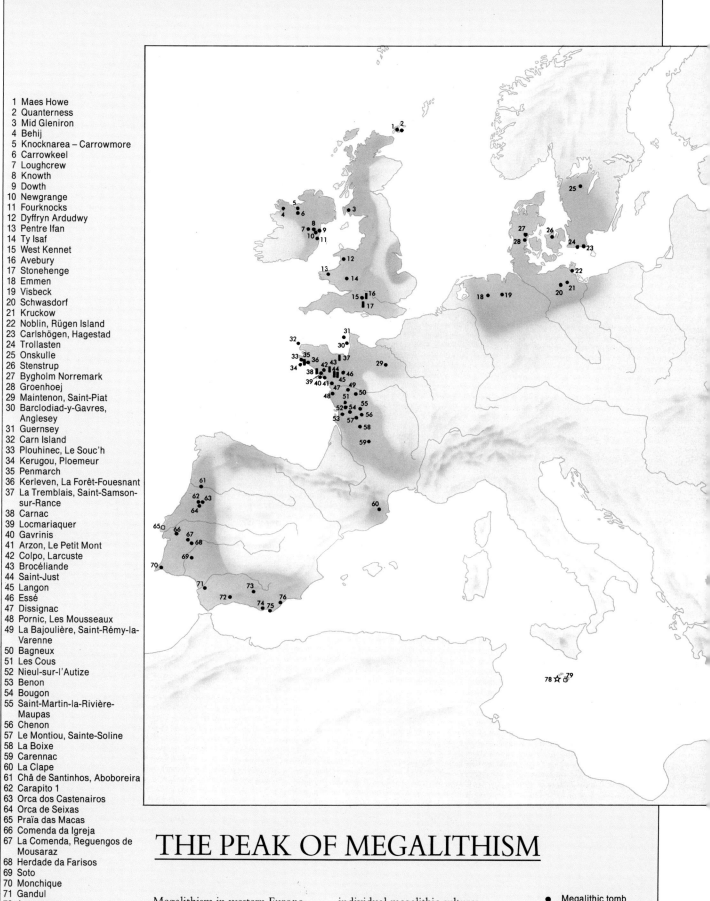

THE PEAK OF MEGALITHISM

Megalithism in western Europe reached its peak during the fourth millennium B.C. The most spectacular monuments were built in the same areas as the first megaliths, forming true individual megalithic cultures with their own architectural and artistic style, and must undoubtedly have been interconnected.

- ● Megalithic tomb
- ▮ Standing stone monument
- ▢ Hypogeum
- ☆ Megalithic temple

127

The Spread of Megalithic Construction

With the coming of the third millennium conditions changed. Structures made of 'great stones' multiplied, spreading further and further as the megaliths colonized new territory: in France this included the Causses, the southern edge of the Massif Central, the slopes of the Pyrenees, and Provence. Most of the collective tombs of the Paris basin also date from this period. These regions did not display the dynamism and architectural innovation characteristic of the preceding millennium. The pioneering achievements of the third millennium are to be found in the islands – the Mediterranean islands, which saw the development of a variety of forms such as tombs, temples, hypogea and other sacred monuments, and the British Isles, where innumerable standing stones marked the boundaries of religious centres.

Megalithic building styles in the Atlantic and Mediterranean islands originally grew out of a series of influences rapidly assimilated and translated into local materials; the innovations were all the more striking. In some cases, such as in the great Maltese temples, these particular forms were conserved for fairly long periods, for increasingly religious functions.

Even before the beginning of the third millennium, megalithic architecture in the islands was developing distinctive features. This was already evident in the case of Ireland and no less so in the standing stones of the British Isles, while the first monuments in Malta also date from the fourth millennium. Consolidation of this individuality can be traced over varying periods of the third millennium, and part of the second; construction styles can thus be identified very precisely with their settings.

British Isles megalithism is outstanding in the abundance of standing stones, and the variety of circular architectural complexes of which they formed a part. These groupings are generally of later date than the great flowering of barrows and tombs; strikingly original, they have no equivalent elsewhere in Europe – strongly supporting the argument that their builders were largely independent.

Circular ditches appeared in southern England during the second half of the fourth millennium, often surrounded by an inner ring of standing stones. This type of open-air monument probably originated in the region's large enclosures characterized by a series of ditches that were not continuous, but interrupted by entrances – ceremonial sites of which Windmill Hill is the best known. These concentric ditches bordered with upright stones might be of very considerable size: the largest, Durrington Walls, is 500 metres in diameter, and stands not far from another similar monument, Avebury, and also

The prehistoric site of Stonehenge, near Salisbury and south-west of London, is the most intriguing of all for modern observers. One of the great trilithons, consisting of two vertical stones supporting a horizontal lintel, beautifully illustrates the fine mixture of monumentality and precision. It rises among a crowd of carved monoliths set in the earth and fallen blocks, all forming part of one of the Neolithic ceremonial centres designed as a reference system marking the course of the sun.

(Photo © J. & C. Bord)

129

The currently accepted view is that the stages of Stonehenge's development may be dated as follows:

Stonehenge I: 3100–2300 B.C.

Stonehenge II: 2300–2100 B.C.

Stonehenge IIIa: 2100–2000 B.C.

Stonehenge IIIb: 2000–1550 B.C.

Stonehenge IIIc: 1550–1100 B.C.

The main axis of the complex passes through the centre of the circle of stones and the Heel Stone, to meet the horizon at the precise point where the sun rises on the day of the summer solstice. This axis is common to all phases of development.

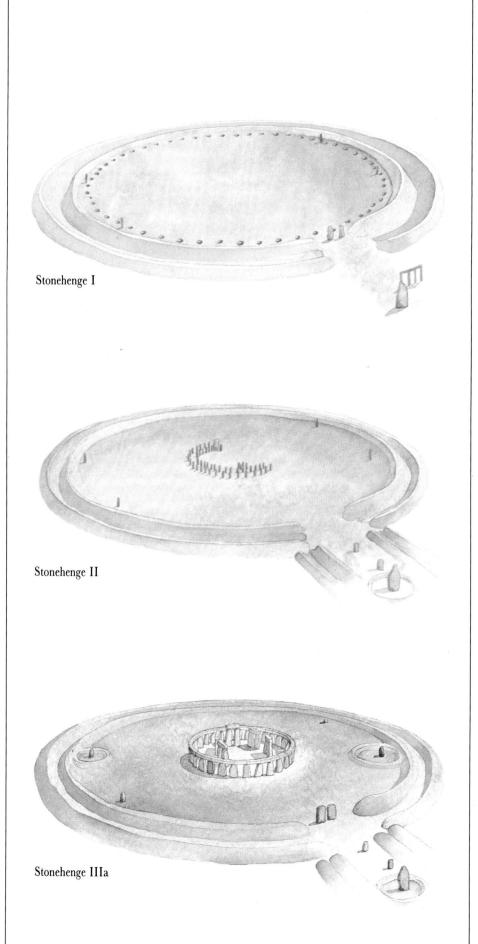

Stonehenge I

Stonehenge II

Stonehenge IIIa

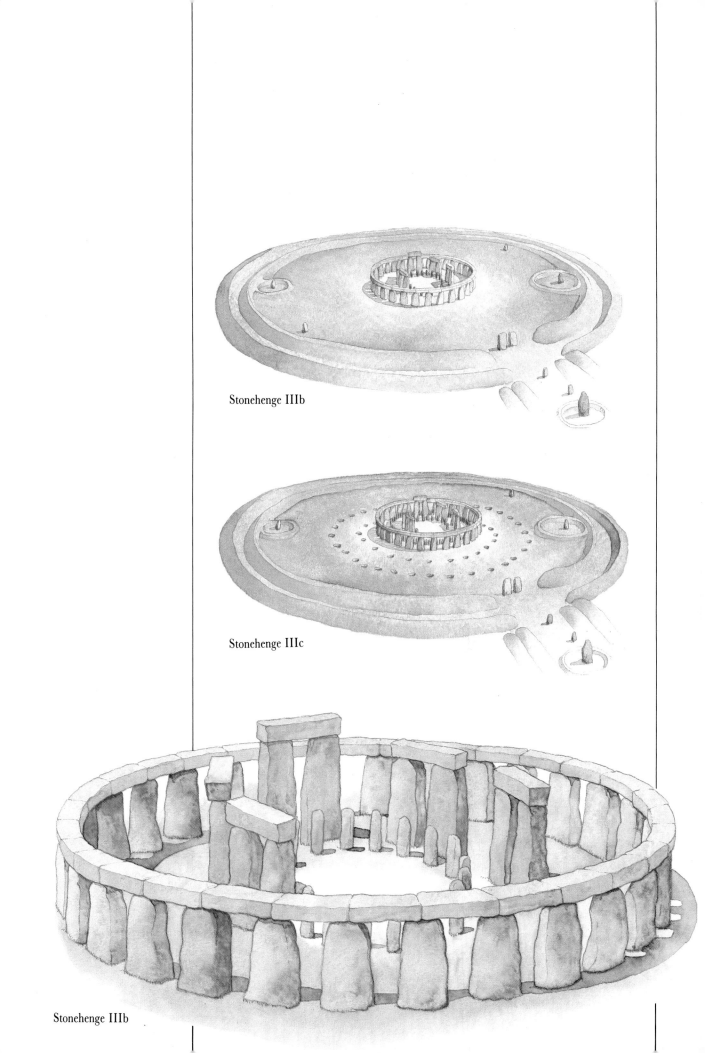

Stonehenge IIIb

Stonehenge IIIc

Stonehenge IIIb

Stonehenge, the most elaborate of all. Such stone circles were also numerous in northern England, a little less so in Scotland, and rarer in Wales and Ireland. The majestic circles of Stenness and Brogar, near the Maes Howe tumulus in Orkney, were built between 3000 and 2800 B.C. The Callanish monument, in the Hebrides, is a tumulus with a small megalithic tomb edged with a ring of standing stones; a ditch surrounds the group, with four double alignments radiating out like a cross, forming avenues, not unlike the structures noted near Stonehenge. At Millin Bay in Ireland a large circle of standing stones surrounds a mound bordered with small blocks set on edge in the ground and containing a narrow burial chamber.

Stone circles are often isolated, more rarely grouped together. At Beaghmore in Ireland there are several, associated with alignments of stones and with post-holes. Certain open monuments show local peculiarities, such as the recumbent stone circles in Scotland, where to the south of each circle two vertical stones frame a third broad slab set horizontally in the ground – a recumbent stone. Aubrey Burl, an authority on this type of construction, has shown that this aided observation of the moon's path.

These Scottish groups were certainly connected with astral observation, but equally they could have been settings for ceremonial ritual, of which traces have been discovered during excavation – various offerings, even burial deposits, more or less well-protected in pits or beneath a stone. They date from the same period as the Clava type of megalithic tomb.

In Mediterranean areas, specific architectural styles multiplied with the monuments, and sometimes occurred only on a single island or within even narrower confines. Close relationships are often apparent between rock-cut sepulchres and megalithic monuments proper, presenting the problem of these great building styles in very precise terms.

Rock-cut tombs or hypogea were more widespread than megalithic monuments: they are found in the Balearics and Sardinia, throughout southern Italy, in Sicily, and in Malta; the hypogea in the Arles region are certainly associated with this group. Most of these artificial caves were built with a circular chamber and a passage of greater or lesser width, and sometimes with an antechamber. Multiple lateral cells are found in Sardinia, for example at San Andrea Priu. The oldest Italian hypogea probably date from the end of the fifth millennium or the beginning of the fourth; in Sardinia they are contemporaneous with the traces of the Ozieri culture, dating from the early fourth millennium.

In Malta at that period hypogea were created inside trenches dug out of the ground. According to John D. Evans, such tombs with

One of the columns at Stonehenge is decorated with two Bronze Age axes and a dagger, symbols of masculine power.

(Photo © R. Estall)

The lintels, or suspended stones – the 'henges' that gave their name to the Stonehenge monument.

(Photo © P. Caponigro)

lateral cells would have served, from 3500 B.C. onwards, as prototypes for the great megalithic building styles: with their Cyclopean enclosures the famous 'temples' (so named because their funerary purpose was not clear) of Ggantija on Gozo and of Tarxien and Hagar Kim in Malta were constructed on a multilobular plan. These were sanctuaries, as indicated by the corpulent female image of the goddess of whom several statues survive. The statue menhir at Hagar Kim is seated, while that of Tarxien, upright but damaged in its upper part, must have been 2.80 metres high. At the same time as the development of monumental structures, certain hypogea such as Hal Safliéni assumed considerable importance. This was a rock-cut tomb with some twenty chambers, containing the remains of 7,000 people! The main hall showed characteristics of buildings above ground, with columns and lintels carved in the rock. Red paintings of cattle, and the terracotta statuette of a goddess lying on her bed found inside, indicate the site's religious function. The temples were abandoned towards the middle of the third millennium, as the population turned to using plain rectangular megalithic chambers for burial purposes. These were similar to the chambers of the Italian group at Otranto, and they remained in use until the height of the Bronze Age, in the middle of the second millennium. Once again standing stones were associated with tombs.

In the Balearic Islands both natural and artificial caves were used as sepulchres, before the construction of megalithic monuments. Some of the artificial caves resembled hypogea of the Arles region, especially the Grotte des Fées. The actual megalithic monuments were coffers; at Son Baulo the monument consisted of a small rectangular chamber at the centre of a stone circle, with a stone hatch-way (port-hole slab) giving access to a small passage. It would have been covered by a horizontal stone slab, but this has now disappeared. Among the

133

objects deposited as grave-goods were pierced buttons and spherical or flat-bottomed vessels dating from the third millennium. It was not until the following millennium that *talayot* towers appeared, and their exact function is not known; they were round (sometimes square), built in cyclopean style with small rooms inside. *Naveta* chambers were linked with death; they were oblong constructions, with a slightly concave façade at the base of which a small entrance led to the sepulchre, a long chamber covered with bonded blocks. The Minorcan naveta of Els Tudons is a fine example of this distinct building style. Equally original was the *taula*: a ring of standing stones on a circular site bounded by a wall, surrounding a massive pillar (4 metres high at Trepuco) supporting a parallelepiped block balanced across it. Twenty-eight taulas have been discovered in Minorca; they are presumed to have been religious sites. All these monuments – talayots, navetas, and taulas – date from the same period, the second millennium.

Corsica's first megalithic monuments appeared during the fourth millennium; these were buried coffers, as at Porto-Vecchio. Made of granite slabs, they might be surrounded by a circle of stones retaining the earth mass of a low mound. During the course of the third millen-

Avebury, north of Stonehenge, occupies an enormous circular site 400 metres across, surrounded (from the centre outwards) by a rampart, a ditch, and a ring of standing stones. The extent of this open construction is typical of the late Neolithic age. The complex is extended to the south by the West Kennet 'avenue', a double line of standing stones leading to a small sanctuary two kilometres away. A similar avenue lay to the west.

(Photo © Fay Godwin's Photo Files)

This 1824 engraving of Avebury includes the points of departure of its two avenues of standing stones. Within the large circle of standing stones were laid out two sets of smaller concentric circles.

(Photo © BBC Hulton Picture Library)

nium construction began above ground of coffers or small chambers, 2 or 3 metres long, which were then covered by fairly large mounds. Such monuments are particularly numerous in the south of the island, and one of the finest is Fontanaccia, on the Cauria plateau at Sartène. In this area some were associated with standing stones, either single or placed in rows; the rows were always aligned north–south. According to the evolution defined by Roger Grosjean, the coffers were the origins of the rectangular megalithic chambers also found on the island. They had a rudimentary corridor opening at the concave façade of the tumulus, as seen at Settiva, which too was associated with standing stones.

Torres, the Corsican equivalent of the Balearic talayot, appeared in the south of the island around the middle of the second millennium. These towers were 10 or 15 metres in diameter, 7 metres high, and built of dry stone. Inside the large entrance a passage led to a chamber roofed by corbelling with small annexes leading off it. Piles of ashes were frequently found inside these structures, which must have had a religious, possibly funerary, significance. The towers were surrounded by a circular, sometimes walled, area and were associated with large sculpted steles representing local warriors. Some third-millennium standing stones, with anthropomorphic features, prefigured steles with carved depictions of swords on them that would date the monument at around the fourteenth or thirteenth centuries B.C. The Filitosa site, deservedly well known, illustrates the scale which such monuments could attain.

Sardinia has many megalithic monuments, of varying types. The links between rock-cut tombs and megalithic constructions have been apparent for some time, and can be explained by the meeting of two

135

At the centre of Callanish, in the Hebridean islands off the west coast of Scotland, a modest tumulus conceals a small megalithic tomb surrounded by a circle of tall standing stones. Four double rows of stones radiate out from the central monument.

(Photo © M. Sharp)

traditions of probably differing origins. The first rock-cut tombs appeared at the end of the fifth millennium. One of the Montessu hypogea had a rectangular chamber, antechamber, and passage, while San Andrea Priu has small lateral rooms or cells; these are related by their grave-goods to the Ozieri culture, dated by radiocarbon methods from the fourth millennium. A few of the hypogea are decorated with schematic anthropomorphic motifs, with arms raised and legs apart: those of the Branca de Modeddu cave recall some of the paintings of southern Spain, while the decorations of the Emiciclo di Sas Concas tomb evoke both the praying figure and the horned emblem, leitmotifs of the Vallée des Merveilles.

The megalithic tradition is more clearly seen in the north of the island, where it developed in parallel with that of the rock-cut tombs. It began with cists; those of the Li-Muri necropolis were placed in the centre of a circular site (6 to 8 metres across) outlined with stone slabs, some quite small, others up to 2 metres long. The date of these cists has not been positively established, but it may be the fourth or third millennium. Although the Li-Muri necropolis appears ancient – in view of the offerings found there – other cists are certainly more recent. The chronology of the circular mounds contained within stone slabs is also dubious. These monuments contain a polygonal chamber approached through a short passage, and covered in massive stones. The Motorra tumulus at Dorgali contained shards which have been compared to pottery found in southern France, and which date from the third millennium (Ferrières and Fontbouisse cultures). The tombs may also be rectangular; the Perta Longa tomb, at Aristis, preceded by a scarcely narrower passage, recalls monuments in Catalonia and the

Aude. Other larger tombs, with a pierced entrance stone at the base of a small quadrangular opening, were forerunners of the famous Bronze Age monuments known as 'giants' graves'.

These giants' graves are very long megalithic chambers. They measure up to 15 metres in length, and are surrounded by a Cyclopean construction with two long curved wings of considerable height, one on each side of a monumental entrance. This entrance would often have a carved stone slab simulating side wings, a horizontal lintel, and an arch above; at the base a small opening was blocked by a stone. Some monuments are very impressive: Li Lolghi at Arzachena (the largest), Murartu, Silanus, Imbertighe, Thomes, Coddu Vecchiu, each with its own unique features. Three stylized anthropomorphic steles were found beside the entrance of the Pedra-Doladas I Silanus tomb, and betyls carved with an outline of female breasts surrounded the Tamuli monument. There are also tombs without lateral wings, as at Su-Cuveccu-Bultei and S'Ena'e Vacca-Omzai. These simpler monuments may have been the prototypes for the giant tombs; there are clear connections between this group of monuments and certain rock-cut tombs with the same layout and the same carved façade, such as the Ittiari group of hypogea at Osilo Sassari. At Orrida, moreover, the monument is a mixture of styles: the chamber was dug out of the rock like a hypogeum, but it has a façade with wings made of large blocks.

The design of the giants' tombs is thought to represent an ox-head, and the wings to represent its horns. The bull cult is suggested by the carved horns above the entrance of the Santu Pedru rock-cut tomb, and by the bucrania carved in relief on the Sennori

Some stone circles near Aberdeen, in Scotland, display an unusual feature: a stone laid flat (known as a recumbent stone) flanked by two standing stones. This may have been a sighting point for observing the path of the moon reaching its highest point in the sky. This monument is at East Aquittorthies.

(Photo © J. & C. Bord)

tomb. All these monuments were in any case collective sepulchres –
the remains of fifty people were found at Preganti, sixty at Las Plassas,
at least twenty-seven at Orrida – but they probably also served
another function. Nuraghi appeared at the same period. In their simplest form they resemble the Corsican torres: towers with a chamber
built in Cyclopean style. Placed at the centre of a walled enclosure,
they probably had a religious purpose. Their complexity, however,
distinguishes them from other monuments; they may have several
chambers – three, for example, laid out like a clover leaf – and several
storeys. Their better condition makes them all the more imposing; the
Santu Antine, Losa, Ruggiu-Chiaramonti, and Palmavera-Alghero
sites, are among the finest and most impressive. It is not surprising that
in honour of these superb buildings the Sardinian Bronze Age has
been named 'nuraghic'. Other stone buildings, known as temples – for
example, at Predio Canopolo – demonstrate the variety and energy of
Sardinian construction in the third millennium.

There was thus a real cultural insularity. Such sites encouraged
original creativity. Some of the architectural styles of the monuments,
and doubtless their functions too, indicate some form of general inte-
gration with current styles, but others also exhibit a local individualized one. This originality is further marked by the remains. Although
open to a wide range of external contacts, the islands preserved their
identity in protective isolation, which would explain why most of such
styles developed fairly late.

Mass Megalithism

On the mainland, megalithic building styles spread inland and
became commonplace – in what might be called mass megalithism.
This popularization affected architectural style as well as funerary
rites, which were no longer reserved for strictly selected individuals
but had become far more widely available. Such new rites must have
been related to the adoption by more egalitarian societies of megalithic forms of expression.

Architecture itself evolved in two directions, starting from the
square modular chamber already known. As Ian Kinnes observed,
either the chamber evolved linearly, and was greatly extended, or
following the dispersal system monuments with a small square chamber became much more numerous.

The tendency to extend chambers can be seen in several regions;
it was accompanied by funerary deposits, frequently substantial, and
meticulous arrangement of the internal space. In northern Europe the
very large megalithic chambers with lateral passage were between 6
and 10 metres long. Built of large irregular blocks like those of the
fourth millennium, they extended in their own way the peak of Nordic
megalithic construction. In Mecklenburg, in northern Germany,

mounds bordered with slabs alternating with dry stones were chiefly of rectangular design orientated east–west, such as the Gnewitz monuments near Rostock. The layout might be trapezoidal, as at Upost near Demmin, or (more rarely) circular, as at Liepen near Rostock. These impressive tombs are found in Denmark, at Frejlev or Blomeskobbel, as well as in the northern Netherlands region of Drenthe, where the Havelte monument dates from the beginning of the third millennium. One of the largest, at Thuine in northern Germany, has a chamber 23 metres long. Two separate groups have been defined: those of Lower Saxony are characterized by an axial passage, and those of Holstein by an off-centre passage, while both types are found in Mecklenburg.

Ireland's 'wedge-shaped' megalithic chambers are so called because the entrance is broader and higher than the inner end. They are found in the west of the country, where 405 have been identified. The mounds are long and narrow, and are surrounded by slabs set in the ground. The Island monument, in County Cork, is distinctive in being surrounded by a row of post-holes, like the court-cairn of Shanballyedmond in County Tipperary. This suggests links between court cairns and wedge-shaped chambers, although the latter are thought to be of later date – the middle of the third millennium. Their origins have been much debated. The presence of bell-beaker vessels in their grave-goods is not sufficient to allow us to attribute the inspiration of the architectural style to the users of these vessels. It has also been suggested that the grave-goods might have been introduced from Brittany or the Paris basin by the first copper ore prospectors. But the distribution of wedge-shaped chambers in limestone regions, from

(Photo © R. Estall)

Intensified by their isolation, Malta and Gozo's unique style of megalithism is clearly visible in the great temples such as Hagar Kim, shown here. Behind the façade of large blocks a passage leads to a honeycomb of several chambers. The funerary function appears to have been secondary to that of sanctuary, in which the prime position is held by the representation of a goddess.

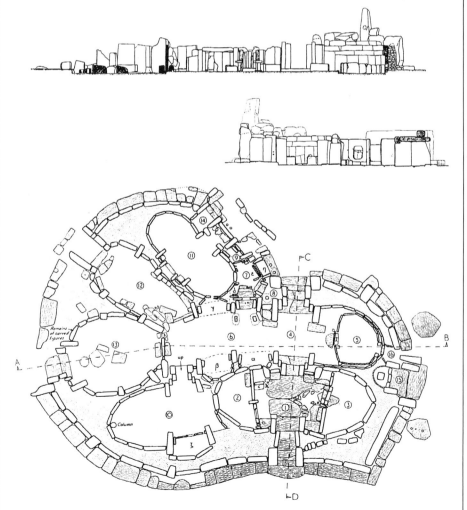

The plan of the temple of Hagar Kim, in Malta, reveals the many-lobed design of the various chambers, in which no traces of any burial have been found – hence the hypothesis that it served as a temple. The two elevation drawings show clearly the megalithic appearance of the façades. It is not known how the monuments were covered.

(Plans taken from *The Prehistoric Antiquities of the Maltese Islands: a Survey*, by J. D. Evans, Athlone Press, 1971)

which deposits of native metal are absent, indicates that any connection between the copper ore deposits of the ancient granite massifs and this type of monument should be regarded with caution. And any resemblance to the very long chambers with short axial corridors seen in France is superficial, proving nothing more than a general tendency to lengthen the rectangular chamber – a tendency seen in other monuments nearer to Ireland, in Cornwall and the Isles of Scilly. Two very long chamber graves (without a passage), in Jersey, resemble Breton monuments more closely than those of the Paris basin, with which they have nevertheless been connected.

The lengthening of chambers over a period of time is so unmistakable that it became effectively a chronological criterion for the monuments of some regions, particularly in western and northern France where architectural style evolved in several directions after the end of the fourth millennium. In the group of gallery graves with a passage entering at an angle into the burial chamber, concentrated in Morbihan and round the mouth of the Loire, the considerably elongated chambers were distinct from their passages. The Pierres Plates tomb at Locmariaquer begins as a gallery 22.5 metres long; facing north at first it then bends towards the north-west and opens out into a chamber. Other tombs are of the same plan, as at Rocher au Bouc, Luffang at Crac'h, and Goërem at Gâvres in its oval mound. All are in Morbihan: all also contain slabs bearing the stylized image of an 'idol'. Radiocarbon analysis dates the construction of the Pierres Plates at Locmariaquer at about 3200 B.C.

Some of the monuments with very long burial chambers have a lateral passage; some twenty of these were built in Brittany and Normandy. The Crec'h Quillé monument at Saint-Quay-Perros in the Côtes-du-Nord is covered by a quadrangular mound surrounded by large blocks; the short passage opens on to the long south side from a megalithic chamber 15 metres long. Close to the entrance is a block with a relief decoration representing breasts and a necklace. Among the grave-goods placed in these tombs have been found narrow-necked collared vessels very similar to certain Nordic vessels: this would seem to confirm the relationship between this side-entry group and those of the Netherlands, northern Germany, and Denmark.

In other monuments the very long megalithic burial chamber has an antechamber on the same axis; the oval-mounded Liscuis II and III monuments at Laniscat are of this type, often with a perforated stone at the entrance to the chamber. This applies to the Prajou-Menhir tomb at Trébeurden in the Côtes-du-Nord, which also displays a good example of third millennium megalithic art: some of its stones bear reliefs of breasts and necklaces, and carved motifs of axes, palettes, and shield 'idols'. The prototype of these monuments must have been the long chamber, almost indistinguishable from its passage, like that at Mané Kerioned at Carnac. Similarly, the Liscuis I tomb has in effect a narrowed entrance while its other features – large parallel sides, short antechamber almost as wide as the chamber, and terminal cell – are typical of the Breton group of very elongated chambers.

The same decorative themes, the same burial chamber design, can be seen in similar megalithic tombs of the Paris basin, the gallery graves, although with one very important difference: the gallery graves have no tumulus, for the collective burials of the Ile-de-France were carried out in a system of trenches dug out in the ground. The existence of a terminal cell is rare, but has been recorded in the Vivez factory monument at Argenteuil, and the small underground niche behind the tomb at La Chaussée-Tirancourt in the Somme is somewhat similar. This burial place was found by chance in 1967; in a trench 3.50 metres wide and 15 long, Claude Masset and Jean Leclerc excavated an 11-metre chamber separated from its antechamber by a transverse stone with a small opening. Since there was no horizontal roofing slab, it has been suggested that there might have been a wooden construction. The chamber was originally divided with small blocks into at least three compartments. More than 350 skeletons were

The statue in the Tarxien temple in Malta originally represented an obese goddess, which must have been 2.80 metres high. This same figure is found seated or recumbent in other megalithic monuments in Malta and Gozo.

(Photo © Roger-Viollet)

Megalithic temple architecture with doors, niches, and roof supports is found inside the Hal Safliéni hypogeum in Malta. This rock-cut tomb was divided into some twenty chambers containing the remains of 7,000 individuals.

(Photo © R. Estall)

deposited there in the course of several periods of use – deposited according to strict criteria of age, social standing or, perhaps, membership of a community. Some of the objects found among the bones belong to the culture known as 'Seine-Oise-Marne' and are attributed to the third millennium by several datings.

The Justice monument at Nerville-la-Forêt (Val-d'Oise) and that of Aubergenville (Yvelines) belong to the same culture; they are classic examples, with their megalithic sides and their port-hole slabs dividing the chamber from its antechamber. The Guiry-en-Vexin tomb in the Val-d'Oise has a magnificent port-hole slab surrounded by the two lateral slabs of the antechamber; a series of blocks covers the chamber, and the walls are made of dry stone. Dry stone was also used for the sepulchre I at Marolles-sur-Seine (Seine-et-Marne), which measures 8.40 by 3.60 metres. This site is remarkable for the traces of incineration of fairly large numbers of bodies, and it seems that a wooden building covered the tomb. Nearby another sepulchre is visible in the form of a roughly oval ditch with a vault measuring 1.20 by 1 metre, containing the remains of fifty-four people – except that the skulls and long bones are missing. The whole was surrounded by a circular palisade. The slab-roofed collective grave at Éteauville (Eure-et-Loir) is an oval chamber edged with slabs and with a dry-stone wall forming an apse. Its grave-goods have affinities with the Seine-Oise-Marne culture, but the design of the tomb is distinctive.

Other tombs of similar date but fairly different in style have been linked with the very long burial chambers with antechambers: these are the Marne hypogea, dug out of the side of limestone hills. At the end of the nineteenth century, the Baron de Baye found dozens of these in the Petit Morin valley. In most, a sloping passage led to an ante-chamber opening into the square or rectangular chamber. Some of the passages are decorated with carved motifs representing an axe with handle and a female idol: the Razet hypogea at Coizard has fine examples of such carvings. Again, the grave-goods belong to the Seine-Oise-Marne culture. Several trepanned skulls were found in these burial sites. The discovery in 1958 of the hypogeum II of Les Mournouards at Le Mesnil-sur-Oger made it possible for André Leroi-Gourhan, Gérard Bailloud and Michel Brézillon to study funerary rites in detail. It held the bones of some forty adults and about twenty children; the bodies – with the head emerging from the enveloping shroud – were deposited with various grave-goods, flint knives, quivers, axes, and some ornaments. The sepulchre was closed with a blocking stone held in place by heavy wooden pegs.

Two more groups of megalithic tombs belong to the family of long chambers with antechamber: one in Belgium and Luxembourg, the other in Germany (Hesse and Westphalia). To the south of Liège the Wéris group consists of a staggered alignment of standing stones and two megalithic tombs: each of the latter contains a rectangular chamber (4.60 metres and 5.60 metres long), a port-hole slab, and an antechamber. The first is buried but the second, built at ground level, would have been covered by a mound. The grave-goods belonged to the Seine-Oise-Marne culture. In 1963 at Stern in Belgium, near the Netherlands border, Pieter Modderman excavated a long wooden

The Trepuco *taulo* on the island of Minorca is distinctive in its circle of upright slabs with, at the centre, this large rectangular pillar supporting a parallelipedal block, 4 metres off the ground. This strange monument, and the nearby *tayalot* tower (background) are both thought to have been sanctuaries.

(Photo © R. Estall)

The Els Tudons *naveta* in Minorca is another unique form of construction linked with megalithism. Its burial purpose seems clear.

chamber tomb, lying at the heart of a site belonging to the strip civilization. He cleared a rectangular stone surface 5.50 by 1.75 metres marked by four post-holes. A row of larger stones indicated a threshold, and quadrangular paving probably indicated the antechamber. Among the artefacts found were arrow shafts with transverse blades, bone arrow-heads, and shards of a bottle with collared rim made of six buttons. Radiocarbon analysis dated the construction of the monument at the middle of the fourth millennium; this is thus another example of the relationship between stone and wood construction – all the more interesting in that here the latter was the first to be used.

The western German group is made up of a variety of monuments. Some are very long chambers with side entrance, which recall monuments in the Netherlands and northern Germany, like that at Rimbeck in Hesse. Others contain a very long quadrangular chamber, generally constructed in a trench but without visible means of access; entry was evidently through the top. The Hiddingsen tomb is of this type, and is nearly 27 metres long. Still other collective tombs, containing between 20 and 250 skeletons, have very similar chambers but with clearly defined access through an antechamber separated from the chamber by a port-hole slab (with a circular hole in it) or a stone with notches cut out of it. These are the third-millennium tombs that were compared with those of the Paris basin and of Belgium. Some were constructed in a trench, others at ground level; the latter were covered by a long barrow edged with large blocks. Some are of impressive dimensions: the Atteln II and Beckum-Wintergalen tombs in Westphalia are 30 metres long, the others between 10 and 20 metres. The best known are the Lohne-Züschen and Altendorf tombs in Hesse. Some are quite short, with chambers of only 5 metres across; these are found in Hesse, at Lohra, and no doubt further east in the Harz and Thuringia areas as well.

The large region from the Vosges to the Franche-Comté and Switzerland is one exception to the rule: the chambers here show no tendency to elongation. Although many tombs have been extended by adding an antechamber, the chambers themselves remain small. The three Aillevans tombs in Haute-Saône are of this type; the chambers are small and square, with sides 2 metres long; a grooved stone separ-

The Filitosa site in Corsica is an assembly of *torres*, towers built in a more or less megalithic style, and Bronze Age statue-menhirs. This religious centre, which may also have been inhabited, remains a mystery.

(Photo © Joly-Cardot)

Three vessels characteristic of Armorican megalithic tombs from the late Neolithic age: the first is collared, and shows some affinity with vessels from northern and central Europe,

the second is decorated with Conguel-style incised zigzags, while the last bears vertical relief motifs in the Kérugou style.

(Musée des Antiquités Nationales, Saint-Germain-en-Laye. Photo J.-M. Labat © Casterman)

ates them from an antechamber walled by two parallel slabs 1.20 metres long. The tumulus of the first tomb, circular to begin with, was enlarged to form a trapezoidal barrow 20 metres long. This first tomb contained the remains of twenty-three people, the second those of about a hundred; the monuments date from the middle of the third millennium. Other tombs, seen as the prototypes of this group, were isolated in the Belfort Gap; the Schwörstadt type megalithic sepulchures are characterized by a port-hole stone and the apparent absence of an antechamber.

In the Petit Chasseur group at Sion in the Valais there is evidence of remarkable architectural development over two millennia. In the fourth millennium the group consisted of cists connected with an alignment of standing stones; in the third a tomb was built which has some affinity with the megalithic antechamber sepulchres of the Franche-Comté – with one difference: the slab separating the chamber from the antechamber was solid and entry was by means of an opening in the lateral stone. The tumulus may not have been very high. The excavators, Olivier Bocksberger and Alain Gallay, think that the sacred area was contained within a plain triangular podium 16 metres long. Two large decorated anthropomorphic steles might have stood in front of the monument; they would have been re-used for the construction of another tomb with antechamber, contemporaneous with the bell-beaker vessels, that is, at the end of the third millennium. Cists were placed against the slabs of this tomb in the Early Bronze Age.

Alongside these typical architectural forms exist others, less typical. The plain megalithic chamber of Lavans-lès-Dôle in the Jura measures 4 metres by 2; buried beneath a round barrow 14 metres in diameter, it contains skeletons placed at four levels separated by stone paving. Seven third-millennium arrow-heads with transverse blades were found among the grave-goods. To the south, in Aquitaine and southern France, the tendency towards longer chambers recurs in various monuments: in Gironde, for example, the megalithic Roquefort tomb at Lugasson is a long chamber, 14 metres by 1.50 metres, and 1 metre high, built at ground level and covered by a mound like the Breton tombs with very long chambers. The increasing height of columns from the entrance to the head-stone are typical of the Gironde group, and this feature is very clear in the monuments of Gardegan-et-Tourtiran and at Montguyon. It is also apparent in several monuments in Aude, notably at Pépiaux, where the Los Fades mound, 36 metres long, covers a rectangular megalithic chamber measuring 24 metres. At Laure-Minervois the Saint-Eugène tomb is made up of a passage, a large antechamber, and a chamber contained within a trapezoid 15 metres long.

147

The Giants' Tomb at Arzachena is typical of one of Sardinia's megalithic monument styles. It is characterized by a façade of large monoliths set in the ground, at the centre of which a large flat stone with carved pediment marks a small entrance in the lower part.

(Photo © R. Pollès)

The five Provençal hypogea at Arles-Fontvieille illustrate another type of tomb: dug out of the ground, these graves have a long chamber, an antechamber with subsidiary niches, and a sloping passage with steps. The largest of them, the Épée de Roland, is 42 metres long. They are all covered with an oval mound and megalithic slabs and were excavated long ago, but nothing was found that could date their construction decisively. They have been connected with other similar monuments in the Balearics and Sardinia, which would justify a fairly early date – late fourth millennium. Rock-cut tombs such as those at Roaix and Les Boileau, in Vaucluse, were used as an ossuary towards the middle of the third millennium; they represent an ill-defined type of burial that is widespread in the Mediterranean area.

Small Tombs in Increasing Numbers

Scattered across the south of France are a great many small tombs isolated in round barrows. There are thousands on the limestone plateaux of Provence (causses), on the southern edges of the Massif Central, and in the Pyrenees. This large-scale megalithism flourished principally between 3500 and 2500 B.C. In Languedoc it was the period of the Ferrières and then the Fontbouisse cultures. At Rouet, in Hérault, the Lamalou tomb has a chamber covered by a single large, horizontal slab, an antechamber, and a long passage. The whole group was buried beneath a round barrow surrounded by kerb stones. Two standing stones, at the entrance of the antechamber and of the chamber, with notches cut from their adjoining edges, form a narrow point which could easily be closed. The Feuilles tomb in the same community has one of the longest chambers in the group – 12 metres in length. Many of these monuments lack an antechamber, and their passages almost always face south-west. Constructed in the second half of the fourth millennium, in the context of the Ferrières culture, and perhaps even earlier in some cases, these tombs were later used regularly by the Fontbouisse people. The Bas-Rhône area has a somewhat different type of tomb; here the passage faces west and is built of dry stones, as are the sides of the chamber. This applies too to the Boussière tomb at Cabasse in the Var, dated at 2500 B.C.

The third region is the causses. This type of tomb was widespread in Ardèche, Lozère, Aveyron, and Quercy. The chambers were megalithic; two large flat stones formed the sides, one slab was used for the head-stone, and a heavier slab the roof. Some have a passage. In the last phase the mound was almost always circular but sometimes

Barumini is one of Sardinia's best preserved *nuraghe*, massive towers containing a chamber of uncertain purpose. It has been suggested that they were religious sites.

(Photo © Yan)

The very long megalithic chambers are known as 'gallery graves'. Those of the Paris basin are underground; this one, the Pierre Turquaise at Saint-Martin-du-Tertre in the Hauts-de-Seine, is a rectangular chamber covered with massive stones. Such monuments usually contain a large quantity of human bones.

(Photo © Tarrète)

trapezoid, as at Cazals and at Larroque. Some mounds contain two chambers. In Ardèche, as in Languedoc, the oldest grave-goods corresponded to the Ferrières culture, that is, the late fourth millennium; in the Grands Causses they belonged to the Treilles culture, of the same period. The Freyssinel tombs at Balsières yielded copper beads and daggers. The origins of this type of construction are unknown.

These monuments are relatively elaborate in their construction, but this is not true of all. Within the same area, from the Pyrenees to Provence, there are also hundreds of much simpler megalithic tombs – what might be called the poor man's megaliths. They are tombs with no clear demarcation between the entrance passage and burial chamber, where the dead were placed in tiny chambers or in coffers and must be contemporaneous with their more sophisticated equivalents. Here may be seen the origin of the cists and caverns of the Bronze Age. There are also small tombs – miniatures – made of dry stones and corbel-roofed, with or without a passage, like those at La Lauve at Salernes in Var, which date from the third millennium.

Monuments are just as varied in the north of the Iberian peninsula. In Portugal Vitor Oliveira Jorge was surprised by the range of monumental forms which he discovered around Porto, in the Serra de Aboboreira. The Basque region has coffers such as Haitzetako-Exabala at Renteria, plain polygonal chambers like Sorginetxe at Arrizala, small rectangular chambers at Ataun and at Aralar, which are representatives of a thousand others in the Pyrenees and which must be fairly late. There are also more or less polygonal passage graves, (Saint-Martin at Laguardia, Forangortea), which appear

150

older and belong to a broad Atlantic tradition. In certain trapeze-shaped passage graves the walling stones overlap, a Portuguese building technique seen at Lanagunilla de Elvillar, in Alava, for example. Other monuments are closer to those of Aude and of Catalonia, with a fairly large rectangular chamber and a passage as broad as the chamber itself and almost as long; the Jentillarri monument in Aralar and those of La Mina and Le Portillo de Eneriz at Forangortea are of this kind in which the height of the structure decreases from the head-stone to the entrance of the passage.

Could the Catalonian megalithic tombs have had their origins in the burial trenches that appeared in the fourth millennium? It is debatable. These graves, from which what is now known as the gallery grave culture is named, are sometimes buried cists made of stone slabs, sometimes half-buried rectangular coffers of some kind. Mass burial does not seem to have been practised here; were these tombs part of an independent development or were they an integral part of the general evolution of megalithism in Catalonia? The absence of precise chronological points of reference makes it impossible to answer, and Miguel Cura-Morera's suggested pattern of evolution therefore remains more or less hypothetical. The oldest monuments would have been round barrows containing a polygonal chamber with a short passage, as at Font del Roure. This type of construction appears in Roussillon; it was already well developed in relation to the supposed prototype of the cist in the trench tombs, but it also belongs to a widespread Iberian tradition. Passaged monuments with rectangular chambers may have been contemporaneous; the long rectangular chamber with a broad corridor appeared later. The Cova d'En Dayna, at Romanya de la Selva, is

The Bager gallery grave in the Netherlands consists of irregular blocks erected above ground level. They were covered by a tumulus, of which a few edging stones still remain.

(Photo © Lanting)

a tumulus 11 metres in diameter, covering a megalithic chamber separated from a passage more than 7 metres long by two upright stones and a carved lintel; the numerous simple chamber monuments belong to the final phase. A 'window' in one of the side columns appears to have been the only means of access. Some of the coffers were completely closed, such as the three examples buried within a mound at Coll de Creus. These third phase tombs, less typical, were widespread in the Pyrenees, where they probably date from the late third millennium.

In the south of the peninsula, rock-cut tombs were used at the same time as monuments above ground, with roughly the same layout; some of these tombs were built with both a dome and passage, such as those at the mouth of the Tagus near Lisbon. In the Palmella and Sao Pedro do Estoril caves two groups of grave goods, mingled inside the tomb, may be distinguished. The first recalls late Neolithic practice in the province of Almeria in southern Spain; smooth, lightly decorated vessels, trapezoidal microliths, concave-based arrow-heads, polished stone axes, conical chalk 'idols', votive adzes made of marble, plaques of carved schist. The second is clearly connected with a later (Chalcolithic) phase, when metal had come into general use. This is the period of bell-beakers, usually decorated, together with bone buttons with distinctive V-shaped perforations, and above all of copper objects, such as awls and arrowheads with almost circular blades, the 'Palmella point'. It is interesting to observe that the fortified dwellings

The Lohne Züschen tomb in Hesse is similar to some of the Paris basin monuments, dating from the second millennium. A very long chamber, edged with stone slabs, lies underground; it is separated from its antechamber by a port-hole slab pierced with a hole known as the 'spirit's hole'. The covering of this type of mass grave was not always made of slabs, small round stones were sometimes used instead.

(Photo © Pfältzer/Roger-Viollet)

One of the Coizard hypogea, in the Marne, consists of a burial chamber hollowed out of the chalk, with antechamber and access passage. These collective tombs have features in common with contemporaneous megalithic monuments, such as the axe with handle motif depicted on both sides of the entrance. Traces of carving into the soft stone with the aid of an antler pick are clearly visible here.

(Photo J.-M. Labat © Casterman)

of the same area, such as Zambujal and Vila Nova de Sao Pedro, also reveal these two cultural phases linked in part with the first use of metal.

These Portuguese tombs and hypogea, and their contents, have been compared with the Spanish monuments in the Almeria region, and their architectural context. In the famous Los Millares group, tomb 19 has a circular chamber originally covered by vaulting, which must have been supported by a central post. It had a small lateral cell, and access was through a passage divided into three sections by port-hole slabs. The tomb lay in the centre of a hemispheric tumulus edged by dry stones. It is characteristic of local megalithic construction, and must date from a little before 3000 B.C. A date very close to this was established from a sample taken from the base of the nearby rampart. This connection between material found at the necropolis and at the fortified site seems to point to a link between the two, dating from the first phase of occupation. As in Portugal, a second, Chalcolithic, phase was marked by the presence of bell-beaker vessels.

The antiquity of the first phase, known as 'Almerian', is confirmed by two dates obtained from tomb 7 at the necropolis of El Barranquete 30 kilometres to the south-east of Los Millares; analysis of the remains of a wooden post from this tomb yielded a date of about 3000 B.C. The contemporary dwellings of Tabernas and Tarajal have

153

Italian megalithic monuments, although rare, resemble others of western Europe. This one is at Bisceglia, in Apulia. Its tumulus has vanished, but the layout of the stones indicates a rectangular chamber.

(Photo © Roger-Viollet)

supplied closely comparable results.

This very ancient dating challenges once again the supposed links between these tombs and certain Aegean monuments – links which were thought to have been connected with the spread of early metal-working. Such links are improbable, however: prospectors for ore did not arrive from the East like settlers needing to build fortified dwellings – they arrived in communities which had long possessed collective tombs and fortified camps, factors which encouraged the development of a metal-based society.

The twin features of lengthened burial chambers and the increasing proliferation of chamber tombs also occurred to some extent in southern Italy. Megalithic burial was only practised here by two fairly limited groups. In the Bari-Tarento area the chambers were like elongated rectangles, sometimes subdivided, measuring between 3 and 17 metres in length. The Giovinazzo tomb still has its 27-metre mound; at Corato the entrance is central, at Bisceglia it is lateral. These were certainly places of collective burial: the remains of thirteen skeletons were found at Bisceglia, and the bones of thirteen more were collected together in part of the Giovinazzo tomb. Chambers in the Otranto region were subcircular in design, without a passage. The architectural styles all appear to date from the beginning of the Bronze Age between 2400 and 1600 B.C. Rock-cut tombs were also in use during the same period throughout the Italian peninsula and in Sicily.

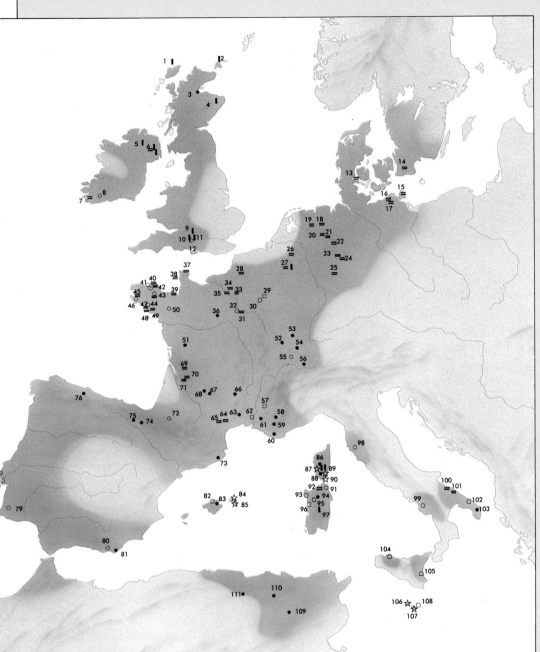

THE SPREAD OF MEGALITHIC CONSTRUCTION

Megalithic construction spread inland during the third millennium from the ancient coastal centres of western Europe, with monuments appearing throughout entire regions. Megalithic building styles in the Mediterranean islands were very varied, distinguished by insular originality and conservatism.

○ Paramegalithic grave
● Megalithic grave
❙ Standing stone
☆ Temple
= Very long grave
▢ Hypogeum

1 Callanish
2 Stenness – Brogar
3 Clava
4 Easter Aquorthies
5 Beaghmore
6 Millin Bay
7 Island
8 Labbamolaga
9 Avebury
10 Stonehenge
11 Durrington Walls
12 Bush Barrow
13 Blomeskobbel
14 Kivik
15 Rügen Island
16 Gnewitz
17 Liepen
18 Thuine
19 Havelte
20 Atteln
21 Beckum
22 Rimbeck
23 Altendorf
24 Lohne-Züschen
25 Lohra
26 Stein

27 Wéris
28 La Chaussée-Tirancourt
29 Les Mournouards, Le Mesnil-sur-Oger
30 Le Rezet, Coizard
31 Marolles
32 Noisy-sur-Ecole
33 Argenteuil
34 Guiry-en-Vexin
35 Epône
36 Eteauville
37 Bretteville
38 Jersey
39 Tressé
40 Prajou Menhir, Trébeurden
41 La Motta, Lannion
42 Crec'h Quillé
43 Saint-Judes-en-Bourbriac
44 Liscuis, Laniscal
45 Lesconil
46 Kersandry, Plouhinec
47 Goerem, Gâvres
48 Mané Kerioned, Carnac
49 Les Pierres Plates, Locmariaquer
50 Saint-Just
51 Bougon
52 Lavans-les-Dôle
53 Aillevans
54 Auvernier
55 Chamblandes
56 Sion
57 Roaix
58 Salernes
59 Cabasse
60 La Lande
61 Orgon
62 Arles-Fontvieille
63 Lamalou, Rouet
64 Pépieux
65 Laure-Minervois
66 Balsièges
67 Larroque
68 Ferme du Frau, Cazals
69 Montguyon
70 Gardegan
71 Lugasson
72 La Halliade, Bartrès
73 Cova d'En Dayna, Romanya de la Selva
74 Artajena
75 Laguardia
76 Oviedo
77 São Pedro do Estoril
78 Palmella
79 La Atalaia
80 Los Millares
81 El Barranquete
82 Sant Vincent
83 Son Baulo
84 Els Tudons
85 Trepuco
86 Settiva
87 Filitosa
88 Fontanaccia
89 Cucuruzzu
90 Tappa
91 Li-Muri
92 Arzachena
93 Anghelu Ruju
94 Mores, Sa Coveccada
95 San Andrea Priu
96 Santu Pedru
97 Genna Arrele
98 Ponte San Pietro
99 Gaudo
100 Bisceglia
101 Giovinazzo
102 Quattromacine
103 Laterza
104 Conca d'Oro
105 Castelluccio
106 Ggantija, Gozo
107 Tarxien, Hagar Kim, Malta
108 Hal Safliéni, Malta
109 Gastel
110 Djebel Mazela
111 Roknia

155

THE SECRET

OF THE

BUILDERS

The Master of the Stones

From today's standpoint, the achievements of the megalith builders look like works of genius. Some of their spectacular monuments have inspired extravagant theories about the techniques they used, particularly for transporting the stones: hauling on runners across frozen ground or over tracks of cereal grains, harnessing hydraulic power...

Although we know very little about the tools and techniques used by these stone masters, recent experimental studies allow us to speculate in ways that, without producing definitive proof, have made a positive contribution towards understanding the megalithic spirit — an impressive combination of effort, patience, and ingenuity.

Such observations have a dual basis; they are inspired by certain European Neolithic sites and their excavation, and also by technologies linked with megalithism throughout the world, and their comparison. The comparative method, open to criticism when dealing with megalithic monuments outside their socio-economic context, is justified in matters of technology.

By definition megaliths are large; they are therefore heavy and difficult to transport. In theory the mass of a stone can be assessed by multiplying its volume by its density; but it is often difficult to make an accurate estimate of the volume of an irregular block, or of the density of a rock that may not be of a homogeneous composition.

Our knowledge of a few known examples of very heavy monoliths can lead us to a fuller understanding of prehistoric megaliths. The heaviest block to have been moved without mechanical aids in modern times is the stone that was transported to St Petersburg on the orders of the Empress Catherine II of Russia, to form the base for the equestrian statue of Peter the Great: it weighed 1,250 tonnes, with a volume of 450 cubic metres and was dragged over six kilometres on a heavy sledge.

The most important monolith from ancient times is undoubtedly the Aswan obelisk in Egypt: 42 metres long and weighing 1,168 tonnes, it still lies unfinished in its granite quarry. The colossi of Memnon ordered by Pharaoh Amenhotep III and set up in the plain of Thebes probably weigh about 1,000 tonnes each; the Nile valley was also the source of the Luxor obelisk given by Egypt to King Charles X of France, who had it erected in the Place de la Concorde in Paris — it is 22.83 metres high, and weighs about 200 tonnes.

The famous dressed and assembled blocks of the temple of Jupiter Heliopolis at Baalbek in the Lebanon were probably set up in about 60 A.D. by order of either the emperor Claudius or his nephew Nero. The base includes stones 10 metres long, weighing about 350 tonnes each, surmounted by a podium or trilithon of three stones, which on average weigh 800 tonnes apiece, and which are between 19.20 and 19.60 metres long, 4.34 metres high, and 3.65 metres deep. The South Stone

These tools found in the quarry at Plussulien are hammers of various kinds, made of trimmed or rough stone. Antler picks were probably also used here, but the acidity of the local soil would have dissolved them. The Plussulien hammers are very similar to those found at Bougon.

(Photo © C.-T. Le Roux)

The Plussulien quarry in the Armorican heartland was used during the Neolithic era for the extraction of dolerite blocks which were trimmed and then polished to make axes. The influence of these was then spread over a very wide area. Fire was used to split the rock. Techniques of striking the rocks were very similar to those used in quarrying megaliths for use in monuments.

(Photo © C.-T. Le Roux)

in the same monument weighs 970 tonnes. Equally vast blocks are not uncommon in Cyclopean walling or harbour installations built by the Phoenicians during the eleventh to the eighth centuries B.C. One such stone, discovered in 1971 in the temple wall in Jerusalem, weighs about 413 tonnes. Some of the lintel stones in Mycenean tombs built around the middle of the second millennium B.C. are estimated at more than 100 tonnes.

Some of the prehistoric megaliths in western Europe are of considerable weight: 350 tonnes for the broken Great Menhir at Locmariaquer, for example, and 180 tonnes for the heaviest stone slab of the Cueva de Menga at Antequera. In the Bougon necropolis the horizontal covering stone for chamber A weighs 90 tonnes, and that for chamber F2 an estimated 32 tonnes; this stone was used as a model in 1979 for experiments in hauling and setting up. The standing stones at Avebury in southern England weigh 40 tonnes each on average, while those at Stonehenge are slightly less heavy – a mere 30 tonnes.

The quarry lying alongside the tumulus F at Bougon was dug out to a depth of 3 metres in the limestone bank. It was partly filled in by quarry waste which hid discarded quarrying tools: antler picks and stone hammers. The excavation trench made it possible to study the various phases of digging and the techniques used.

(Photo © J.-P. Mohen)

The Olmecs, Mayas and Aztecs of America used blocks of between 20 and 60 tonnes for their steles and altars. A statue found at Teotihuacán near Mexico City weighed 227 tonnes, and the blocks of some Cyclopean Inca walls up to 200 tonnes.

The *moai*, the Easter Island statues weighing up to 300 tonnes, offer a final example: one unfinished figure, barely cut out from the solid rock, is 20 metres long. The greatest moai ever erected is that of Te Pito Te Kura – 9.80 metres high, with an estimated weight of 80 tonnes.

Petrographic and geological analysis of the stone can suggest theories for the origin of the blocks. Several searches for outcrops close to the sites have disclosed quarries used in prehistoric times, which in some cases confirm their origins; quarry tools can also help us to understand extraction techniques. The nature of the materials involved determines very precisely both the layout and the style of construction. In France, megaliths are absent from the sands and clays of the Landes and Sologne; Touraine, on the other hand, has natural supplies of fine sandstone, which prehistoric builders used for large rectangular Angevin-style chambers. In the Beauce the fine-grained limestone appears in the form of massive blocks, which were used for building rectangular or polygonal burial chambers. In the Eure valley, further to the west on the borders of Normandy, the simultaneous use of regular sandstone slabs and irregular blocks of conglomerate puddingstone reflects local geological variations. The standing stones to the south of Angers in Maine-et-Loire consist of volcanic rock, and those to the north of Armorican sandstone. In the south-east a modest outcrop of hard secondary rock was exploited for further standing stones, while there are many funerary chambers in the Senonian and Eocene sandstone region. To the east, standing stones and megalithic chambers rest on sandstone, while the presence of limestone and lacustrine millstone determined the building of several burial chambers.

Prehistoric peoples sometimes used erratic blocks found near the construction site. Roughly tabular blocks, with the kind of blunt ridges often seen on granite, are the result of surface erosion of ancient massifs: the Armorican massif, visible in the outcrop near Carnac, is one example. In northern Europe moraine blocks were shifted by the glaciers of the quaternary ice ages; these blocks were used to cover many of the burial chambers of northern Germany, Denmark, and

At the bottom of quarry-trenches, half filled with trimming waste, prehistoric men abandoned their tools. This antler pick was found in the quarry beside the tumulus F at Bougon in the Deux-Sèvres. Stone was extracted from a series of conical pits. The bottoms of two such pits are seen here.

(Photo © J.-P. Mohen)

161

In 1979 a series of experiments took place in the tumulus F quarry at Bougon, in which blocks were extracted from the rocky bank with simulated prehistoric stone hammers and antler picks. Moderately-sized blocks were then brought to the tumulus under construction on a sort of litter.

(Photo © J.-P. Mohen)

southern Sweden. Stones like these were used in the state in which they were discovered, so the problem of extraction did not arise.

The search for the necessary blocks might however involve travelling some distance from the selected place of construction. The Roche aux Fées monument at Essé consists of about 40 blocks, some weighing 40 tonnes, from an outcrop at least four kilometres away. The granite or amphibolite-pyroxenite slabs of the Dissignac monument near Saint-Nazaire were transported five kilometres from the coast, while the great covering stone on the Gavrinis tomb was brought from about the same distance: this granite, with its very strongly marked grain, occurs in the Locmariaquer peninsula, while the bedrock of the island consists of clear fine-grained granite, like the other slabs of the monument. Stonehenge is once again unique: the eighty blue stones of the second phase of construction are dolerite from Pembrokeshire, more than 200 kilometres to the west. During the third phase, the great trilithon sarsens – a form of sandstone – came from local outcrops of glacial moraine at Avebury, just over thirty kilometres away.

In limestone terrain quarries had to be established to provide building materials, either slabs or dry stones. At Bougon the quarries were discovered within the necropolis itself, in the form of large trenches hollowed out close to the tumulus, and almost completely filled in afterwards. Albert Hesse's resistivity surveys have established the outlines. The Callovian site's limestone rock lies on two levels, upper and middle. The thin (30–40 centimetres) upper layer was extracted from shallow sections surrounding the earliest tumuli, such as the E tumulus dated at about 4000 B.C. The middle layer, much thicker, provided the basic material for the site's three great mounds. The rock was extracted from conical pits 3 metres deep, close to the monuments. The pits intersect, forming vast excavations which were more or less filled in by quarry waste, limestone gravel alternating with layers of red clay soil.

The partial filling in of the large quarry running beside the west side of the F tumulus has been studied stratigraphically, and has yielded valuable information on Neolithic extraction techniques. Five successive phases of digging are visible in a cross-section of the pit. The first grave is the deepest, and lies next to the mound. The quarry was extended away from the construction, in trenches of decreasing depth. As digging proceeded the waste material was used to fill in some of the preceding grave; a partial longitudinal section has exposed the funnel-shaped pits. Quarrying tools were discovered at the bottom of the graves, in the bottom layer of debris – several picks and a double pick, or rake, made of deer antlers. Traces of wear are visible at the tips of the tines and on the main stem, at the point where it would be held.

The stones used to build the Bougon tumulus were quarried using trimmed stone hammers to loosen the blocks, and antler picks to scrape out the loosened rubble between the hard layers.

(Musée des Antiquités Nationales, Saint-Germain-en-Laye.
Photo J.-M. Labet © Casterman)

These tools are very similar to others found in the ditch of the first Stonehenge monument, and in the shafts and galleries of Neolithic flint mines in northern France (Nointel, Hardivillers), in Belgium (Spiennes), and in England (Grimes Graves). Marks from such picks can still be seen on hypogea walls in the Marne, and at Bougon they were used to pick and scrape away the split layers of rocky banks to expose blocks of solid rock which were then loosened with axe-hammers made from stones roughly chipped to shape brought from an

163

outcrop five kilometres to the south. Stones extracted in this way, without the use of fire, are of fairly regular parallelipiped form. They were used to form kerbs both inside and outside the mound, acting as a type of chest to be filled up with stone-trimming waste and forming the bulk of the monument. English sites have yielded up many bovine shoulder-blades, used as shovels to clear away debris from the extraction process, and a single aurochs' shoulder-blade abandoned in the gravel mass of tumulus C at Bougon may have been used for this purpose. The finer particles must have been carried in baskets or leather bags.

A series of experiments carried out in the tumulus F quarry at Bougon in 1979 demonstrated the efficiency of prehistoric techniques. Deer antlers were formed into picks, with the rear tines cut off with flint blades. These picks were used to scrape out and enlarge the natural cracks in the existing rock, then to extract blocks of 10-20 kilograms, and finally to remove the waste material. They turned out to be flexible, strong, and extremely effective; moreover they became worn in the same way and at the same places as the Neolithic tools.

Accretions and flint nodules, either used as found or bevelled, were used next to loosen blocks cut out with picks in the quarry. They were also used to smooth the surfaces and edges of some slab columns, and to carve out grooves, windows, and some of the angles seen on similar prehistoric slabs in the necropolis. These hammers, weighing a kilogram or two, were only really effective if they were used with a regular repetitive movement which did not demand particular

A rocky bank on the Chaumes plateau at Exoudun, 4 kilometres from Bougon, has been identified as the source of roofing slabs for some of the necropolis tombs. In an experiment using the same tools as in prehistoric times – stone hammers, antler picks, wedges, and wooden levers – a stone weighing about half a tonne was extracted from this bank in about an hour.

(Photo © J.-P. Mohen)

164

Choosing and Extracting the Blocks

strength. Thus little by little the surface of the rock was pulverized; small flakes were detached, creating characteristic cup marks on the rough-hewn Neolithic slabs of some chambers. Many of these stone axe-hammers were discovered in front of the Gavrinis cairn, and had been used in decorating the slab stones of the tomb. Hammered blocks were found in the body of the monument, and innumerable fragments from this decorative process evoke the meticulous care of the prehistoric stonemason at work.

Surface decoration by chip-carving stone produced two different effects. The first was a line tracing a sign or a known object, such as the axe with handle. The second consisted of pitting the surrrounding surface so as to outline a motif in 'false relief' (a form of excised decoration) – as used to show up the breasts on female figures. The two techniques were used at the same periods, each tending to be used for particular motifs.

Such hammers must have been used to carve out the tenons and mortices of the Stonehenge trilithons, as well as to produce the entasis effect on these trilithon columns – the lateral bulge reducing progressively towards the top, to give an illusion of greater lightness to the standing stones. The same device was to be used for the columns of Doric temples in Greece 1,500 years later!

The Bougon quarries could only supply slabs of modest dimensions. Weighing between 100 and 200 kilograms, they could be fixed to a sort of litter and carried by six or seven people. The larger pillars of the great megalithic chambers, also from the middle Callovian era, are of a quality unknown at this site; they may have come from the Pamproux region, five kilometres to the north. The metre-thick stone covering the chamber A (7.50 by 5 metres), is a coralline clayey rock of the Tertiary system found in the clay outcrops to the east of the necropolis. A block of this size cannot have been easy to uncover or transport, although it was probably not particularly difficult to extract, despite its hardness: by removing the surrounding clay it would have been possible to manoeuvre the block with the aid of wedges, props, rollers, and levers made of tree-trunks.

Slabs of another fairly hard rock, Bathomian flint limestone, were used to cover some of the Bougon megalithic chambers. The slab of the F2 chamber, for example, measures 6 by 3.50 metres and is 1.50 metres thick. This 32-tonne block must have come from the nearest outcrop at Exoudun four kilometres to the south, where a very compact and thick rocky bank forms a cliff carved away by the Niort valley of the river Sèvre. Traces of Neolithic dwellings are plentiful higher up the valley: shards, flint flakings, and fragments of grinding stones are concentrated together on the edge of the plain. This site may have formed a spur limited by a ditch and rampart now vanished. At the beginnning of this century there were still lintels and stone field gateway slabs close by, a practice that must date from much older times. An enormous stone abandoned in the same place may have been a prehistoric megalith. It was on this plateau of Chaumes at Exoudun that the experimental extraction of a large slab was carried out in 1979.

Since the layer of soil is shallow and irregular, the bedrock layer is visible here and there, as well as the cracks in it, and removing the earth revealed a slab of good quality stone of the required dimensions, outlined by natural cracks of varying widths. These were enlarged and deepened on two or three sides, using deer-antler picks and limestone hammers to dig out a trench. Where the block had to be detached from the rock stratum, notches were cut out in it, into which dried hornbeam wedges were forced; they were then soaked with water so that they swelled, while at the same time they were driven further in with stone hammers. A final blow resulted in cracking, and the stone was freed. Another wedge would disengage it so that a roller or lever could be slid underneath to remove it. The extraction of a block of about half a tonne at Exoudun took three people one hour.

The simplicity of the undertaking explains why so few traces of such work can be seen on Neolithic megaliths; some interesting traits do, however, remain. The choice of rocks, often very precise and dictated by the exact function of each stone (covering slab, pillar, kerb) indicates the great mastery of prehistoric quarrymen, who knew all about local geological variations and how to meet the demands of the 'architects'. When it came to cutting up the stone, gashes recently noted on the edges of the breaks in the Grand Menhir at Locmariaquer confirm the accurate onslaught on the weak points of the block, and perhaps even the use of wooden wedges, indicating a sound understanding of the seams of the rock. The technique of sawing the stone with a thread and grains of sand was only used in prehistoric times to produce small artefacts such as axe-blades and decorative items.

There is nothing in these techniques that contradicts known facts concerning ancient and traditional quarrying methods. Monoliths were roughly squared up on site with very simple instruments, stone hammers and wooden rollers. The Egyptian obelisks were carved out of the solid rock itself, as proved by the immense the Aswan obelisk still lying unfinished in its quarry. These blocks were squared up with lumps of stone weighing 5 kilograms used with both hands as a heavy hammer; an hour's work of this kind was enough to pulverize granite five millimetres thick. Trimming and polishing a large obelisk has been estimated to require 400 men for fifteen months.

Excavation of the Champ-Chalon monument at Benon in Charente-Maritime has revealed (foreground) the quarry pit that supplied the small slabs for the rectangular tumulus which is being cleared (further back). To the right can be seen the access passage to a circular chamber.

(Photo © R. Joussaume)

Eight hundred metres from the Baalbek sanctuary, in the Sheikh Abdallah quarry, an enormous stone has remained in place since the first century A.D. It still shows the rough-hewing corresponding to the lifting and cutting designed to separate the block from the body of the rock; as the underside was cut in a broad groove rollers were slipped beneath to bear it once released, and prepare it for removal to the sanctuary. More recently, on Easter Island, six quarrymen used stone picks to carve a large statue 5 metres tall; the work took them a year.

To this day quarrymen in the limestone region of Poitou, in the granite Ile Grande in Brittany, and their colleagues elsewhere have the same perfect understanding of their stone, its texture and veining, its faults, its weight, its resonance, colour, brightness – they have all the

Ropes, Tree-trunks, Muscles

expertise needed to master it in every respect – as their equally expert predecessors of 5,000 years ago.

One of the challenges of megaliths is the deployment of blocks of considerable weight; the construction of earth or dry-stone monuments already demanded collective labour on a grand scale. Successful undertakings of this size required the combination of several elements, found whenever people gathered together to work enthusiastically on a site set up for the glory of the group or the clan. Maurice Leenhardt describes the erection of the central post of a dwelling hut in New Caledonia – a considerable undertaking. The operation could not succeed without advance planning, diplomacy and technical skill. The combined clan selected the tree on the mountainside and cut it down three seasons later with stone axes and firebrands. Plaited ropes and creepers were prepared for haulage. Family teams were assembled; a track was opened through the forest, and faggots of wood spread for the tree to slide down. Everyone crowded together to haul on the ropes, and priests between the rows of hauliers blessed and encouraged them. At the end of each line, 'masters' directed and controlled progress, while the magician performed his rites to ensure the success of the operation.

The same participants, or very nearly the same, can be identified in Egypt, in the famous scene on the tomb of Djuti-hetep at El Berschi: a stone colossus 7 metres high and weighing some 60 tonnes, placed on a sledge drawn by ninety men spaced out along ropes, directed by 'conductors' and encouraged by priests, all at the command of the Pharaoh.

The simplest way to move a megalith without using modern machinery requires the assembling of three elements – ropes, logs, and manpower – which is what happened for the Bougon experiment of moving a 32-tonne block.

Ropes are indispensable for dragging very heavy stones over a long distance; the technique of using levers alone to push the block is only effective over short distances and with stones of moderate size. The ropes maintain both the traction and the balance of the block, which must be held and directed accurately; a broken rope may lead to an accident. Prehistoric ropes consisted of plaited vegetable fibres and nearly all have disintegrated, though discoveries in European bogs and lakes do indicate that ropemaking was a daily domestic activity both in the Neolithic era and after the beginnings of metalworking.

The oldest rope extant, a fragment 30 centimetres long, was found in 1960 by Father Glory in the Lascaux cave near the shaft of the Galerie des Félins; it is about 17,000 years old, and consists of three twisted threads of vegetable fibres plaited together. By Neolithic times

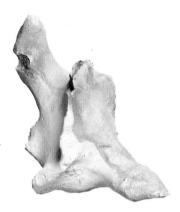

In the Nointel mines in the Oise, flint nodules (bottom) lying in the chalk, were dug out with trimmed flint picks (top). The marks are still visible on the sides of pits and galleries.

(Photo J.-M. Labat © Casterman)

The work of the Neolithic miner was very similar to that of the quarryman. Pits and galleries were dug into the limestone to extract flint nodules. The Spiennes site in Belgium near Mons, was used in a semi-'industrial' manner.

(Photo © M. E. Rahir - D.R.)

fibre-plaiting techniques were more fully developed, however, and a fairly large variety of threads, cords, nets, plaits and esparto-ware has survived from this era. Most European remains date from the third and second millennia B.C. Although occasional animal fibres have been found, such as horse-hair nets, vegetable fibre is much more common, and particularly wood fibre: lime, elm, birch, willow, and sometimes bark from fir or lime trees. Woody fragments were soaked in hot water and beaten to separate the fibres. Neolithic people also sought out the long flexible roots of fir, ivy, and wild clematis; these too were soaked and beaten to make the fibres supple. Threads were made by twisting, followed by plaiting. Lakeside sites have yielded good examples in Switzerland (at Auvernier, on Lake Neuchâtel) and in France (Le Bourget lake).

Comparison with other societies helps us to a better understanding of the ropemaker's technology and his value to society. In the Egypt of the Pharaohs, in the third and second millennia B.C. – approximately the same time as the megalithic age in Europe – ropemakers formed a specific caste. They can be seen clearly in the relief carvings on the Weh-hetep tomb at Meir. The wide variety of ropes had many uses, including the manufacture of many objects: strings for traps and nets, tethering cords for animals, strings to hang up meat to dry, to attach handles to tools, to construct rafts and reed huts, strings for bows and musical instruments, belts, necklaces, sandals, ropes for boats and monumental building-sites.

The Skills of Ropemaking

Some of the ropemaking techniques seen in Africa are undoubtedly very similar to those of the megalith builders. Ropes were used for all sorts of purposes: in order to make finer threads, for netting, for example, vegetable stalks were plunged into marshy mud, after an initial soaking, and macerated for several days. The workers who twisted the fibres were virtuosos of their craft. The inner faces of two fine strips would be stuck together. 'Next,' according to Father Glory who wrote up these observations, 'the ropemaker rolls them in a spiral on the right thigh, pressing down with the palm of his right hand. With the left hand he holds out the two threads as they twist on themselves under the pressure of the right hand moving from the hip down towards the knees. Next, under the pressure of the reverse movement from knee to hip, the two threads combine together and twist evenly.' This produced a thread 3 millimetres thick. Then 'the left hand takes up three threads which the thumb twists against the fore-finger while the right hand, grasping each of the fine cords, works in a twisting movement to tighten them and even out the roll. Swiftly, depending on his skill, the workman piles up on his right twenty to thirty metres of cord per hour.' These cords might be cables 30 or 40 millimetres thick, for moving felled trees or building materials. They were made at times and places fixed in advance, at special gatherings of many families; the social aspect of a major collective undertaking, such as the construction of a megalith, would thus be apparent from the first preparatory stages of the work.

Easter Island is treeless today, but fossil pollen studies have indicated the presence of trees between the tenth and seventeenth centuries A.D. This is the period when the great statues were set up – probably therefore erected with the aid of rollers, wooden levers, and bark ropes.

Traditional rope manufacture in the Poitiers area of France, both domestic and factory-based, first used flax – which produced the best ropes, supple and strong – and also the very long creepers found in certain local areas of brushland. The high quality of such ropes has been verified; a string half a centimetre in diameter can raise and support a bucket of water weighing ten kilograms. The flax ropes used for the Bougon haulage experiment were 3 centimetres thick, and their total length was 600 metres, representing a mass of 200 kilograms.

Wood also seems to have been an essential material for setting up megaliths, as shown in numerous comparable documents – used for the haulage-sledges of Egypt and Syria, the Baalbek rollers, the round-log roads of New Caledonia and the levers of Easter Island. In Neolithic Europe wood was the basic building material. Strong posts made the framework for walls and roofs; the many post-holes found during excavations, and the numerous traces surveyed in lake sites, are revealing on this point. Near Bougon, with its abundant deciduous trees and particularly oaks, wood was certainly in use 5,000 years ago to transport megaliths and also, at the beginning of this century, was still used for heavy burdens in the same way.

The hypothesis of a vehicle with wooden wheels has been discounted; the few completely wooden wheels known from the end of the Neolithic period, found in Switzerland and in Italy, would not have been sufficiently robust to transport such weights. Haulage sledges would have required a relatively flat track to slide along; this technique seems too elaborate. There are no traces at Bougon of any construction of a track of this type, despite searches round the necropolis mound. On the other hand, the notion of a track has been retained – more precisely, a movable track: two parallel 'rails' made of oak logs squared off on two sides to provide a smooth surface for traction and avoid ground irregularities, stones, and molehills, or loose shifting areas where the load might sink in. This track, three times the length of the block to be hauled, was removed from behind the block and replaced in front as it was dragged along. But more was needed: along the track a system of rollers was arranged with, once more, evenly shaped oak logs 40 centimetres in diameter. The block, its flat underside already smoothed, moved over them by rolling them along.

Wooden aids were also needed to haul and erect the block: large levers, elm logs 10 metres long, oak blocks to wedge up the levers, and a whole series of sleepers and poles to manipulate the wood and bear the ropes. Ash handles were made for polished stone axes, such as those found in lake sites. Experimenters have selected genuine polished axes of unidentified origins (therefore of modest archeological importance), and fixed them by exerting pressure, without tie or glue, to the bulging end of the handle. Two flint axes, and one made of dolerite, a hard rock, were used to cut down the trees. The structure of the polished axe was very effective because following dynamic principles the shock waves registered regularly in the stone. The flint axes, fairly late since they were known around 3500 B.C., wore down only slowly as small chips detached themselves. They were remarkably efficient: a tree some 30 centimetres in diameter could be felled in an hour with two flint axes striking alternate blows. The stone axe blunted more quickly and the blade required frequent sharpening with a sandstone polisher and an abrasive; this however was the type of axe used consistently from the most remote times. It was also used to square off logs for the demountable track and to strip the bark off certain tree-trunks.

The labour force was the next problem. A small theoretical calculation came first: what strength was needed to pull a 32-tonne block on rollers? Physicists established that in this case the load was best divided by 12, and because of irregularities in the rollers, which consisted of

The flint nodules extracted from the Nointel mine were chipped away, as is clearly visible, to make rough axe shapes which were then polished.

(Photo J.-M. Labat © Casterman)

THE GREAT OX OF GAVRINIS

The Gavrinis capstone as it was in 1983 showing the ox with long curved horns and the axe-plough motif broken by a fracture in the block. The capstone corresponds to the middle part of the great decorated menhir, two fragments of which were found in the tombs of the Table des Marchands and Er-Vinglé. This monolith, some 14 metres high, must have been erected close to the Grand Menhir Brisé at Locmariaquer before being pulled down and reused in other tombs of the region.

(Photo © Glotain/Direction des Antiquités préhistoriques de Bretagne).

One of the finest discoveries of recent years occurred during renewed excavations at Gavrinis in 1983. When Charles-Tanguy Le Roux removed the covering stone from the chamber he was astonished to discover carved motifs: the ox with large curving horns was unique at that time, and a second pair of horns appeared to indicate another animal beyond an apparently deliberate break in the rock. On the exposed surface Le Roux identified in addition an axe-plough more than 3 metres across, also interrupted by a break in the rock. The distinctive grain of the stone linked it with the enormous standing stones of the broken Great Menhir at Locmariaquer. Close to the Great Menhir Le Roux identified the same stone as at Gavrinis, covering both the Table des Marchands and also a more damaged section on the Er Vinglé tomb. Measurement of the breaks proved that these three large fragments were sections of the same monolith. An unidentified design on the Table des Marchands turned out to be the front feet and the head of the second ox the horns of which were uncovered at Gavrinis. Before being broken it must have been erect, like the Locmariaquer menhir and possibly close to it.

What is the meaning of this kind of re-use, and particularly of these deliberately broken stones? Using blocks again in other monuments symbolizes the endurance of a cult whose rites would suffer complete destruction of some of its sites.

logs with the bark left on, the figure of 10 was fixed as the optimum. The mass of the ropes, assessed at 200 kilograms, had also to be taken into account; there was also some friction, equivalent to at least 100 kilograms. The total mass to be dragged therefore totalled at least 620 kilograms.

Then another question arose: would animals or people be best for hauling, and how many would be necessary in each case? Oxen were the obvious choice of animal – they are tractable creatures whose pulling power has been estimated at 80 kilograms apiece. But their power is only marginally cumulative; oxen roped together in pairs on a yoke co-ordinate their efforts with difficulty. Although the yoke was known in Neolithic times, ancient iconography displays no examples whatever of animal traction.

Not all megalithic blocks were left in their rough state. The stone was often hewn to form doorways. This example is in the Romaña de la Selva tomb in the Spanish province of Gerona. The columns were squared off to make a neatly-fitting monolith structure.

(Photo © Roger-Viollet)

The doorway dividing one of the chambers in the Montiou tumulus at Sainte-Soline in Deux-Sèvres from the passage is carved all over. The limestone slabs of the walls are trimmed and fitted with great care. The whole structure was probably roofed with a stone slab.

(Photo © J.-P. Mohen)

The only relevant recorded case is the transport of the Mussolini monolith, which was drawn in 1928 by sixty oxen yoked in pairs in three rows. This operation was helped by the use of wooden rollers and by a track descending gradually down to Rome. When the equestrian statue of Henri IV was transported in 1808 to its setting on the Pont-Neuf in Paris the respective capacities of animals and men as hauliers were demonstrated with great clarity: the mass of the bronze statue was estimated at 25 tonnes, and that of the timber frame and the runners at 15 tonnes – a total of 40 tonnes to be hauled. The foundry workshop in the Faubourg du Roule was several kilometres from the statue's destination; eighteen pairs of oxen hauled the burden. A great crowd gathered along the route: 'Paris suddenly took on a festive air. There was unprecedented spontaneous popular enthusiasm,' commented Charles J. Lafolie in his *Mémoires Historiques Relatifs à la Fonte et*

à l'Élévation de la Statue Équestre de Henri IV (1819). Problems arose in the Avenue de Marigny when the convoy reached a cambered roadway: the burden threatened to topple off its runners. The oxen were inadequate, and a 'considerable reinforcement' of horses was added; but the operation was delayed. As it moved into the Avenue des Champs-Élysées the delay lengthened considerably, and anxiety grew.

> Everyone wondered if the obstacles were insurmountable; finally, some workmen offered their help. At first théy were refused, then it was decided to try this new method. Ropes were fixed to the cross-beams of the trailer, and the workmen seized hold. The oxen were hastily removed and a thousand arms took up the strain. The monument shifted, it no longer moved at walking pace, it flew, and in less than half an hour it reached the Tuileries crossing . . .

It was therefore decided not to use animals at Bougon: but how many people would they need? At Stonehenge Richard Atkinson had a 4-tonne replica of a blue stone pulled by students; forty hauled while twenty more placed the rollers and directed the runners. Atkinson's estimates appear generous: ten men per tonne, and five to oversee the steering. The Bougon calculations indicated that substantially fewer would be needed; the theoretical approach must be tested. It remained to be established whether both men and women would take

Stone could be trimmed to imitate wood very effectively. This door, with hinges, is in the Fontenille passage grave in Charente. The lower hinge is embedded in the socket of the sill. To the right, the arched door-case is visible.

(Photo © J.-P. Mohen)

Bougon: What can be Learned from Experience

part in the experiment, or only men, as indicated in various ancient sources. Without going further into a debate for which the Neolithic era was not fully equipped, it was decided to stick to the pattern handed down from antiquity.

Near the site where a half-tonne stone had been extracted on the Chaumes plateau, a 32-tonne block was hauled along. First a genuine block had to be found, of the same dimensions and mass as an actual Bougon stone, the slab covering the F2 chamber. But the dynamite used in the local quarries did not allow for the extraction of stones of such a size, and a block of concrete corresponding to the stone had to be used. Mass, volume, and shape were rigorously copied. In order to allow for the difference in density between concrete and limestone and still retain the same volume, a mass of polystyrene was placed inside the block, which measured 6 metres in length by 3.50 metres across and 2.30 metres high.

It took two days to fix the 200 kilograms of flax ropes in place, under the guidance of an expert in ship's rigging. This involved making up a large net, wrapping it round the block and linking it to four parallel haulage ropes, each 100 metres long. Jute cloths were placed at the corners, to prevent over-rapid wear on the stretched ropes. As the block was somewhat irregular in shape, wooden wedges were pushed between the block and the ropes so as to take up the slack.

Preparation for the experiment first brought together a dozen or so people, who spent three months preparing data on every aspect of the trial. In the final two weeks all the materials were assembled, practical conclusions were drawn from theoretical and archeological surveys, the sizable labour force had to be trained and the framework was constructed. Fifty Bougon archeological diggers contributed to the exercise, and local people were contacted as well.

Nearly 500 people arrived on the morning of 28 July 1979, some to haul the block and others to watch. Five separate teams of between six and eight people practised moving the oak rollers and rails, each weighing (300 kilograms), and replacing them in front of the block, while another team was charged with holding up the ropes with large poles.

At the first attempt to move the load the ropes stretched, but a jammed roller prevented the block from moving forward. The roller was levered away and replaced. At the second attempt: 230 men hauled, and while twenty more pushed from behind with short levers. The ropes stretched again, the block trembled, and with a shriek from the rollers it moved forward five or six metres, accompanied by tremendous shouting and applause.

Each of the materials used in construction imposed its own character. Here irregular large blocks cover the tomb buried within the earth tumulus of Ramshög near Hagestad in southern Sweden.

(Photo © Märta Strömberg)

Several short hauls were thus achieved during the morning. As the block moved forward, the rollers and rails taken up behind the megalith were put down again in front of it, and in this manner it advanced some 40 metres. One stage was even achieved with only 170 men pulling. At first they held the rope at shoulder height, but then tried it waist-high, walking backwards, and this seemed more effective.

To everyone's surprise this operation – so often considered 'superhuman' – was achieved with ease. None of the rollers was crushed by the weight of the block; the ropes stood up well, and showed no particular signs of wear. There was one problem, however: despite precautions taken to keep the block moving in a straight line, it began to deviate during the second and third stages. On both occasions one roller was crooked. A 10-metre lever manipulated by twenty men was used to shift the block back into place while the faulty roller was removed. Traction was maintained. Once again, a sound understanding of materials and their practical application was as effective, if not more so, than massive strength or elaborate machinery.

It was also by means of such levers, each operated by twenty

177

Lifting Megaliths with Levers

people, that in the afternoon of this same day, 28 July, the 32-tonne block was raised up without the use of a ramp. Three large levers set along one of the short sides of the block first lifted it about 50 centimetres; wooden props and wedges were slipped underneath, and the levers were then used in the same way on the other side. Thus by interplay of levers and a system of interlocking beams, the block was gradually lifted to a height of about a metre, and could have been raised further. Prehistoric people were therefore capable of lifting a covering stone to the top of the supporting columns to set it in place.

Erecting standing stones demanded very different efforts. Here the stone had to be tipped up to set it vertically on its end; its stability had also to be maintained by systematic wedging.

The manipulation of large oblong stones demands widely differing methods, according to their size and mass. Naturally less preparation is required to set up a one tonne block than the 350 tonnes of the broken Grand Menhir at Locmariaquer! The old Breton quarrymen knew how to manoeuvre moderately sized blocks by using wedges, rollers, levers, and ropes to move them sideways on their points of balance and imbalance close to the centre of gravity. Thus even small groups of men could roll or shift blocks sideways by working first on one side and then the other.

A ditch was dug at the place where the stone was to be raised, to receive the base of the monolith and the wedge stones; ditches like this have been found in the excavations of the Grée de Cojoux alignment at Saint-Just in Ille-et-Vilaine. Richard Atkinson has suggested that at Stonehenge, logs were driven in around the ditch sides, which were liable to receive the weight of the block obliquely as it was tipped up, to consolidate them.

The great difficulty in this operation was to bring the megalith up slowly. The movement has to be completely controlled so as to avoid slips and crushing, breaking the stone, or fatal accidents. There must have been accidents, although there are few examples of stones broken while being set up: the technique must have been very effective. Wooden frames were first envisaged, with a sand pit into which the monolith was tipped down; the stone was then gradually brought to the vertical as the sand shifted from under it. A model of the machine was built, and proved effective with a 'mini-megalith'.

In 1924 the engineer Stone published his observations and reconstructions for erecting the Stonehenge monoliths, working on models built to a 1:12 scale. Hauled to the edge of a wedging-up ditch, the stone tipped and slid under its own weight down to the bottom, where it lay obliquely. Ropes were then fixed to its upper end and hauled using a system of three logs fixed in a tripod and holding a pulley to

The dry stone of limestone areas was soon put to use. Stone slabs were piled up and wedged against each other; the passage walls of the tumulus A at Bougon were made in this way. These stones are weathered by frost, that is, successive rain and frost have gradually split them apart.

(Photo © J.-P. Mohen)

form a derrick, enabling the megalith to be raised with minimal effort. It only remained to set the wedging stones in place, and to fill in the ditch. In August 1985 the Prat-Ledan monolith near Plabennec, weighing 18.5 tonnes and 7.50 metres long, was set up in this way, with the aid of about a hundred people from Brest.

Other scholars have imagined something more elaborate. A ramp and wooden planking would surround the megalith more substantially, and they argued that it would be simultaneously pushed and hauled to the vertical with hoists. A fine example of this technique was recorded in the sixteenth century. At the request of Pope Sixtus V the architect Domenico Fontana embellished three squares in Rome by erecting obelisks; the largest was 32 metres tall, at St John Lateran. The setting up of the obelisk in St Peter's Square is illustrated in a Vatican fresco, so detailed that the architect Lebas was able to use it in

An experiment in megalith moving, at Bougon in 1979. Three large levers were operated together to lift a block weighing 32 tonnes; each was worked by a team of some twenty people. One side of the block was raised and held with wedges. The same operation was then repeated on the other side, and so on.

(Photo © Coll. J.-P. Mohen)

1833 when he was preparing to erect the Luxor obelisk in the Place de la Concorde in Paris. Such operations were carried out, so the chronicle relates, in an atmosphere of anxiety and amazement. In the Vatican the architect insisted on absolute silence, on pain of death, while the monolith was erected.

Was this technique, known to Vitruvius in the first century A.D., used in prehistoric times? It is impossible to say, but the technique used for the Grand Menhir at Locmariaquer must have been much practised to enable such a colossal stone to be set up: a remarkable achievement!

Recent digs have shown that terracing, masonry, and the assembling of materials played a very important part in the construction of many monuments. Megaliths themselves were often only a framework or a simple skeleton; occasionally they are missing altogether, as in the case of long barrows without chambers.

In ancient times the soil was first either raked or levelled. Traces of this preparatory work have been recorded in several places. At Stonehenge the circular bank of the first phase of construction rested directly on the chalk. At Bougon the ground was raked before the first rows of tumulus stones were set up, while clay soil was used to even out the base of the mound F, filling in hollows in the limestone bedrock. This clay sediment also appears mixed with small chalk pebbles; this base layer was therefore prepared in advance.

The bulk of the stones or earth in the mounds and cairns was sometimes very considerable. The volume of stones at Gavrinis has been assessed at nearly 5,000 cubic metres, equivalent to 10,000 tonnes. Bearing in mind that one man can transport perhaps 100 kilograms per day, the mound required 100,000 man–days, or three years' work for a team of one hundred men. Other cairns are even more immense; the volume of the Barnenez cairn is over 6,000 cubic metres while the Mont-Saint-Michel tumulus at Carnac comprises 20,000 cubic metres. These are among the most ancient monuments, and date from about 4000 B.C.

These enormous accumulations of broken stones are planned architecturally. A series of concentric or simple boundary kerbstones retained the banks as they were constructed to form a monument, preventing them from spreading and blurring the mound's outline. Excavation of the Barnenez monument in the 1950s revealed the prime importance of walls or external kerbs for defining the cairn and establishing a barrier between the world of the living and that of the dead. The internal kerbs were the framework, forming the steps of a monument which resembled a type of Mesopotamian ziggurat. The earliest Egyptian and pre-Colombian American pyramids have been linked in this context, but obviously such similarity relates only to technological convergence. The stepped monument is the simplest architectural form allowing any real height, with the steps acting as both buttress and scaffolding.

The art of dry-stone building reached its peak in several circular

Two hundred people were needed to pull the Bougon block; it moved forward on log rollers which spanned two portable rails made of squared-up tree-trunks. A team following behind with small levers helped to set the block in motion and kept it moving in the right direction.

(Photo © Coll. J.-P. Mohen)

On Easter Island, Thor Heyerdahl's team replaces a moai on the Anakena site, using methods thought to be very similar to those used by the islanders. The pile of stones plays an essential role in lifting the statue, economizing on wood which was thought to have been in short supply. Since that experiment it has been established that large coconut palms, now unknown on the island, once grew there. They were probably extremely useful in setting up the enormous statues.

(Photo © D.R.)

How to Build a Megalithic Tomb

burial chambers beneath large mounds roofed by corbelling in western France and the south of the Iberian peninsula. These coverings, also known as 'false domes' or 'vaults', made it possible to protect the tomb without the need for a stone slab, by piling up cantilevered flat stones. This type of construction, looking like the inside of a beehive, was stabilized by the cairn's mass of gravel. It appears to be extremely ancient, dating from the late fifth millennium: at the mounds of La Hogue and La Hoguette in Normandy, the Barnenez monument in Brittany, and at Bougon and Le Cous at Bazoges-en-Pareds in central western France. The magnificent corbelled chambers of the Iberian peninsula, at Los Millares in Spain and Monte de Outeiro in Portugal, appear distinctly later (third millennium), and thus are totally unconnected with the earlier examples. The same applies to the original forms at Newgrange, where the vault stones are especially fine, and to Maes Howe in Orkney, where the stones are arranged with particular care.

Many of the megalithic chambers themselves were very well built. The image of the 'dolmen table' standing on spindly pillars does not reflect the reality of the original. The sides of the chambers were blind, made of slabs sometimes complemented with dry-stone walls. Studies of several Portuguese, French and Irish monuments indicate that there were four stages in the construction of a megalithic chamber tomb. First the ground was prepared by raking, or by levelling with a

182

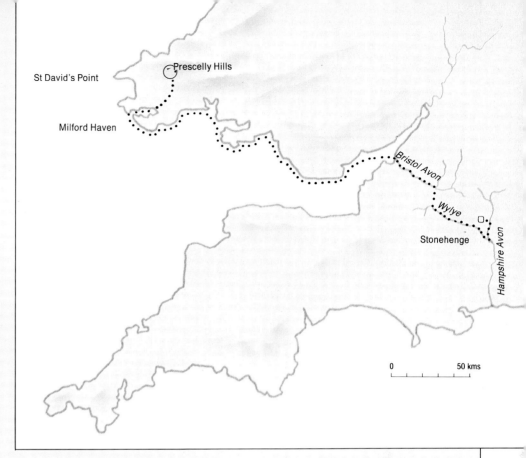

BRINGING THE STONES TO STONEHENGE

The 80 'blue stones' used in Stonehenge's second phase of construction, in the second half of the third millennium, are dolerite from Pembrokeshire, more than 200 kilometres away. The blocks, weighing several tonnes each, were brought from the Prescelly Hills along a mainly sea and river route, as suggested by Richard Atkinson. According to this theory, the 'blue stones' reached Stonehenge along what would become 'the avenue' some centuries later.

The great trilithons were erected during Stonehenge's third phase, around 2000 B.C.. They are sandstone, or Avebury sarsens, where the blocks were found abandoned among glacial moraines. Weighing up to 30 tonnes, the sarsen stones were brought more than 30 kilometres to Stonehenge.

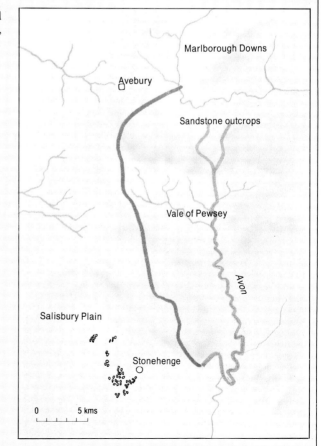

183

Ropes were needed for moving the megaliths. In France, some prehistoric fragments made of plaited vegetable fibres have been preserved in Lake Grésine in Savoie. The care with which they were made rendered them very strong.

layer of clay; a slab placed on the ground would determine the shape of the chamber. Next came the first elevation of the cairn: the chamber and its passage were marked out by kerb stones, then the walling slabs were set in position, in some cases resting directly on the raked ground or, more commonly, fixed in a small trench cut into the rock. The upper part of the stone was placed against the kerb and it was propped up on the inside. The slabs might interlock, as in the Angoulême-type chambers with grooved stones, or overlap as in the Portuguese chambers of Upper Beira. They were always placed in a precise order: often the head-stone came first and the passage last, as in the Hérault megalithic chambers. Most of the pillars were set vertically. However where the horizontal covering stone was particularly heavy the side stones were placed obliquely, like buttresses, the better to withstand the lateral thrust. In the final phase the horizontal covering stone was set in place; it was raised level with the top of the columns and shifted on beams to its final position. The tops of the columns are often shaped to meet the slightly irregular underside of the covering stone: a detail that might indicate that the stone was held up on props above the columns so that their shape could be adjusted where necessary. Once the stone was lowered into place it locked the whole design by its weight. When this key operation was complete the inner props of the chamber could be removed through the passage that had already been built. The cairn or tumulus was then finished. The downward thrust of its bulk and the strength of its kerb stones combined to ensure that the whole structure was completely stable.

In northern Europe, northern France, and Portugal, the inner arrangement of the chamber was the next stage. In the third millennium, compartmentalization with small stone slabs seems to have been widespread. Stone paving might divide two layers of burial.

The means of access was usually complex, reflecting rites that varied from one monument and period to another. The entrance was most often dry-stone walled, but the stage at which it was sealed is not known. The most striking method of entrance was surely the notched or perforated slab (porthole slab) placed at the passage opening. This distinctive architectural feature was very widely used, for it has been found from the European Atlantic zone to sites as far away as the Caucasus and India. It appeared in Europe in the fourth millennium, and became commonplace during the third. Fine examples can be seen in Portugal and southern Spain (Los Millares). In the gallery graves of the Paris basin, stone plugs were inserted in the hole in the entrance stone. At Fontenille in Charente a stone door with hinges and pivots was set into the tomb's passage.

The re-use and subsequent arrangements of monuments were more common than was once thought. They have been identified in

almost every recent thorough excavation. Sections of kerbs may have been restored or consolidated by banked up stones, or a passage entrance finally sealed by piling gravel over the façade, as can be seen at Gavrinis. Some extensions also seem to have been designed purely to increase the size of the monument, however, such as the large rectangular extension of the tumulus C at Bougon, and the trapezoidal extension of tumulus F – the funerary function of both these additions appears to be of secondary importance. At Barnenez the second monument is similar to the first one and lies next to it, increasing the volume of the monument without affecting the function of the first cairn. It can also happen that the first monument disappears completely within the mass of a later mound, and in some cases the second tomb differ markedly from the first. Might this represent a later superimposed religion? Or should it be regarded as a development of the same religion, the first monument being seen as a sort of shrine? And finally, how should we assess of the re-used decorated stones in the Morbihan tombs?

Composite monuments, those that were reused or added on to, had a life lasting through the centuries. Perhaps some of them were like our country churches, which display elements of Norman, Gothic and Renaissance styles. They emphasize the need for extreme caution over dating and theorizing about the different uses to which the same monument might be put over periods sometimes separated by one or two millennia.

Alignments and circles of standing stones may also display successive phases of changing use spread over several centuries. Digging in part of the Grée de Cojoux alignment at Saint-Just, Charles-Tanguy Le Roux was able to observe the evolution of a site that had been in occupation from 4500 B.C. onwards. The first standing stones were blocks of quartz; then a mass of long low stones was set up enclosing their bases. Further very large schist boulders were next placed on this mass, and wooden posts completed the monument. At the end of the third millennium a mound covered part of the group: a funerary chest has been found, containing bell-beaker vessels and an early Bronze Age urn as well as two coffer tombs.

The famous monument at Stonehenge has been meticulously surveyed and several stages of construction have been distinguished, spanning a millennium. Apart from the technological aspect, the most impressive point about this site is the homogeneity of the overall conception down through time; within a permanent circular base the precise axis established for focusing on the rising sun at the summer solstice has remained unchanged. The different reference points must have been marked out on the ground with the aid of ropes used like a giant compass: then the important points would have been marked by setting up monoliths, many of which were hewn into shape. While the installation of the blue stones clearly represents the second phase and the trilithon constructions the third, the latter required the removal of some of the blue stones and their subsequent replacement. The trilithon structure, it should be said, consists of two upright stones with a third stone placed like a lintel spanning the gap between them. The precision of the trilithon adjustment has already been mentioned, as well as the aim of lightening the shape of the columns by tapering the outlines. All these observations combine to demonstrate that the construction was very carefully worked out both in its conception and in its execution.

Organization, Patience, Ingenuity

Modern knowledge of the techniques employed by builders of megalithic monuments eliminates all esoteric theories. Today we can appreciate the high degree of work organization, the creative ingenuity of the master builders, and the incredible patience needed for the realization of such great undertakings.

Many aspects still remain obscure, however. Experiments certainly demonstrate the feasibility of certain constructional techniques, but bring no absolute certainty as to whether they were used. Above all they raise interesting questions, in terms of human endeavour, regarding these first great buildings of western Europe and their construction.

We can be certain that the effectiveness of means and techniques was the essential criterion of megalithic working sites. Very few blocks seem to have been abandoned during the course of operations. At Exoudun, near Bougon, a stone lying at the bottom of a fairly steep slope below a rocky outcrop may be an example of clumsiness. In Brittany monoliths were apparently abandoned on site at Lescogan near Beuzec-Cap-Sizu, and at Sévéroué near Saint-Just. In England, one of the monoliths probably destined for Stonehenge seems to have been abandoned without any apparent reason. Such exceptions confirm the care of prehistoric builders for carrying a task through to its proper conclusion, a task characterized by the efficiency of the workmen and the use of simple but highly appropriate methods.

But what was the purpose of all this work?

The undisturbed interior of the
megalithic chamber H of the great
Barnenez monument reveals clearly
how the stones were wedged
together to create an indestructible
building. This view shows the
decorated head-stone.

(Photo B. Acloque © CNMHS/SPADEM)

Ancestral Society

Megalithic architecture needs open spaces. Its buildings were designed to be seen, often from far away, and before attempting to grasp their importance to both builders and users, it is important to try and imagine their geographical settings. Was the climate the same as it is now? Where did the shoreline run? How big were the forests, the open stretches – heaths, moors, meadows, cultivated fields? How did human beings try to make their mark on nature, and how were megaliths placed in this first modification of the landscape? Such questions are particularly pressing because, almost everywhere in western Europe, megaliths seem to be linked to the Neolithic era's shift from the immemorial hunting culture to a society of farmers and 'gardeners'.

Natural surroundings are in a constant state of evolution; changes of climate can be identified over fairly long periods, together with their effects on plant, animal, and human life. The last Ice Age saw the spread of steppe or even tundra landscape, home to the hunters of mammoths, bison, horses, and reindeer. This glacial period reached its maximum coverage 18,000 years ago. Vast quantities of water were held in glaciers and ice-sheets, and the sea level was some 120 metres lower than it is now. The subsequent warming of the climate and the melting glaciers, raised the sea level, a general phenomenon marked by numerous variations which can be traced up to modern times. The Ice Age ended about 11,000 years ago, and the warming continued through the post-glacial period to a climate of peak humidity slightly warmer than our own, 5,000 years ago, known as the 'Atlantic' period.

The landscape changed gradually over the years, from cold and arid steppes characterized by fir trees and birches, to forests where conifers predominated at first, followed later by oaks. The time of maximum oak-tree coverage, some 7,500 – 8,000 years ago, saw the first signs of neolithization in south-east Europe and the Mediterranean basin; this was the beginning of the changes which led to the Neolithic age. In this 'New Stone Age' the early hunter-predators, dependent on nature's untamed resources dictated by the rhythm of the seasons, developed into producers. They began to domesticate the world around them, living off livestock and agriculture, and exploiting its mineral wealth in the use of pottery, and later metal. Such innovations became part of society's general evolution as they increasingly affected and influenced it.

Improved methods of food storage meant that the earliest farmers could spread the consumption of their reserves over longer periods, and plan their harvest for the appropriate season. As the land's animal and vegetable yield increased, so smaller areas were needed for survival; groups settled and used the land as they needed it. Megaliths were

The Brogar circle of standing stones on the Orkney Mainland, north of Scotland, is a relatively late monument forming part of a megalith complex of tombs and circles. It is visible for many miles across wide-open countryside, and an observer standing at its centre can scan an immense horizon.

(Photo © Sheridan/Artephot)

The Villard megalithic tomb at Le
Lauzet-Ubaye in the Alps was built
on the upper part of the slope rather
than at the top, so that it could be
seen from a long way off in the
valley. This setting is classic in
mountainous lands throughout
western Europe.

(Photo © Sauzade)

part of that use, in accordance with ancestral traditions of land-
clearing, planting, and building. In the south of France the new pattern of life became established very quickly, and in conditions which
are now reasonably well understood. The fairly late appearance of
megaliths here was no doubt at least partially due to the enduring
importance of another very ancient and widespread form of collective
burial, that of funeral caves.

The Neolithic style of life became established in southern France
during the fifth and fourth millennia, and appears to have played an
active part in changing the landscape. Woodland growth was partly
destroyed by burning off for cultivation and by the constant onslaught
of livestock, particularly goats. The oak forests suffered and were
mainly replaced by box trees, by fields and meadows, and cleared land
lying fallow. In the Mediterranean climate, however, the unprotected
soil was quickly exhausted and could support only poor heathland
bushes. In the Jean-Cros shelter at Labastide-en-Val in Aude, Jean
Guilaine and his team studied the food remains of the shepherds who
drove their flocks every year from their villages in the plains of Languedoc up to the heights of the Massif Central. Such circumstances
brought together two quite widely differing types of land culture – the
agricultural and the pastoral.

The burial places of the earliest agriculturalists of the western
Mediterranean were modest: simple ditches dug in caves, beside the
walls of a shelter beneath rocks, or out in the open. Most such burials
contain a single crouched skeleton, but a few group burials are known:
for example a sepulchre at the Gazel cave at Sallèles-Cabardès in
Aude contained a woman and a five-year-old child, huddled together.
In the cave of La Baume-Bourbon at Cabrières in the Gard, bodies
were placed directly on the ground in a space which was not easy to
reach. In the Fontbrégoua cave at Salernes in the Var, six skulls and
three jaw-bones showing traces of incision were found in dwelling
strata; perhaps these are the marks of secondary rites, or of cannibalism. Burials sometimes show individual details such as the stones
placed to form a cist at Reillane (Alpes de Haute-Provence) and in the
Gazel cave.

Most of these funerary rites were practised throughout the Neolithic and Bronze Ages; many cave burials are contemporaneous with
hypogea and the megalithic monuments which were introduced fairly
late, towards the end of the fourth millennium and during the third,
usually in limestone areas yielding large slabs of stone. There were
dozens of megalithic burials in the valleys of Provence and the coastal
plains of Languedoc and Roussillon; hundreds of megalithic tombs are
still visible on the limestone plateaux which form the southern edge of
the Massif Central, from the Rhône valley to Périgord. The monu-

The Vernic megalithic tomb at Plouescat in Finistère is submerged at high tide; the sea level has risen since prehistoric times, covering vast areas such as the Gulf of Morbihan.

(Photo © Ed. Jos)

ments of these groups in the Ardèche, the great Causses, and Quercy usually stand near the edge of a plateau or dry valley. The pastoral nature of these areas is clear, not only because it still exists today but also because the local ecology offers little alternative: the shallow soil and lack of water mean that crop cultivation is unreliable, and the terrain must have been as bare in Neolithic times as it is now. Did men and their herds play some part in the development of this arrid landscape? In any event, they certainly maintained it in this state.

Land brought under Control

Megaliths should not be seen simply as tombs for shepherds, however: some archeologists consider that these sepulchres were aligned on long tracks, the drovers' roads used for flocks at the time of transhumance. In fact the regional character of the contents of the tombs, and the relative proportions of men, women and children placed there, prove that what we see here were small communities – pastoral, certainly, but complete; and it would be very interesting to know more about the open-air dwellings and how they differ from cave-shelters.

This description of southern France applies equally to other Mediterranean regions. In the Iberian peninsula megalithic monuments are part of a completely Neolithic culture, with knowledge of ceramics, agriculture, and animal husbandry. In the dry lands of the south, regular water supplies for carefully maintained gardens were maintained by irrigation systems. In the third millennium tombs were sometimes associated with fortified dwellings, as at Los Millares, constructed in steep and stony areas better suited to livestock than to cultivation (a plain's activity), and specialized crafts developed,

191

especially copper working. These high narrow plateaux dominated vast open landscapes.

The wish to mark the land as distinctively as possible also seems to have determined the setting of megalithic monuments in the Mediterranean islands; the monument was intended to be visible from a great distance, the centre of a broad vista of land or sea. Some of the imposing Maltese temples built facing the sea exemplify the visual focus offered by these constructions. In early Neolithic times the sea became a great highway as navigation made it possible to reach hitherto almost unknown islands; the wide distribution of obsidian knives from Lipari or the eastern Mediterranean is evidence of this traffic.

Over 15,000 years, as the atmosphere warmed up, the sea-level rose spectacularly – from 100 metres below the present level during the glacial period to 40 metres below by about 7000 B.C. This was happening from the time of the Flanders transgression until about 4000 B.C., the date of the first megalithic monuments. But at this time, and

The tumulus E tomb at Carrowkeel, in County Sligo in Ireland, dominates an enormous expanse of landscape. It is visible from a great distance across terrain which was densely populated in Neolithic times, with spread out forest, fields, and pastures.

(Photo © Anthony Weir/J. & C. Bord)

during the following millennium, coastal areas now beneath the sea were above the water-line. Breton archeologists have found megaliths with submerged bases – the Lehan-en-Tréffiagat standing stone, the fairly late (early third millennium) tombs of Lerret at Kerlouan and Kernic at Plouescat, in Finistère. The standing Lilia megalith at Plouguerneau, in the same area of Brittany, is lower-lying, with its base some 7 metres below the highest modern tides. There are similar examples in Brière at the mouth of the Loire and further south in the Poitou marshes, and in the Rochefort area of Charente-Maritime there are megaliths lying beneath the peat. In the Gulf of Morbihan the rising sea level has appreciably altered the landscape. Present-day islands were part of the mainland when the megaliths were constructed – the double group of standing stones on the foreshore of the little island of Er-Lannic is regularly flooded by high tides. The hundred or so tombs seen today round the gulf and on its islands were built on high points dominating the channels of the Auray and Vannes rivers. Many other islands, such as Carn Island at Ploudalmézeau, Guennoc island at Landéda, and even the Channel Islands of Jersey and Guernsey, were also heights dominating broad stretches of coastal plain which now lie submerged. The rising of the waters has led to fresh erosion and created beaches which did not exist five or six thousand years ago.

Pollen analysis of the ancient soil beneath the mounds helps identify the flora of the period before their construction. Just before the great megalithic cairn on Carn Island was built (in 4000 B.C.) the oak was the dominant tree, but pines, limes and elms were also present. Hazel pollen indicates open country, confirmed by the abundance of grasses – half of all the pollen and spores were Graminaceae and Compositae mingled with the plantain that flourished in the wake of ground clearance.

The ancient sub-soil near the Dissignac tumulus reveals that there were few trees in the area. The considerable density of pollen traces from plantain, mugwort, and thistles reveals the extent of the clearances. Agricultural effort is also apparent from the presence of cereal pollen, as well as charred grains of corn. The search for open country is clearly evident at Barnenez, where the imposing monument is set on a spur facing the sea, the greatest open vista of all. Visible from great distances over land and sea, it dominates the vast horizon. Inland in Brittany, colonization of the land must have been gradual, and was followed later by megalithism.

However the search for raw materials, such as the dolerite mined at Plussulien in the Côtes-du-Nord from the middle of the fourth millennium onwards, and for fresh lands needed as a result of a substantial population growth, would explain why the elms retreated and cereals appeared in the Arrée hills around 4000 B.C. As far as can be established, it appears that Neolithic fields – perhaps rather more like gardens – were quickly abandoned. The population does not appear to have been entirely settled, shrubby growth recolonized the cleared ground, and fresh terrain was cultivated. Unmistakable traces of forest clearance by burning off near Dol-de-Bretagne and at Plouguerneau have been dated to around 3000 B.C. Studies of fossil pollen suggest that the Breton countryside at the beginning of the Bronze Age was heavily populated, well into the interior. Deforestation continued; pastures and fields gradually took over from natural oak groves or, in some places, the hazel spinneys that had replaced them. Pastoral activity also tended to modify the landscape, and the retreat of the elms may also be due to the intensive use of their foliage for animal forage. Little is known about the livestock, since the generally acid Breton soil does not preserve bone; but a few exceptions indicate that there were dogs and sheep at Téviec and Hoëdic, in the Gulf of Morbihan, from the early days of the fifth millennium. The Neolithic fauna at Machecoul in Loire-Atlantique were mainly domestic animals: small oxen, primitive pigs, sheep, and dogs. There were a few wild animals – boar, deer, bear, and horses.

Dwellings far from the Tombs

It would rewarding to know where to find the hamlets and villages in this landscape transformed by human efforts and marked by megalithic monuments. Unfortunately, there are almost no traces of such dwellings. Certainly the immediate surroundings of the oldest megalithic tombs, on the heights were uninhabited: no vestiges of residential use have been found close to these monuments. There are a few indications, however, that people preferred to settle on the light and fertile silt lands in the valley bottoms, near fresh water and not far from the sea. Thus at Le Curnic-en-Guissény in Finistère there are the remains of hearths with a quantity of charcoal, grinding stones and pestles, shards, shaped flints, fragments of polished axes – traces of a settlement that lasted for a thousand years. Of the actual dwellings nothing remains except a few trenches and a solitary post-hole.

Equally eroded, more or less seasonal settlements have been recorded in Brittany, at Pleubian in the Côtes-du-Nord and at La Butte-aux-Pierres, in the Grande Brière. On the little island of Er-Yoh in Morbihan there are paved areas and low walls between the rocks, side by side with numerous hearths, and near Quiberon the detached spur of Croh-Collé had small dwellings behind a low rampart. The total is meagre. So where did they live, the Neolithic peoples in the Carnac area? How many were there? What is the implication of the abundant remains at Er-Lannic and are they the remains of a dwelling or of a shrine?

British stone circles often stand in bleak; treeless country, on mountainous plateaux. This one on the Penmaenmawr massif in North Wales is typical of the pastoral world of the late Neolithic and early Bronze ages.

(Photo © M. Sharp)

Breton burials provide little more in the way of information; most of the bones have dissolved in the soil. The megalithic tombs undoubtedly represent an important cultural element, but were they the only places of burial? The example of neighbouring regions – Normandy and western central France – would appear to indicate that they were not: there must have been other, additional, burial places. Sited where they could be seen from great distances, the long barrows of southern England are fine examples of prominent landscape settings, magnificently illustrated by the position of Stonehenge. In the Wicklow Hills in Ireland megalithic monuments were not built on the actual hilltops, but on the upper slopes visible from the valleys; similarly the megalithic mounds in Orkney are visible from five kilometres away all round.

In a country that was originally heavily wooded, the oldest monuments date from the time of the first clearings in the early fourth millennium, when climatic conditions were at their most favourable. A slight cooling followed, which brought about a further retreat of the elms, already threatened by woodland clearance.

Pollen from the Irish site of Fallahogy near Londonderry reveals a fairly complete state of Neolithic evolution. For forty years deforestation and rural colonization had very noticeable effects, which diminished over the next four centuries; then a phase of total abandonment appears to have lasted for another four centuries, followed by a second phase of forest clearance. Another Irish site, Ballynagilly in the Tyrone area, has yielded a few dwelling structures as

195

Erected near the shoreline, this megalithic monument was visible from neighbouring heights and from the sea. All that remains of it today is the central chamber built of large blocks.

(Photo © A. F. Kersting/Artephot)

well as the history of the area over 1,700 years (from 3800 to 2100 B.C.) In the early years there was little woodland clearance, but this became much more intensive around 3200 B.C., while cereal culture developed and the numbers of elms declined. Traces of a house dating from this period, have been identified: it measured 6 by 6.50 metres, and was built with oak planks around an indoor hearth. Occupation was contemporaneous with several megalithic court-cairns scattered across the surrounding countryside. Then, about the year 2700 B.C. and for the next 400 years, the forest grew up again. Was the site abandoned? Did population numbers drop? Finally, for two centuries after 2300 B.C., there was intensified human activity, until the moment when the first Chalcolithic bell-beaker vessels appeared, and the site was then eventually abandoned.

At Newgrange archeologists have surveyed grass mounds that were used during construction of the monument and which must have come from the immediate locality: by then the terrain was cleared of woods and corn was cultivated, but brushwood was beginning to invade the fields. A similar pattern has been established near another Irish tumulus, Townleyhall. The charcoal found beneath the barrow came principally from hazels, which probably grew after the beginnings of cultivation. Traces of furrows have been discovered beneath

The Earliest Farmers' Fertile Land

the body of the South Street tumulus in Wiltshire, and similar traces were found at the Belderg Beg site in Ireland. The furrows crossed each other at right angles; the ploughing is more likely to have been aimed at levelling the cleared ground than at cultivation of a field.

Variations in sea-level have modified parts of the Denmark coastline, as in Brittany. In the fourth millennium northern Jutland was an archipelago, while in the south the land encroached on the present shoreline. Megalithic tombs seem to have been erected during two different periods, and indicate the pattern of colonization. Until 3000 B.C. the tombs spread inland, across country that was still fairly heavily wooded; cereal crops were grown on burned-off ground, fresh fields were needed every year, and the community was semi-itinerant. Later the population concentrated on the hillsides overlooking the sea, and became settled, no doubt thanks to more advanced agricultural techniques such as the swing-plough; they also benefited from effective storage methods and a more open sea-orientated bartering economy. This is the period of intensive flint mining in northern Jutland, Ålborg, Hov and Bjerre. The population would have increased where conditions were most favourable. Most of the ten Danish third millennium mounds under which traces of ploughing have been found are on the coast; so too are the depictions of ploughing pecked out on the rocks of southern Sweden, for example at Tanum Tegneby.

At the Danish complex at Sarup, a series of megalithic chambered barrows surround a large camp with discontinuous ditches. They lie on hills overlooking the sea, and are grouped in sub-sets covering areas two or three kilometres across. The terrain thus marked out by these monuments was cultivated.

The first farmers preferred light sandy fertile soils, on outcrops between banks of moraine or river gravels. Traces of the villages of central European ribbon culture, dating from the fifth millennium, are grouped round deposits of loess. In the region of Ingelstorp and Hagestad in southern Sweden, large megalithic tombs are either surrounded by better soil, or very close to it; here there was a clear connection between megaliths and agriculture. Other smaller tombs scattered across less fertile soil belonged to communities more concerned with pig- and sheep-rearing, or deer hunting. In this region groups of people with different ways of life seem to have been contemporaneous at certain times.

Megalithic buildings thus became part of a landscape that was no longer entirely natural. The systematic exploitation and development of animal, vegetable, and mineral resources – leading to animal husbandry, crop-growing, ceramics, and soon metallurgy – created a type of rural environment still visible in some countries. The boundaries of

The seven houses of the village of Skara Brae are very close to each other, and have separate rooms. A narrow lane provides access to each house. This third-millennium hamlet thus housed at least seven families, which seems to have been typical of this northern region where settlements were widely scattered.

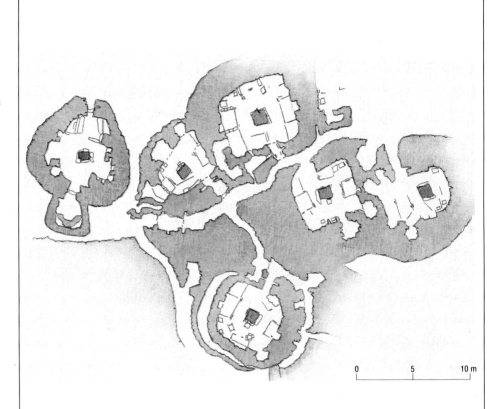

rural territory, more limited and constricting than those of the hunter, strengthened the sense of identity with the land and encouraged its defence. The need for rare primary materials – obsidian, jadeite, amber, soon followed by copper and gold – combined with the improved means of locomotion and navigation that led to colonization of the Mediterranean islands encouraged long-distance travel. The beginnings of mastery of far-flung seas and lands had appeared in Europe.

The domestication of ecological and geographical areas had thus established itself among the innovations of the Neolithic Age, and its centre the megalithic monument expressed in the clearest possible manner the focal identity of the place and the need to control the earth's surface.

Unlike Madagascar where megalithic tombs were at the very heart of the village, megalithic monuments in Europe were generally set a little apart from known dwellings. All the well-known megalithic sites – Bygholm Norremark in Denmark, Newgrange and Knowth in Ireland, Quanterness in Orkney and Stonehenge in England, Barnenez, Gavrinis and Carnac in Brittany, Antequera in Spain, Tarxien in Malta – stand well away from villages or any other living area. This, of course, is why so little is known of the dwelling places of the faithful who attended these sacred monuments, and why it is so difficult to identify them.

The interior of a well-preserved Neolithic house in the village of Skara Brae, on the Orkney Mainland, reveals the hearth, the bed, a kind of cupboard, a small window-space, and so on. Neolithic people used stone chiefly for tombs, designed to endure for ever, and only rarely, as here, as a material for everyday life. The use of stone in Skara Brae can be explained by scarcity of wood in these northern regions of the British Isles. We do not know how the houses were roofed – probably with wood and thatch.

(Photo © Sheridan/Artephot)

Very few megaliths stand amongst traces of domestic settlement; those that do appear to be anachronisms. At Soubise in Charente-Maritime, the three megalithic La Sauzie tombs date from several centuries before the late Neolithic traces and domestic structures that surround them. The long barrow wedged between the ditches of the inner enclosure of Hambledon Hill in England must also predate the digging out of the surrounding banks.

At Los Millares, on the other hand, the megalithic necropolis extends over 900 metres at the crest of a high promontory between the citadel and two small third millennium forts. Recent excavations have confirmed that all these structures date from the same period. It is exceptional for domestic and funerary structures to be associated in this way; indeed, this heavily fortified semi-feudal settlement seems very distinctive. It relates to the early stages of an artisan economy

Perishable Dwellings for the Living

based on copper, which is not found in other megalithic zones of western Europe. Be that as it may, the civil architecture of Los Millares, with its dungeons and small dry-stone towers, is very similar to the construction of circular megalithic tombs roofed with corbelling.

The search for dwellings corresponding to megalithic monuments in the Atlantic zone is difficult; erosion and silting up have in turn destroyed or concealed remains. In Brittany, for example, very little is known about villages, or even about the houses where megalithic people lived. At best, the site of a house is discovered through a few trimmed flints or shards, or exceptionally through bones from animals consumed, or shells; but structures are rare and unhelpful, as are the rubbish pits. Considering all the observations together, however, can lead us to a few useful deductions.

There seem to have been two distinct types of ground occupation. One was substantial, frequently surrounded by a fence or a ditch; the other was less extensive, more spread out, and no doubt seasonal. Both types appear in the Bougon area in the third millennium. The fortified camp or enclosure possessed a religious function which is also found in the British Isles. The houses themselves were made of light materials, as indicated by the foundations of the circular living huts at Bougon; other houses may have been larger, however, like that at the top of Fort-Harrouard overlooking a megalithic tomb in Eure-et-Loir.

The information to be gained from these examples is meagre, but one thing is clear: namely, the contrast in western France between the perishable materials used for houses, where the only foundations were post-holes, and the durable stone materials used for the megalithic monuments.

This duality of materials seems an essential factor in understanding the function of the monuments: the latter were intended to endure for ever, while the houses functioned only for a generation or two. Some authorities would like to see the megalithic tomb as the funerary imitation of individual dwellings; it seems, however, that through their very choice of materials, the prehistoric peoples of western France were seeking rather to construct genuine shrines, not only for the dead, but for the faithful of innumerable generations to come.

The village of Skara Brae lies on the west coast of the largest island in Orkney, to the north of the British Isles. It dates from the same period as the megalithic tombs such as Maes Howe, and religious monuments such as the circles of standing stones at Brogar and Stenness. The exceptional state of preservation of this village stems from its construction in small stone slabs, which give it an undeniable resemblance to the megalithic tombs of the area – although there the finish is of far higher quality. Discovered in 1850, the village became famous after Gordon Childe's digs between 1927 and 1930. David Clarke's later surveys, in 1972 and 1973, have refined the observations. Some of the houses built with carefully fitted stones have survived the passage of time, thanks to the piles of rubbish that partly concealed them.

The village was in use between 2400 and 1800 B.C. Only some flattened traces remain of the first phase of construction, lying beneath other layers – square or semi-rectangular houses with central hearths, bed bases, and side compartments. Eight houses still exist from the well-preserved second phase, built to the same design as the earlier ones, but with walls surviving to a height of 3 metres. Inside are not

TERRITORY AND BOUNDARIES

The Prehistoric monuments near Stonehenge lie in five regularly spaced groups representing the three main styles of construction: long barrow, camp with circular ditch, and large ring of standing stones. All lie in open limestone country between wooded clay banks, and accurately mirror the patterns of settlement around 2000 B.C. in an area covering no more than about 100 kilometres at any point. Each of the five concentrations is known as a 'territory', about 20 kilometres across. Each contained between 3000 and 8000 individuals under the leadership of one family who arranged the construction of the largest funerary monuments. Were there any links between political and military powers, under this divided system? The central site of Stonehenge, whose construction demanded considerable numbers of workers, can be seen as a symbol of the unifying strength of a very powerful prince. The single tomb under the mound of Bush Barrow, built near Stonehenge at the beginning of the Bronze Age, may mark the grave of one of these important individuals, buried with his treasure and his sceptre. At Stonehenge the

divisions between temporal and religious powers may have been blurred. The isolation of ceremonial sites such as the great circles of standing stones, the complexity of initiatory knowledge based on celestial observation – everything seems to indicate that the two sources of power were separate, even if religious faith depended on the protection of temporal strength.

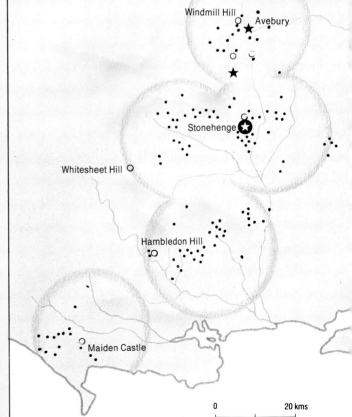

- • Main circles
- o Camps with ditches
- ★ Long barrows

0   20 kms

only hearths and beds, but also cupboards and shelving, still set in the walls with small stone slabs. Apart from one which may have been a workshop, the houses lie close to one another. The remains piled up outside and inside give a clear picture of life in the third millennium. Some of the many stone and bone tools were used to work skins, others for wood, and still others for weaving. Barley was cultivated, cattle and sheep husbandry flourished, and there was sea-fishing. Other similar sites have been discovered in these islands: Rinyo on the island of Rousay, for example, and the Links of Noltland on Papa Westray.

What might link the 'mortuary houses' found in the unchambered long barrows in Scandinavia and the British Isles with the few dwellings excavated in the same areas? In Ireland the remains of domestic houses indicate a rectangular design, visible in the form of a small foundation trench punctuated by post-holes, with an internal hearth. The house at Lough Gur in County Limerick measures 6 by 10 metres; the one at Ballynagilly in County Tyrone is smaller, 6 by 6.50 metres. With its walling of oak planks, it dates from about 3200 B.C. The best preserved house layout is at Ballyglass in County Mayo: it is rectangular, measuring 9 by 4.50 metres, with a small niche at the back. As these traces have been discovered beneath a megalithic chamber tomb, the problem arises of the links between the dwelling and the tomb. In this case the dimensions and materials of the house are very different from those of a burial chamber.

Behind the palisade façade of some of the long barrows lie traces of rectangular houses rather than megalithic chambers; the most important examples in Great Britain are at Grendon, Normanton

It is not uncommon on Neolithic Sites to find a large sandstone mortar on which grain could be crushed with a sandstone or granite pestle. The flour obtained was dampened and kneaded to make a dough that could be baked: the earliest known bread.

(Musée des Antiquités Nationales, Saint-Germain-en-Laye.
Photo J.-M. Labat © Casterman)

202

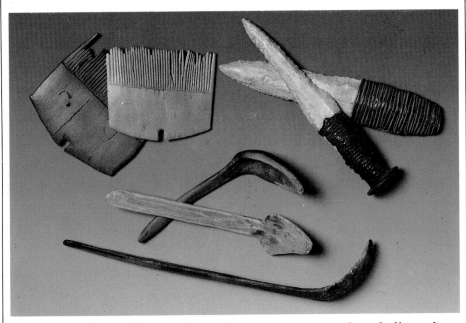

Down, and Street Houses. As we have seen, some writers believe that
these wooden constructions may be the prototype for megalithic
architecture, for example in Ireland. Similar timber constructions
were still being built fairly late in the third millennium in Denmark. In
these countries the 'houses of the dead' (mortuary houses) were religious buildings with clearly marked characteristics; they cannot be
confused with dwelling houses, which were generally longer.

What did the megaliths mean to societies capable of marking the
countryside so clearly with their presence? The combined effort
needed to set up these great stones must have had considerable social
implications in its need for a common plan, diplomacy, technical
skills, favourable religious conditions. Various strategies could have
been employed to organize the gathering of several hundred able-
bodied people to haul and lift the huge blocks of the fourth and third
millennia. Perhaps these men belonged to the community ruled by the
person requiring the stone, or perhaps they gathered from various
communities linked in certain ways – through treaty, kinship, social
protection, economy, or religion. They may have enjoyed a certain
amount of freedom, or they may have been slaves and dependent on
others, as prisoners or war or through birth into a lower social class.
The standardized design of Neolithic houses indicates a largely egalitarian society: but could this not have included a dominant family,
even if it lacked some or all of the material signs of power? The role of
an élite appears necessary, indeed decisive, in the construction of
megaliths – decisive too in the maintenance of the dogma, of distant
and often complex origins, that the monuments represented. The

203

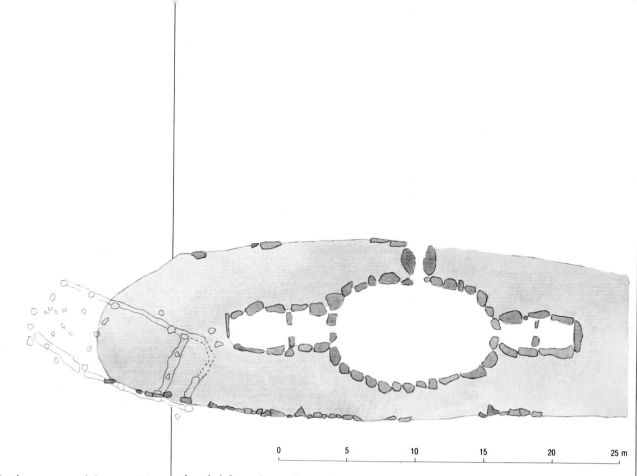

```
0        5        10       15       20      25 m
```

It has been suggested that megalithic tombs were seen as the houses of the dead, the counterpart of the dwelling of the living. Traces of a quadrangular house buried beneath a tumulus at Ballyglass in County Mayo in Ireland, with chambers and internal courts, indicate clearly the difference between the two types of construction.

burial function of certain megaliths allows us at least to find out more about a few of these individuals: those who acquired the status of ancestor.

The role of ancestors is apparent in the design of the monuments, conceived in the light of rituals that sustained the ideology and reinforced the spirituality of the site. In this respect it is reasonable to consider the exact impact and function of such monuments.

It is generally accepted that the changing way of life characteristic of neolithization was accompanied by profound social upheaval. The settling of human groups, the building of the first villages, and population growth probably entailed the development of more complex social codes and more highly structured societies. Paradoxically, the somewhat monotonous dwelling designs have led to theories of egalitarianism; there have even been suggestions of a 'primitive communism', a theory now refined, particularly by Alain Testart. In 1986 he returned to an analysis according to which, contrary to previous beliefs, the earliest societies were not all nomadic. Some, already settled, represented heavily hierarchical groups with social inequalities; for the techno-economic foundation of these societies rested on a highly developed system of food storage.

Neolithized Society

Society in the Mesolithic hunting cultures of western Europe seems to have been based on small groups of people, yet many studies have found indications of well developed structures, on the lines of the first Neolithic communities. The Tardenois people of northern France, for example, generally settled on sandy soils, in clearings, just as the first farmers of the early Neolithic Age sought out loess (a fine grey loam) deposits in temperate Europe. Around the eighth millennium the sites of Star Carr in England and Mullerup in Denmark were bases where surplus food was stored and craftsmanship developed with the use of selected materials.

THE DIFFERENT MODELS OF SOCIETY

	1	2	3
Population	small ±100	average ±1000	large ±10,000
Area	3 km diameter	10 km diameter	100 km diameter
Food supply	hunting, fishing, modest farming	large scale hunting, farming, plough cultivation and stock-rearing	large scale hunting, intensive farming and stock-rearing, manuring, transhumance
Production	flint, bone, pottery, textiles	artisan: semi-precious stones	artisan and industrial flint, metal
System of contact	medium distance, intermittent	medium distance, regular	long distance, regular
Use of territory	scattered, or hamlets	mixed, camp and farms	centralized main camp, other camps, farms
Worship and burial	small collective megaliths and individual graves	large collective megaliths and individual graves	individual megaliths and other individual graves

DAILY ACTIVITIES
OF A NEOLITHIC VILLAGE

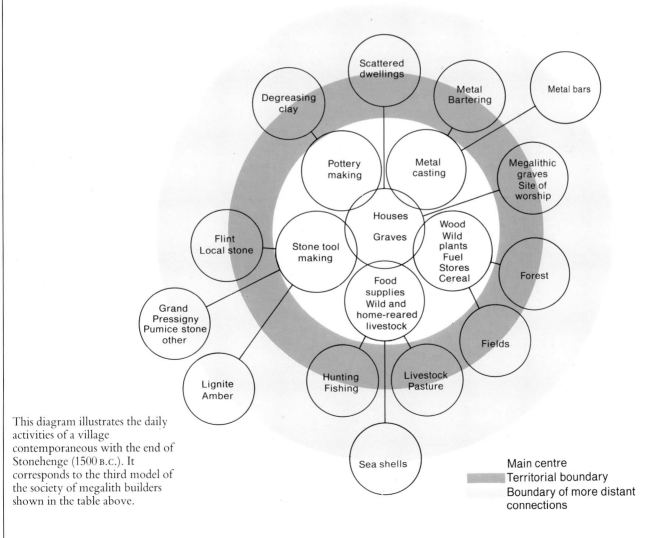

This diagram illustrates the daily activities of a village contemporaneous with the end of Stonehenge (1500 B.C.). It corresponds to the third model of the society of megalith builders shown in the table above.

Main centre
Territorial boundary
Boundary of more distant connections

During the sixth millennium in the Morbihan area of France, a few domestic animals such as dogs and sheep appeared at Téviec as part of a relatively settled society fully adapted to a coastal way of life. Enormous piles of sea-shell or *kjoekenmodings* (their Danish name), contained kitchen waste and also sometimes burials, including stone coffins enclosing several skeletons lying under deer antlers. These heaps of shells have been recorded along the coast of western Europe from Denmark (at Maglemose, for instance) to Portugal, where the finest group is at Muge. This development of the western coastline corresponds precisely to that of the megalithic monuments, the first of which appeared some centuries later. What can have happened, during these few centuries, that could explain the birth of monumental building in stone? There had been one fundamental change: people had abandoned the hunter's way of life for that of farming.

The first village societies of western Europe must have benefited greatly from the Neolithic innovations that had been brought in much earlier further to the east and south. Such societies were certainly not all alike, and some remain deeply marked by hunting and gathering activities. The cave paintings of eastern Spain, dating from about 6000 B.C., show hunters with bows, women using sticks to turn the soil in the fields – but also archers drawn up against each other, classic images of war that seem to coincide with the Neolithic Age. The same motifs are seen in some megalith paintings in western Iberia. Woodland hunters lived in northern Europe too, in the cave sites of Zalavrouga in the Soviet Union. At Vedbaek in Denmark, individual pit graves were linked with a village of hunters of the same period as the earliest megaliths. These hunters began to use pottery, then turned to agriculture.

The great megalithic monuments themselves appeared in the context of a completely Neolithized society; they are associated with landscapes that had been transformed by farming since from the fifth millennium. The megalith builders were familiar with pottery, also polished axes, and a relatively settled way of life in the first hamlets and villages. The essential link between megalithic construction and a fully Neolithized society has been described by Humphrey Case and Colin Renfrew, for Ireland and England respectively. Since Neolithic development occurred a little later in the islands than on the mainland, megalithism must also have appeared there later. The tendency towards settlement and gradual acculturation spread from east to west, until it met the sea. The time came when there were no fresh lands to colonize. With the growing competition between hunters and farmers, and between the farmers themselves, there was an increasing need to mark out lands more clearly, mobilizing forces for an imposing symbolic construction.

Ceremonial axes varied in their shapes as well as in their basic materials: axe with terminal knob (top), perforated axe-hammer (left), small, thick fibrolith votive axe (centre, left), green-stone axe with pointed butt (centre, right), and chloromelanite axe with curved and extended cutting edge; this last is from a grave at Pauilhac in Gers.

(Musée des Antiquités Nationales, Saint-Germain-en-Laye.
Photo J.-M. Labat © Casterman)

Richard Bradley offers a different explanation. Many megalithic monuments, particularly among the older examples, are tombs. In certain societies such as Madagascar and imperial China, funerary rites constituted the most highly developed of all institutions and regulated public and private life. The time and value devoted to them bore no relationship to economic and social conditions. In this system, ancestors were the indispensable intermediaries between the living and the gods, who were seen as the masters of the natural elements on which the survival of the group depended. Thus the megalithic monument belonged not only to the living but also to their ancestors and the gods.

Ancestor worship, practised by a great number of societies, is based on this type of transference. In farming communities close to the soil and heavily dependent on the cycle of the seasons, natural forces such as rain, storm, hail, the sun, and the moon, understandably

207

This polishing stone from Fyfield Down in Wiltshire is one of the many stones found out in the fields showing the grooves and scoops left by the burnishing process. Polished axes for woodcutting were brought here for sharpening.

(Photo © Fay Godwin's Photo Files)

occupy a primordial place. Farmers were more dependent on the elements than were hunters; in a society under demographic pressure and with only limited resources, expression acquired greater force with the growing economic and metaphysical distress that it symbolized. A bad harvest, the exhaustion of food reserves, the impossibility of seeking fresh resources in other jealously guarded lands, the need to retain or even defend lands that were already too limited – all such factors strengthened social links. This was the moment for intervention by the person linked to their ancestors, who because of his intimate knowledge of divine forces, and the prestige which this privilege conferred on him, had the right to supervise reserves. The megalithic monument was the setting from which the chief drew authority to protect the group and to justify, with the support of ancestors and gods, his right to this authority.

In the search for the social context of megalithic monuments, archeologists have had to consider not only the relevant dwellings, but also the strategies developed to control access to different resources: raw materials had to be obtained for stone tools, ornaments, and ceramics. There are very few places where it is possible to identify a complete Neolithic settlement with its various zones of use, but a few famous sites nonetheless represent quite varied social styles. These are of three main patterns.

First, the simplest: scattered rural dwellings, with a sparse egalitarian population which can be seen united in a small megalithic tomb built at the centre of its limited territory. The second pattern also indicates a dispersed – but larger – rural population of craftsmen, who could assemble for important collective work under the direction of a few individuals, perhaps from a single commanding family. It was the dead of this family who were placed in the large megalithic tombs. The ruling family then had further religious monuments built: their territory expanded, and alliances developed with neighbouring groups. Finally, the third pattern: the appearance of a prince at the head of a federation of lands which were themselves ruled by families or lesser princes. The prince dominated a substantial rural and artisan population, with both isolated and centralized houses. Large religious centres, megalithic to a greater or lesser extent, were much frequented.

The island of Arran in Scotland is typical of the first model, the simplest. It does not appear to have developed further. Colin Renfrew and his team have shown that the eighteen modest megalithic sepulchres built near the shore, where the land was fertile, were burial sites for all the members of these small communities. No trace of a village has been found: each community no doubt lived scattered round the megalithic tomb, the centre of their lands and symbol of the group. Made up of a few dozen individuals – estimates vary from thirty-five to seventy – the group probably followed an egalitarian lifestyle. This was around the year 3000 B.C.

The presence of these small, 'segmented', social groups with little established hierarchy has also been noted in Orkney on the island of Rousay. Similarly, the remains of 394 people found in the Quanterness tomb correspond to burials taking place over five hundred years, here of men and women belonging to a single community of about twenty people. The construction of the monument would have required some 10,000 man-hours, representing for example one hundred men working for one hundred hours. Such labour was not an impossible task. The inhabitants could have spread the construction of the grave over several years, or could have sought help from neighbours. People here lived by growing cereals and by hunting. The pottery found on several sites indicates that they lived in hamlets like those of Skara Brae and Rinyo. Several monuments of the Quanterness type were used in the same way, at the same time, in the Orkneys.   Around 2400 B.C. the second pattern of society seems to have taken root in this region: the first graves were abandoned, supplanted by large tombs or other imposing monuments reflecting a more hierarchical society, with larger territory and a larger population. The Maes Howe megalithic tomb, an architectural masterpiece, thus replaced on its own the tomb at Quanterness and several other

Among the ceremonial objects found over a large area and offered to ancestors at the end of the Neolithic Age were these long flint dagger blades from Le Grand Pressigny (Indre-et-Loire). The blades, sometimes more than 30 centimetres long, were shaped from rough-hewn nodules known as 'pounds of butter'.

(Musée des Antiquités Nationales, Saint-Germain-en-Laye.
Photo J.-M. Labat © Casterman)

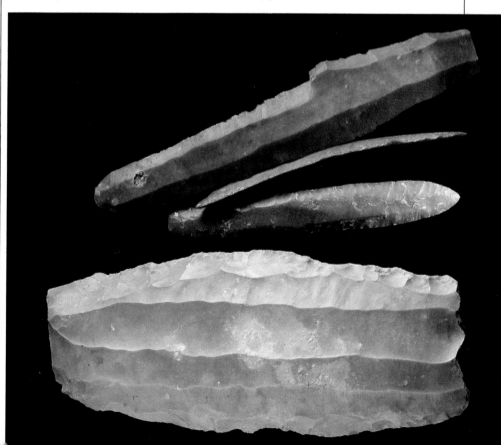

In this Swedish megalithic tomb at Draghy, two bodies have been placed side by side in a cavern which had already been used: the older bones were pushed to the corners of the chamber. This is a fine example of a re-used megalithic tomb. It is not known what period of time separated the two deposits, but it may have been several centuries. Re-use proves the enduring nature of the monument, even when actual burial rites changed.

(Photo © Antikvarisk-Topografiska-Arkivet, Stockholm)

local tombs. The two great standing stone circles of Brogar and Stenness emphasize the abstract style of this new type of architecture. Within the megalithic tomb itself, the bodies to be buried were selected. Ceremonies which were no longer strictly funerary became more important.

In southern Sweden Märta Strömberg has recreated the pattern of settlement in the Ingelstorp and Hagestad area. What she describes is fairly close to the first model, that of the Arran settlement; twelve megalithic tombs were built at distances varying from two to six kilometres apart, each apparently lying at the centre of a unit of territory. The little niches of certain tombs were probably designed for one family, or for a particular social or sexual division. The pattern changed in the Bronze Age, and cemeteries with flat individual tombs appeared within the same territorial limits. The coastal complex at Sarup in Denmark is similar to the Swedish example. In Ireland, isolated megalithic tombs found all over one region belong to different groups of the scattered population of an egalitarian society. In the Boyne valley, on the other hand, the tendency to group monuments together to form a necropolis is linked with the growth of a hierarchical society whose more centralized organization links it to the second pattern.

The finest example must be the Knowth necropolis, with its first small monuments followed by the construction of the great central mound surrounded by other tombs, much more modest. It is interesting that actual architectural styles vary very little with this development. The same pattern can be seen at Newgrange, not far from Knowth. Unfortunately little is known about the dwellings connected with these monuments, and it is therefore impossible to verify what seems likely: the existence in this area, at about 3000 B.C., of a highly structured society consisting of several thousand people and which also probably established enormous camps.

Some centuries later, conditions in the Wessex region of southern England corresponded to the third pattern. Colin Renfrew has distinguished five 'territories' there, each about twenty kilometres in diameter and defined by one or more camps with barrows and discontinuous ditches. The essentially rural population consisted of between three and eight thousand people in each territory; it was made up of families, of which one dominant family organized the building of the mounds. The central setting of the Stonehenge territory, with its impressive monument demanding considerable manpower for its construction, no doubt reflects the position of the individual who dominated this territory, and perhaps also the other 'great families'. Bush Barrow, very close to Stonehenge, contained an individual burial with particularly rich grave-goods, which could well

Excavation of the megalithic chamber of the Togarp monument near Tommarp in southern Sweden revealed compartments divided up by setting small stones into the ground, and reserved for specific sectors of society. The organization of the burial space probably reflects the society of the living.

(Photo © Märta Strömberg)

have been the tomb of one of these great princes. Their power must have been both political and military, as indicated by the offerings. Was it also religious? The stone circles – including Stonehenge – lie in four of these territories, at a distance from dwellings and graves. Colin Burgess suggests that religious power was reserved for the priests, ancestors of the druids described by Julius Caesar – priests whose powers were strengthened in about 2,000 B.C. when the *cursus*, the long straight avenues, the circular ditches, and the standing stone monuments were greatly increased in number.

The Champ-Durand fortified camp at Nieul-sur-l'Autise in Vendée was surrounded by concentric ditches, now filled in. They were detected by aerial photography. Excavation made it possible to reconstruct the system of ramparts and gates, giving an idea of the scale of collective work involved. What was the function of this type of enclosure? Was it a response to a defence need, an assembly site for economic or perhaps religious purposes, or a combination of all three?

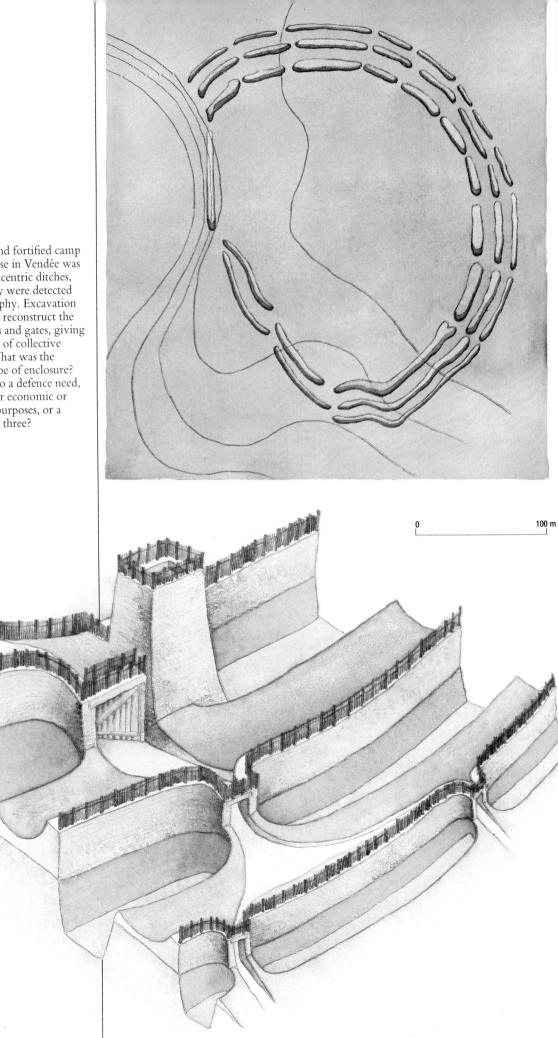

0   100 m

One Dominant Family, or Several?

In his surveys of burials beneath southern England's long barrows, Richard Atkinson drew attention to the very small number of skeletons discovered; they could not possibly represent the entire community of a territory. How were they selected? In their studies of the bones in the Lanhill tomb in Wiltshire, anthropologists noted resemblances between individuals – doubtless a single family. The power of this group lay in the fertility of the soil, the exploitation of flint mines, and much bartering. This again is a fine illustration of the second type of society, which thus appears to have developed at a very early stage. In effect the large scale of the first monuments of Normandy, Brittany, and central western France, indicates collective labour undertaken by a considerable number of people about 4000 B.C., yet the tombs themselves contain the remains of very few of them. This selection, and the monuments' architectural grandeur, can surely be explained by the theory of a society ruled by one or several families.

The discovery of the Bougon Neolithic territory indicates that the five mounds of the necropolis occupied a central position, isolated from the two substantial dwelling areas which were arranged a few hundred metres to the north and south. Although unfortunately no trace survives from the period of the first tombs, more recent Neolithic remains have revealed much: the selection of the dead was evident from the time of the first passage graves, where there were never more than a dozen skeletons. This selection remained important throughout the fourth millennium, during which the great megalithic tombs were built. It became less strict around the middle of the third millennium, at the time when the graves were re-used. The presence of several layers of dwelling zones, probably fortified, suggests that there were at least two communities living on the two sides of the necropolis, both associated and competitive: the tombs' passages seem oriented towards these two living areas.

If the dead of the megalithic tombs were selected, it would be logical to find other bones in other burial contexts. In fact, as excavations become increasingly meticulous and extensive, archeologists are discovering human remains in the houses or nearby. Secondary and fairly complex funerary rituals can be deduced, as in the megalithic tombs. This is what happened at Fort-Harrouard in the Eure valley, where the middle Neolithic layers, rich in human bones, are of the same date as the megalithic tomb built at the foot of the site. There are many examples of piles of human bones deposited outside megalithic tombs at a period when the tombs were in use. The causewayed camps of western Europe were often burial sites, and there are probably more individual ditch graves scattered about the countryside than anyone has estimated. The Chassey cists of the Parc du Château at Auneau in Eure-et-Loir, or the ditches of the same period in the Toulouse area,

213

A wooden bow, a very unusual preserved item, and flint arrow-heads found in collective offerings in one of the hypogea near Coizard, in the Marne. The bow and the axe are symbols of male power.

(Musée des Antiquités Nationales, Saint-Germain-en-Laye.
Photo J.-M. Labat ©
Casterman)

would seem to indicate this. This observation confirms the social function of the megalithic tomb.

In the late Neolithic Age the more collective nature of hypogea and certain sepulchres corresponds to the first pattern of settlement, but for a larger population. This characteristic is evident in the Paris basin, and became spectacular in the Vaucluse artificial ossuaries (Roaix, Les Boileau), where the abundance of skeletons must be the result of massacres.

In southern Spain the fortified settlement of Los Millares is directly linked to the megalithic necropolis. Although there is no way of identifying any one larger or richer tomb that would indicate a hierarchical society, the very elaborate rampart of the fort alone indicates an already powerful social structure. The small fort of Zambujal in Portugal appears to have been associated with a large megalithic tomb dominating the surrounding countryside, and would reflect the centralization of power around 2000 B.C. These two Iberian examples thus illustrate the movement from the second pattern to the third.

Most Neolithic societies appear to have been more or less egalitarian; some however seem to have had a centralized organization from the earliest times – this probably applied to the first great monuments of western France, dating from the fifth millennium. Later, at the time of Stonehenge, the authority of the prince is confirmed by the large barrows with individual burial and personal offerings. And yet there appears to be no simple correlation between the size of the monument and the degree of hierarchy within a society: human beings, whatever cultural pattern they create for themselves, are capable of overwhelming energy in fulfilling their ancestral rites. The giant mounds of central western France and of Brittany also appear to illustrate this collective faith 'which can move mountains'. The opposite is also true – there are many human cultures, in other times and other places, which have felt no need to erect great blocks of stone. To what extent, then, is the construction of megalithic monuments linked with any particular society? Certainly such building demands a structured society, but the connection between megalith and society reveals a whole range of complexities. We only know that there was no single megalithic society, but several; thus the megalithic monument appears as a striking form of social expression, chosen by various different groups which adopted material and spiritual means to achieve this type of building.

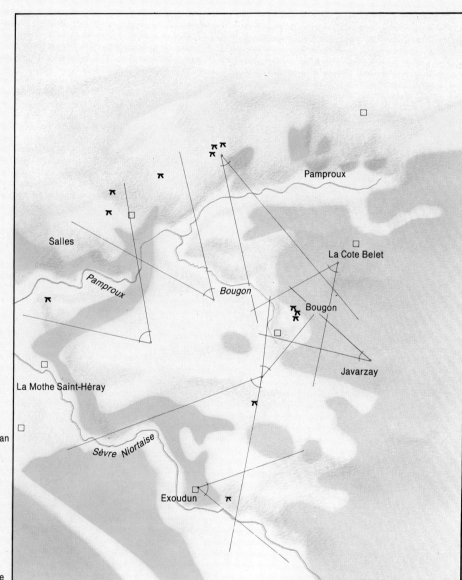

Siderolithic

Bathonian flint

Lower Callovian
Middle and Upper Callovian

Oxfordian

Primary

⊼ Barrows and dolmens

◁ Principal viewpoints

☐ Remains found on surface

Salles

Pamproux

Pamproux

Bougon

La Cote Belet

Bougon

Javarzay

La Mothe Saint-Héray

Sèvre Niortaise

Exoudun

A SITE AND ITS REGION

The Bougon necropolis lies at
the heart of a 'territory' about
ten kilometres broad between
the valleys of the Pamproux and
the Sèvre Niortaise, an area
crowded with megalithic
monuments. The original rock

beds have been identified for
most of the stones in the
necropolis (megalithic stone
slabs, stone for tools, for
ornaments, and for cleaning
pottery), as well as the builders'
dwellings. Exoudun and its site

dominate the valley of the Sèvre
Niortaise, the source of the great
slabs of 'Bathonian flint' used at
Bougon, four kilometres away,
which was why the site was used
for the 1979 trials in hauling and
erecting megaliths.

215

Ancestor Worship

Social power could also be expressed in another way: in the construction of enormous camps surrounded by large trenches. Some of these camps are linked with megalithic monuments, particularly in western Europe; others belong to very different cultural or geographical landscape. In a settled but perhaps widely scattered community, the monumental centre symbolized group cohesion and protection.

Ancestor worship has been practised in many different cultures, It has been observed in action in Madagascar and in China. What role did these ancestors play in megalithic monuments? Ancestors are those who, having passed the threshold of death, are in possession of the secrets of the gods. They were chosen and recognized by a certain number of descendants who turned to them for authority. The three aspects of this cult – death, selection, and group protection – can be identified in megalithic tombs. There is considerable evidence that the individuals buried in these tombs had been carefully selected: there are examples among the oldest monuments, and also some of the largest – around ten individuals were buried in the French tombs of the fifth millennium, only a few in the oldest Iberian sepulchres, six on average in the English long barrows. A little later on the island of Rousay, the largest monument at Knowe contained only three skeletons. In southern England the mounds of the Severn–Cotswold group of tombs, some of them of considerable mass, sheltered on average no more than about sixteen bodies.

The size of the monument has nothing to do with the number of individuals buried or cremated there; there is probably a closer connection with the importance of the people placed in the tomb, or with the importance of the intercession confided to the dead by the living. Many megalithic monuments continued to be venerated for hundreds of years without any more dead being added; it may be that the individuals buried there soon became the mediators for several generations.

The collective nature of ancestor worship appears to explain several characteristics of these tombs. The secondary rites, so important in the mortuary houses of northern Europe, imply that the collective ceremonies extended over a long period. During this time the dead person gradually lost all individuality to acquire the eternal collective status of ancestor; and the solidarity of the ancestors representing a single community is clearly visible in the deposit of objects. In these tombs or hypogea the grave goods are those of the group and not of individuals – this is the interpretation placed on objects introduced into the megalithic tomb of Aillevans (Haute-Saône) and in the hypogeum II of Les Mournouards in the Marne; these are bows and arrows, axes, and a few ornaments, placed to one side of the skeletons near the entrance. And in the Tomb of the Eagles, in Orkney, the

Artefacts found in the Argenteuil megalithic tomb may have formed part of collective offerings. Vessels, flint knives or daggers, polished axes and horn shafts, flint arrow-heads and a curved stone quiver pierced at both ends, as well as various beads and pendants, can be identified

(Musée des Antiquitiés Nationales, Sainte-Germain-en-Laye. Photo J.-M. Labat © Casterman)

offerings appear to have been deposited not for one of the dead in the tomb but for the group of ancestors whose totem must have been an eagle.

In the third millennium more collective funeral practices certainly involved the whole of the population, but the dead buried in the megalithic tombs were still probably seen as ancestors: the little lodges into which some bones were laid may signify that there was also a hierarchy or classification of ancestors. At Gnewitz in northern Germany five wall niches measuring 1 metre by 2 are spaced along the

217

A flint arrow-head was found embedded in a human vertebra in one of the rock-cut tombs at Les Ronces at Villevenard in the Marne. It is not unusual to find late Neolithic skeletons shot through with arrows. Battle casualties, perhaps, or sacrifices?

(Musée des Antiquités Nationales, Saint-Germain-en-Laye. Photo J.-M. Labat © Casterman)

walls of a very long tomb. Bones were brought here of skeletons which had no doubt been exposed elsewhere, and were separated into the niches according to criteria that distinguished one family or age-group from another. In France it is not unusual to discover several hundred individuals gathered together at this period: 350 at La Chaussée-Tirancourt. Recent excavations have shown that there, too, strict rules regulated each burial, each move of the remains, each sealing of a phase of use. The southern region of the Iberian peninsula provides several examples of collective graves with more than a hundred skeletons, and the hypogeum of Hal Safliéni in Malta, dating from the same period as some of the temples, contained the remains of 7,000 dead. In this case, although the collective and egalitarian characteristics appear overwhelming, the construction of the great temples suggests in contrast a highly hierarchical society. Political or religious power is not apparent in the burials of Hal Safliéni, however.

It is obviously very difficult to understand and describe what Gordon Childe calls 'the fossilized behaviour patterns of extinct societies'. Recent discoveries reveal a variety of social settings, human groupings with more or less thoroughly structured organization, but all neolithized. At such times, when the inhabitants of western Europe were becoming settled and established in limited territory and scattered hamlets, megalithic monuments were the equivalents of major fortified dwelling sites, expressing symbolically the need for social cohesion and divine protection. The props of this setting were the ancestors, a genuine institution capable of mobilizing group energy. Such monuments provided the site for ceremonies which deflected the anguish of loss, or of epidemic illness, in a destructive world.

The material constraints implied by the building of the most imposing megalithic monuments indicate a highly organized society, probably hierarchical. Other monuments might correspond to societies which were certainly complex, but of differing types. Some, in northern Europe, appear to have been relatively egalitarian in the third millennium, while others in the fifth and fourth millennia in western France were more hierarchical and must have had ruling families. Still others, in the third millennium in the Paris basin or on the Causses, appear more highly collectivized. Monumental tombs and temples were built in largely centralized Mediterranean societies in the third and second millennia. Finally, the princely system was known in both Brittany and in England at the beginning of the Bronze Age, coinciding with the last of the megaliths.

The diversity of contexts suggests that the megalith builders were motivated by spiritual instincts as well as by concern for social order. Two societies at a comparable level of complexity did not always adopt the same strategy as the basis of their stability. Ancestor-based religion, linked with megalithic constructions which were more specifically funerary, represents only one answer among many. Differing ideologies – what is known as 'natural forces', for example – appear to have developed in England with the stone circles. Finally, ideologies more closely allied to economic factors such as the semi-industrial exploitation of flint and axe manufacture, must also have been able to supply the surplus energy capable of activating a whole culture.

The double male burials at Les Chatelliers-du-Vieil-Auzay in Vendée suggest the possibility of human sacrifice: one of the men seems to have died by violence. Three third-millennium graves were set in a long barrow near dwellings. Two vessels were deposited for each head in the second grave. In two of the three, the bodies had been carefully laid out, either head to toe or side by side.

(2 Photos © P. Birocheau/J.-M. Large)

THE SACRED

WORLD OF

MEGALITHS

Ceremonial Centres

The role attributed to ancestors in the construction of megalithic monuments was inseparable from religious expression; it is only our modern society that differentiates between the two. Religious belief and patterns of thought in traditional societies generally look on creation as a coherent whole. The possibility that all human activity may reflect a cosmology, a system of mythic explanation embracing the essential aspects of the universe, must be considered in order to understand the past. According to this approach, megaliths are not simply connected with death in some cases and with the sun in others. Rather, all reflect human life in differing degrees, its social, economic, ritual, and spiritual aspects, though it is difficult for us to understand the expression of the sacred in megalithic monuments. The modern observer is reduced to interpreting a handful of symbolic offerings, some funeral rites, and a few symbols carved, chipped out of, or painted on certain stones, and to observing the majesty and orientation of the monuments.

Few of the monumental sites remain undisturbed since prehistoric times – but a few do still remain. Generally the peripheral sectors of the monuments, which have most easily escaped destruction, are the first areas to be explored. Despite decay, some areas have remained intact and help to explain the purpose of the monument.

In some chambers the offerings are particularly rich: at Mané-er-Hroeck searchers counted 106 axes, 49 beads and pendants, a discring; in others, nothing. Any apparent disarray of the remains may simply reflect the complex history of their abandonment.

Many chambers show signs of internal divisions, indicated by small flat stones; some, placed vertically, mark the outlines of small niches or compartments designed to take offerings, while others were laid flat to separate layers of bones. Some complete human skeletons were huddled so tightly that they appear to have been bound in a bag or a shroud; this has been observed in several places, particularly at Les Mournouards where archeological material such as shards, trimmed or polished stones, and deer-horn artefacts were placed together at the entrance of the grave, and have been interpreted as a collective offering. One of the little niches in the Mid Howe tomb in Orkney contained six pots and a flint knife; these too may have constituted a collective offering. At Knowth and Newgrange in Ireland, a large carved and decorated stone resembling a concave circular altar table was placed at the centre of several of the tomb's lateral chambers. It was accompanied by carbonized grain and the remains of burnt human bones. The emptiness of some tombs such as those at Ascot-under-Wychwood, and Lugbury in Wiltshire, and of some niches of the Mid Howe type, may indicate that bones were removed at the time of some later rite.

The tomb in the Mid Howe megalithic monument on the island of Rousay, in Orkney, is subdivided by large stones set transversely. Some compartments were empty, possibly indicating that the bones that had been there were subjected to ritual manipulation.

(Photo © M. Sharp)

The passages leading to the tombs were quite often used for deposits. In such cases remains have been discovered beneath the stones used to seal the passage; these may consist of a complete human skeleton or simply a skull or jaw-bone, as at Bougon. Haphazard fragments of bone may also be found, flint flakes, or a few shards. Several explanations have been suggested for such passage deposits: the corridor may have been used as an extension for a congested chamber, or perhaps as a secondary place of burial, an annexe – for a later burial, for instance – or it may have belonged to a monument designed as a single unit, and dispersing the objects would enable each part to be sanctified. In Frances Lynch's words, the passage thus became a place of spiritual communication rather than a means of access for the living.

Deposits of offerings in front of the façade confirm the functional importance of this area, also known as the 'forecourt', at the foot of the external kerb. This is exactly where the most famous decorated block was found at Newgrange. In Jutland 7,000 shards were similarly discovered in 1940 in front of the Groenhoef monument at Horsens. The original vessels had been placed on the surrounding blocks of the tumulus, on each side of the passage entrance. There was a similar

The megalithic tomb of La Chaussée-Tirancourt in the Somme is made up of a series of compartments corresponding to a division of human bones according to social or family criteria.

(Photo © R. Agache)

discovery at Katbjerg, in the same region, in front of another circular monument. Here there were not only shards but also burnt flints, polished axes, arrow heads, and amber ornaments. During the excavation of this Jordhoej monument, Poul Kjaerum observed that the passage leading to the corridor entrance was itself empty. These two examples indicate the importance of external areas open to contact with the faithful; many offerings were placed near this point. But why was the way in towards the tomb's corridor bare of offerings? Was this pathway left clear for certain of the living who could go inside the tomb, or was it for the ancestors to come and go along it?

After the burial period, which was probably fairly brief, the grave was closed. Next came the very long period of veneration. In fact many megalithic chambers possess a sealed access corridor: fitted stones were used to block and hide the entrance of the tomb, blending in with the external kerbs. The Bougon tumulus shows systematic sealing of the passages, which must have taken place shortly after construction and the first use of the monuments. Traces of offerings have been discovered in front of the external kerbs.

At Gavrinis, early twentieth-century excavators found access to the chambers blocked by a quantity of stones in the corridor. Charles-

Tanguy Le Roux's digging since 1980 has revealed imposing external kerbs and a forecourt where he found fragments of pottery, trimmed flints, chips of dolerite, and polished axes. A deposit of ashes suggested that wooden structures had been burnt, perhaps when the forecourt itself was sealed. Gravel and sand covered both the forecourt and the carefully constructed façade. This total sealing of the monument, reducing it to the appearance of a simple mound, occurred frequently in Brittany and central western France. At the base of the standing stones can be found not only the wedging stones but also traces of the ceremonies carried out before the final stages: ashes, charred stones, shards, flint chips or tools, polished axes, grinding stones and pestles. Two sites in Finistère have yielded almost complete vases, of the same style as those placed in the megalithic tombs.

Ceremonies also sometimes took place at the alignments. Postholes have been found close to the standing stones at Saint-Just in Ille-et-Vilaine; stakes were set in them to complete the monument. Towards the middle of the third millennium, burial coffers were added to the group; standing stones were not usually associated with death but, as ceremonial sites, they were apparently sometimes linked with funeral rites. The first investigators of the nineteenth century discovered human bones at the foot of some of these stones.

In some of the monuments surrounded by a ditch – now filled in – archeologists have found deposits of offerings: vessels, flint tools, human bones (frequently scattered and more rarely intact skeletons). Such discoveries, for example at Nieul-sur-l'Autize in Vendée, have encouraged the conclusion that these great third-millennium sites also

The apparently haphazard accumulation of human bones inside one of the compartments of the Chaussée-Tirancourt tomb was in fact dictated by precise criteria, revealed in part by scrupulous inspection at the time of excavation. For example, one small cell contained the assembled bones of six children.

(Photo © C. Masset)

had a ceremonial function. When the sanctuary at Stonehenge was begun towards the middle of the third millennium, a circular ditch was dug out and lined along its inner edge with a ring of fifty-six pits, in which have been found the remains of incinerated human bodies. Not all the ditches and standing stones of open-construction monuments reveal a funerary element, however; where such a feature exists, it appears simply to emphasize the monument's ceremonial role.

The world of death adopted very diverse aspects in megalithic tombs, indicating ceremonies which may have been very persistent, perhaps performed immediately after a death but also frequently later, at a time of commemoration or fresh funerals. What we are discovering now – traces of cremation, a few scattered bones – are only the remains from these long-lived practices. The joint work of archeologists and anthropologists has made it possible to reconstitute certain burial rites.

It is rare to find skeletons lying in anatomically correct positions in the collective burial chambers, although it is not unknown, particularly in some third-millennium constructions which have in effect become ossuaries. At Roaix in Vaucluse, for instance, thirty-five dead people were simply thrown in on top of each other: there appears to have been a massacre. The bones in most other tombs, particularly those dating from ancient times, display an apparent disorder that has occasionally been interpreted too readily as indicating secondary

The Days of the Great Ossuaries

In the Roaix hypogeum, in Vaucluse, intact skeletons were discovered with, to one side, a series of skulls (below, right) which had been deliberately placed there during secondary rites.

(Photo © J.-P. Mohen)

The Boileau hypogeum in Vaucluse was discovered in 1984. The roof of the cavern had fallen in on the layer of human bones, most of which were still intact. A large number of bodies had obviously been placed in this ossuary on a single occasion. The few offerings included small vessels, a few arrow-heads, and some items of adornment.

(Photo ©J.-P. Mohen)

burials; skeletons already *in situ* may have been relegated in preparation for a fresh burial.

This is what appears to have happened in the hypogeum II at Les Mournouards. Some sixty bodies wrapped in bags gradually accumulated there, and as space became limited the remains were pushed to the sides of the chamber. In many other cases, however, the disorder of the bones appears to be the result of later ritual manipulation connected with much more complex funeral rites.

The Mid Howe tomb in Orkney is divided into twelve compartments. Two were empty, while the others contained skeletons pushed up against the sides, as well as a pile of the remains of fifteen individuals, six being represented only by the skull. Not far away, at Knowe of Yarso, a tomb divided into three sections contained the disarticulated bones of twenty-nine people, a group of four in the first two compartments and twenty-five in the third; twenty-two skulls without jaw-bones were ranged along the wall. In the Ramsay monument the fourteen compartments contained nothing but the incomplete remains of three individuals, while the Isbister tomb contained the remains of 431 people. Archeologists studying the grave at West Kennet in England were able to prove that bones had been removed and only some of them replaced: the others were placed along the walls. The study of Scandinavian prehistory has yielded similar observations, recalling the rites described in nineteenth century Madagascar where in certain circumstances the ancestor would be shown in procession, sometimes reduced to a few bones.

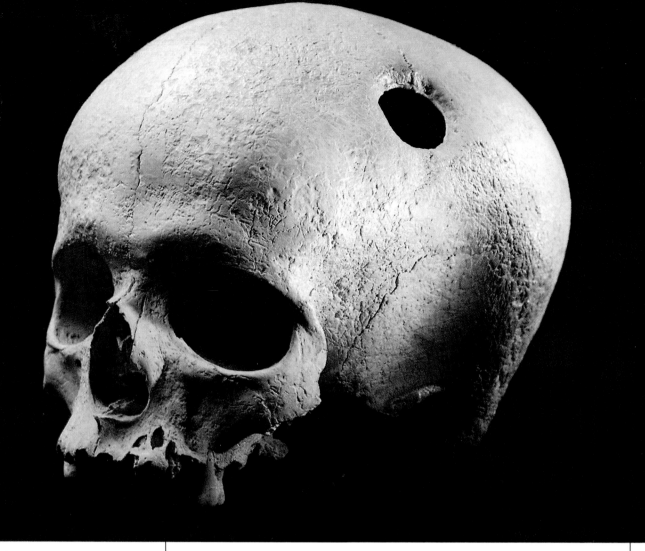

This trepanned skull was found in one of the hypogea in the Petit Morin valley in the Marne. The slight ridge of scarring appears to indicate that the subject survived the operation.

(Musée des Antiquités Nationales, Saint-Germain-en-Laye.
Photo J.-M. Labat © Casterman)

It often appears that bones were carefully sorted out inside the tomb: skulls together, as with the fifty found in the upper layer at Roaix, and the long bones also sometimes collected together at one side. Such selection was not always based on anatomy, sometimes the remains of children were separated out. At La Chaussée-Tirancourt the bones of six children were grouped together in this way in a niche within the tomb. In the long chambers with niches in southern Sweden (Ingelstorp) or in northern Germany (Gnewitz), the remains of one particular social group were kept separate. Most of the skeletons in these niches were incomplete and must have been brought from the place where the body had first been laid. In this area the timber mortuary houses – as at Tustrup or Vrone Hede, in Denmark, for example – may have been used to receive the corpses at the time of the funeral before removal to the megalithic tomb. The remains of such 'houses of the dead' have also been discovered beneath the Nordic and British mounds built over them after their collapse. The exposure of the dead was practised in many civilizations (and is so still). A wall painting at Çatal Hüyük in Anatolia, dating from the sixth millennium, appears to depict one such funerary house, outside the city, surrounded by vultures. The dead were exposed there until the spring, when they were buried on ledges made of dried earth from their own houses.

One of the burial chambers in Bougon's tumulus B contained about ten cranial sections brought back and lined up in two rows.

The Moment the Dead became Ancestral Relics

These skulls were associated with a few long bones but no other human bones; discovered in 1980, this tomb confirmed that selected dry bones were sometimes brought into megalithic tombs, as relics.

Ritual seems to have accorded an important role to skulls. There are no models of skulls, like those in early Neolithic Jericho, but trepanning may be seen as an original form of skull worship. Such skulls are not unusual in third millennium megalithic tombs and hypogea; those from the Rodez group in southern France and the Marne hypogea have shown that trepanning was carried out on living people who survived the operation, as proved by the ridged scarring. This may have been another manifestation of the ritual treatment of bones, practised here on living subjects to gain admittance to the inner circle of ancestors. It also appears that other trepanned individuals did not survive the operation. Cranial discs perforated and worn as pendants may also have been taken from dried skulls.

These and many other observations give revealing glimpses of a world that is strange to us, where multifarious funeral rites appear to reflect a complex after-life which was very much present for the living. When for example two skeletons are discovered in a particular position in relation to each other, as in the fourth and third millennia in central western France, it is possible that one at least of the two may have been sacrificed. Such burials have been found at Bougon in front of the kerbstones of the great rectangular C2 monument: an adult and a child were buried there together, to the north and the south, probably also to the west and the east. In the long barrow of Les Châtelliers-du-Vieil-Auzay in Vendée three double burials of adult men were found, dating from the third millennium. Not only were these dead buried in pairs, side by side or head to toe, but at least three of them died violently: one man in tomb number 5 had an arrow in the fourth lumbar vertebra and the skull of the other had been accidentally crushed, as had also happened to one of the men in grave number 2. Thus the bodies of the dead, and then their bones, were placed in the monuments on the same footing as offerings. They appear to have had the same symbolic properties: the dead person gradually lost his individuality and became an ancestral relic.

A new image of death thus began to develop: the megalithic monument was no longer a simple cavern where corpses were piled up – it became the ceremonial centre for the worship of certain human bones treated as true relics. This is confirmed in the burial caves of southern France, such as the Boucle chasm at Corconne (Gard), or the Tortue aux Monges cave near Narbonne. The most spectacular example is the Baume de Fontbrégoua at Salernes (Var), where Jean Courtin discovered six craniums incised with flint, scattered over several

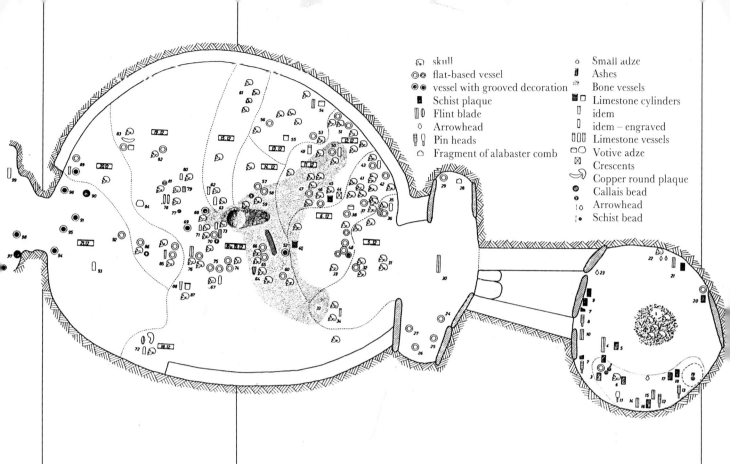

🐚	skull	๐	Small adze
◎๐	flat-based vessel	𝄢	Ashes
◎●	vessel with grooved decoration	⚏	Bone vessels
■	Schist plaque	■□	Limestone cylinders
▯▯	Flint blade	▯	idem
◇	Arrowhead	▯	idem – engraved
▯▯	Pin heads	▯▯▯	Limestone vessels
⬠	Fragment of alabaster comb	◠◡	Votive adze
		⊠	Crescents
		⤳	Copper round plaque
		๏	Callais bead
		⸬๐	Arrowhead
		⸬●	Schist bead

Plan of the double burial chamber at Praia Das Maças in Portugal, showing the distribution of archeological remains. Despite appearances, they were placed according to very precise criteria. In the small chamber to the right, offerings were spread out along the walls and human bones gathered in the middle, while vessels were placed in the antechamber. More obscure was the placing of funerary deposits in the large chamber which deliberately left some areas empty.

(*Les Monuments Préhistoriques de Praia das Maças et de Casainhos*, by Y. Leisner, G. Zbyszewski and O. da Veiga Ferreira, Lisbon 1969)

square metres. The archeologist suggested the possibility of cannibalism, interpreted here as the ultimate ritual approach to assimilating the dead.

What were these offerings discovered in the burial chambers, in the access passages, in front of the tumulus kerbs, or sometimes at the foot of standing stones, as at Saint-Just? Axes, rings, necklace beads of polished stone, flint daggers, pottery; sometimes intact, but usually in fragments, they appear to have suffered the same fate as the human bones, also generally disarticulated and broken: they must have undergone several phases of a complex ritual and occupy a secondary position there. In such cases the fragment is as important as the complete object, and its presence as significant for the prehistorian as for the archeologist.

One of the most abundant artefacts is the polished hard stone axe, often discovered whole because of its durability and resistance to impact. Miniature fibrolite axes, a marbled beige in colour, also appeared; they date from around 4000 B.C. in central western France (Bougon B and E) and in Brittany, where they have frequently been found in barrows at Carnac and where they probably originated. These very hard items, between 2 and 10 centimetres across, are usually highly polished, particularly at the blade-edges which show no signs of wear. Some indeed are too small and flat to have been of practical use. Some were sawn, cut in two and perforated, and were worn as pendants.

The 'Carnac' style axes, however, might be as large as 46 centimetres across; made highly polished of black chloromelanite, eclogite and jadeite, they too were unused. Their splayed-out blades might be concave on the edges, making polishing more difficult. These axes have been found in the Saint-Michel barrow at Carnac, and in neigh-

Official axes had no functional purpose: their slenderness, their carefully polished surfaces with no signs of use, the perforation of some for use as pendants, all indicate that these were votive offerings. Here, at Arzon, the scarcity of the raw material – jadeite – and the collection of seventeen axes in the same deposit emphasizes the symbolic value of these axes, which appear as carved motifs on some megaliths.

(Musée des Antiquités Nationales, Saint-Germain-en-Laye.
Photo J.-M. Labat © Casterman)

bouring monuments dating from the fourth millennium. Polished axes have been found at the base of the Manio standing stone in Morbihan. The stone itself is carved and decorated with five wavy lines, and five axes were placed blade-upward round its base. Polished axes made of green jadeite, as found for example in the Carnac region, indicate clearly the need for an important votive object, shaped like a domestic tool but not used as such, to be placed in tombs. Many such axes measure about 20 centimetres; their fairly slender shape and pointed heel recall the drawings on the passage stones at Gavrinis. They were very carefully polished, with no traces of use on the blade. Sometimes the heel was perforated, as appears to be shown on one of the Gavrinis representations. Isolated hiding places such as at Arzon or Quiberon yielded some of these axes in a pit.

The Armorican axes may have been made of local jadeite; the other stones used may have come from the Alps. These axes reached English sites at Cunzierton and Sweet Track in Somerset; one fragment has even been found at Cairnholy in Scotland.

Morbihan symbolic artefacts included other luxury objects, delicately polished jadeite or serpentine disc-rings. The ring from the Mané-er-Hroeck megalithic tomb is made of green serpentine, 7 milli-

metres thick and 100 millimetres external diameter. It was associated with a jadeite axe and two pendants of green variscite.

Breton megalithic tombs might also contain dolerite axes from quarries at Plussulien in the Côtes-du-Nord, where mining began around 4000 B.C. and continued for 1,500 years. The different phases of manufacture have been reconstructed: after detaching a block from the basic rock the craftsman took an hour to rough out the basic axe shape, and another hour to trim and refine it. He needed between two and four hours to smooth it, and then the polishing took two or three days. An average size dolerite axe thus represented considerable effort. These artefacts spread all over modern France and overflowed into Belgium and England, without being connected with any particular type of tomb. Bradley has shown that 'luxury' axes were fairly widely spread across three regions of the British Isles: Cornwall, Scotland and Cumbria. Their diffusion must therefore have been easy – and their possession much desired. They may have circulated in the form of gifts passed from hand to hand. A certain concentration on the

These polished green stone disc-rings from megalithic monuments in Morbihan may be bracelets. Like the ceremonial axes, they appear to have been symbols of great wealth.

(Musée des Antiquités Nationales, Saint-Germain-en-Laye.
Photo J.-M. Labat © Casterman)

edge of the zone of diffusion seems to indicate that what was seen as an 'exotic' precious possession was subject to greater political supervision in these areas. There are even copies of the axes made of soft stone such as limestone, like the two examples at Woodhenge near Amesbury: their value lay only in the design they reproduced.

The Treasury of Grave-Goods

The later megalithic chambers of the British Isles often contained an especially distinctive item: a pile of weapons made of hard stone. This has been recorded both in collective tombs (Knowth in particular) and in individual burials. It probably represents the attribution of personal power. The dagger made an appearance in certain third-millennium tombs; one found at Le Grand-Pressigny was shaped out of flint blades. Soon they were made of copper, and then, in the following millennium, of bronze. Daggers were carved on some of the Stonehenge stones; they are associated with axes, and belong to the same scale of values.

Much sought after for necklace beads and pendants, variscite is a green phosphate mineral formerly known as 'callais'. It occurs naturally at the mouth of the Loire, and in Catalonia. It seems likely that the variscite for objects found in the Morbihan and Poitou tombs came from the Nantes area. Catalonian variscite was used in quantity in Neolithic times in northern Spain and western Languedoc, but the origin of the variscite used for the beads and pendants found in Portuguese megalithic tombs is not known.

Amber was little used in Neolithic times, except in Scandinavian tombs; although beads and pendants found in the megalithic burials at Los Millares were made from amber, its supposed Baltic origin has not been confirmed. It became much more widely used in the individual burials which extended the megalithic tradition at the beginning of the second millennium, both in Wessex and in Brittany.

The idea that offerings placed in megalithic tombs were essentially of symbolic value is reinforced by the nature of some of them: anthropomorphic plaques made of carved schist, decorated bone idols, and zoomorphic amulets found in Portugal and southern Spain. The rarity of their material and the quality of finish indicates their great value. Other objects appear commonplace beside them, though the chips or blades of flint, bone-working products, small stones, and fragments of a sandstone grinder may have had a more precise significance which remains unknown today. It was amongst such offerings that the first metal ornaments and weapons appeared, towards the middle of the third millennium. In southern France, near the gold-bearing rivers of the Hérault, Gard, and Gardon basins and in the Cévennes, a few gold and copper beads have been found from the many necklaces deposited in the tombs, and some decorations which

Some of the votive fibrolith polished axes found among the collective offerings in the Bougon necropolis tombs, in Deux-Sèvres, are extremely small, barely 2 centimetres across. The bone pins were probably used as personal ornaments.

(Musée des Deux-Sèvres.
Photo J.-M. Labat © Casterman)

must have been sewn onto clothes. Small jewels have been discovered at Saint-Eugène in Aude, at Cazevieille in Hérault, and at Arles-Fontvieilles in the Bouches-du-Rhône. Dozens of copper daggers have been found at Freyssinel, at Balsièges in Lozère, and in areas nearby – but these were not weapons. They must rather have been symbols of power, similar to those worn on the chests of certain statue-menhirs of the period, like the one at Sion. Copper awls and pins have also been found, and lead beads and pendants in tombs in Hérault.

In the south of the Iberian peninsula, gold, copper, and silver help to emphasize the precious nature of the offerings: prospecting for ore in the regions of Almeria and Rio Tinto in Spain, and near Zambujal to the north of Lisbon, appears to have preoccupied the communities of the time.

The use of copper spread right across western Europe around the year 2000 B.C. Inside tombs these metal objects were often associated with the vessels known as 'bell-beakers'; they were found in the new collective tombs, as in the Portuguese rock-cut tombs and the coffers of the Sion necropolis, and may also have been deposited in secondary burials. In western France, the Netherlands and the British Isles, bell-beaker ware and metal offerings were gathered together in individual but still traditional megalithic graves.

Pottery too was an important element of the offerings. It has been found in the oldest monuments in the form of shards, or more rarely as complete vessels, which were never very large, and can in no way be confused with the storage-jars found in dwelling sites. It is difficult to know if the vessels of megalithic monuments, often finely shaped and decorated, had any specific function. The stem vessels, also known as 'perfume-burners' or pedastal urns, are a fine example of these particular shapes whose purpose eludes us. They have been found in tombs in France as well as in dwellings attributed to the Chassey culture, dating from the second half of the fourth millennium. In southern France the vessels are almost all cylindrical, while in Brittany or the Paris basin they may be cubic in form. All have a large hollow or 'cup' on their upper surface, and the rims of many carry a geometric pattern of triangles or rectangles cross-hatched, squared, or dotted.

The large hollow dishes with a base found in northern Europe perhaps fulfilled a similar function; they belonged to the funnel-beaker culture which, in about 3000 B.C., partly coincided with the Chassey culture. Such vases were also highly decorated, and appear to have been luxury items.

Another very individual shape appeared a few centuries later; this was a small bottle with a rimmed neck, which was found in abundance in Scandinavia and which appears to have been imitated in Brittany. Indeed, a few rather rough and poorly baked examples were found in megalithic tombs with very long side-access chambers, such as at Mélus in the Côtes-du-Nord.

'Flower pot' vases of fairly rough manufacture, found in the Paris basin, were characteristic of the very long megalithic barrows and hypogea of the Seine-Oise-Marne culture.

It was in about the year 2300 B.C. that the drinking vessels known as 'bell-beakers' appeared in certain megalithic chambers; some had been introduced when the tomb was re-used, in both Portugal and Brittany. This type of vessel is easily recognizable through its curved bell-shaped outline, the quality of its manufacture, and the horizontal decorative bands. They have also been found in individual graves, both megalithic and otherwise, for example in Great Britain. It has occasionally been suggested that these luxury vessels were for funerary use, but some shards have also been found among the remains of dwelling houses – with, admittedly, more widely varied shapes.

Thus although it was relatively abundant, the pottery deposited in megalithic monuments remains puzzling: were the footed bowls actually small altars? No one knows. What was contained in the other vessels? Was it a viaticum? an unguent? a liquid offering? That too remains unknown. All the vessels have two points in common: their moderate size and their high quality in comparison with domestic ware.

Polished hard stone maces were ceremonial weapons found in the most recent of the Irish megalithic monuments.

(Photo © Dublin National Museum)

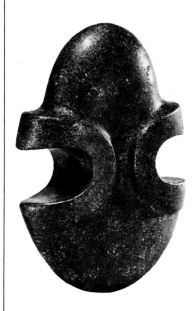

235

Portuguese megalithic graves have yielded plaquettes with anthropomorphic, probably female, designs. This example, with a fairly typical owl-face, was found at Montemar-o-Novo.

(Musée des Antiquités Nationales, Saint-Germain-en-Laye.
Photo J.-M. Labat © Casterman)

An unusual item among the offerings deposited in Iberian megalithic graves: sandals. This pair, made of two polished limestone plaques, was found in a rock-cut tomb at Alapraia in Portugal.

(Musée des Antiquités Nationales, Saint-Germain-en-Laye.
Photo J.-M. Labat © Casterman)

Apart from its function, pottery displays characteristics of manufacture and decoration which are typical of certain social groupings. Birgitta Hardh has identified the regional variations of vessels deposited in the megalithic tombs of southern Sweden; the offering of the vessels is an additional element that personalizes the monument in a collective manner.

The animal world is generally only sparsely represented among such grave-goods. Animals chiefly appear in the form of ornamental items such as beads and pendants made of perforated teeth or shells; at Bougon, for instance, bovine incisors and the canine teeth of boars, dogs, wolves, and bears make up the majority of ornaments. The identification of these animal remains emphasizes the predominance of untamed wildlife and of noble game, the opposite of what is seen in dwelling areas where domestic animal remains predominate.

When the Bougon megalithic chambers were first explored, in 1840, investigators reported finding in chamber A a complete dog skeleton lying by the side of a child's body, implying that these were two companions. This deposit dates from the middle of the third millennium, and from a phase of re-use. To date, it remains unique. John Hedges has drawn attention to the presence of eagle bones in Orkney; his book, *Tomb of The Eagles*, seeks to demonstrate the existence of totemism in Neolithic society. Clearly a general rule cannot be drawn from a single example, but it must be conceded that some creatures such as cattle, dogs, bears, and eagles were at the centre of a certain amount of specific human activity, and that they thus helped to strengthen the cultural identity of the group.

Bovine bones figure among the rare animal offerings, and pictures of cattle can be seen in megalithic and cave art, first in Brittany and then in Italy, Sardinia, and Sweden. Three bovine skulls were placed at regular intervals in the English tumulus of Beckhampton Road, and other animals appear to have played a part elsewhere. At the centre of the funerary chamber of Barclodiad-y-Gavres, in the island of Anglesey, the charred remains of a hearth were mixed with bones of reptiles and amphibians. Similar remains have been found in the graves of Scandinavian Bronze Age 'sorcerers'.

The evidence thus tends to show that many of the offerings placed at the foot of megaliths and inside the tombs were not everyday objects simply brought from the village.

Sculpted and polished stones in Ireland and schist crooks decorated with carvings in Portugal have so far been found only in funerary contexts. Jadeite axes were placed in non-funerary hiding places, but in both cases these objects of great symbolic importance represent artefacts of everyday life, remaining the preserve of a small number of people. Although these objects were originally designed for the living, the aim was to legitimize a temporal authority equally acceptable in the after-life: symbols of the gods could only be confided to those whom the gods favoured and who held the power to intercede with them. These prestige artefacts were intended to impress when presented to seal an alliance or treaty, or to assure protection, and might be dedicated to a living person or a community, one of the dead or a group of ancestors, one particular god or the whole pantheon. Through its secret and sacrificial nature such a gift reinforced the intimate link between the donor and the deity.

Even in cases of a personal gift, however, the collective nature of such offerings remains clear in western Europe during the fourth and third millennia; later, in the second millennium, offerings of a personal nature were enclosed in individual burials beneath a barrow. The period of this change coincided with the last great megalithic monu-

ments such as Stonehenge. These sceptres, this jewelry made of amber and gold, proclaimed to the gods the new social status of the prince, unknown in Neolithic times.

Many of the stones were decorated. This art was more widespread and more varied than was first realized: 120 ornamented stones were found in the western Iberian peninsula, 210 in western France and the Paris basin, 470 in Ireland, together with some small groups, generally of later date, such as the cists in Hesse in Germany and the Kivik tomb in southern Sweden. There were too the axes and daggers shown on five of the Stonehenge columns, and the decorated blocks in Scotland, related to cave art which was quite widespread in western Europe but which is still not well known. The anthropomorphic stone slabs in the Swiss Valais recall the statue-menhirs of southern France. Malta has a unique group of temple decorations and carvings. The elements of this art are varied, and include paving in passages and chambers, standing stones, and small objects. Depending on the region, the artists used paint, engraving, chipping, rubbing down, or carving.

Such shapes and marks have been studied. Their creators – the builders or the users of the megaliths – employed a language linked with architectural and ritual expression; it remains largely enigmatic, but what we do understand of it throws light on the different groups of monuments, their functions, and the relationships between them.

In Malta and in Sardinia, megalithic art reflects insular peculiarities. The temples of Malta and Gozo contain a fairly large number of female figures made of stone or terracotta; the enormous statue at Tarxien, which is broken, is some 3 metres tall. Another, much smaller but very well known, shows a sleeping woman lying on a bed. All

Gold items first appeared in the megalithic graves of Morbihan: above, the band, a bead, and three ornaments are from the Kerouaren monument at Plouhinec; bottom, long gold beads mixed with green variscite beads were found in the Grah Niol tomb at Arzon.

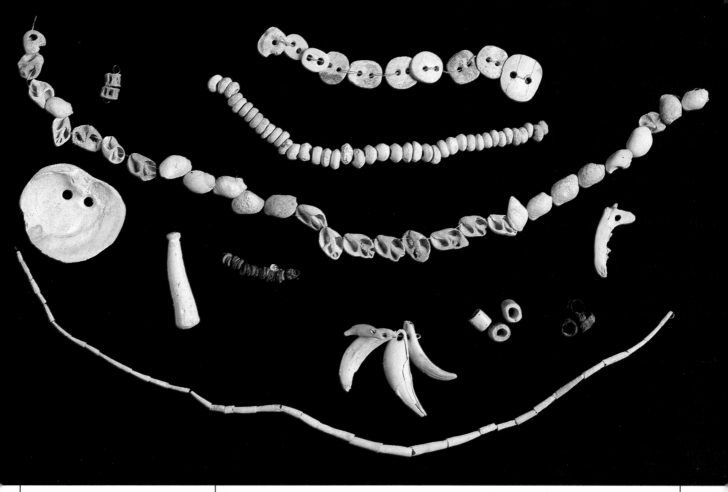

Ornaments placed as offerings in the hypogea of the Petit Morin valley in the Marne include (bottom to top): mollusc shells, dogs' teeth, shells, and perforated fish vertebrae. The cranial discs with double perforations are directly connected with the practice of trepanning. Such discs were sometimes copied in shell or limestone.

(Musée des Antiquités Nationales, Saint-Germain-en-Laye. Photo J.-M. Labat © Casterman)

represent corpulent women, naked or clothed. There are also some sculpted phalluses. At Tarxien the lintels are decorated with scrolls or a frieze of horned animals, either rams or oxen; one of the walls also displays two large sculpted bulls and a sow. Two rock-cut tombs in Sardinia (Branca di Modeddu and L'Emiciclo di Sas Concas) are decorated with schematic anthropomorphic motifs reminiscent of the praying figures of Iberian cave art, and at San Pietro, another artificial cave, two large horned cattle are carved above the entrance. All the marble statuettes and idols on this island are female; some of the stones surrounding the giant Tamuli tomb have breasts, as does the Genna Arrele statue-menhir, while one of its neighbours bears a praying figure motif on the breast. The dagger carved beneath the belt may have been added later, giving the figure a masculine character. In Corsica it is difficult to know if the most ancient statue-menhirs are contemporaneous with the megalithic tombs; most can be reasonably accurately dated to the Bronze Age, through the weapons and particularly the swords shown on the front wall.

The decorated megaliths of the Iberian peninsula are concentrated in the west–north-west Portugal, north-west and south-west Spain; they include stone slabs in passages and chambers, and some standing stones. The Portuguese group of Viseu is uniform: the motifs are painted in red, sometimes on a cream base, such as the two human silhouettes visible on one of the Juncais slabs now in the Lisbon national museum. Black is also used in the painting. One stone in the Queiriga burial chamber depicts a hunting scene painted in red, in which the archers and their dog confront a herd of deer; although there are no direct links, this naturalistic scene, rare in megalithic art, recalls paintings in the Spanish Levant.

Ornaments found in graves in Aveyron include limestone and shell beads, perforated teeth, a few jade or quartz beads, and the earliest copper ornaments. Two small winged beads are also typical.

(Musée des Antiquités Nationales, Saint-Germain-en-Laye. Photo J.-M. Labat © Casterman)

Animals are seldom represented in megalithic art: a very dubious reindeer has been recorded in Portugal, and two horses are incised on a block at Cubillejo de Lara de los Infantas, near the source of the Douro. Near Viseu the head-stone of certain monuments bears the painted representation of an 'animal skin'. A saw-tooth motif appears on other stones, forming a kind of garland. Some stones are entirely covered with dotted interlocking lines, and so-called 'serpentiform' curves, either painted or carved.

Amongst these painted or chipped out figurative representations can be recognized a form of tall-footed cup (at Baião near Porto), and a knife (at Monte Corzan near Corunna); a short-toothed comb painted on a stone at Antelas, at Oliveira de Fradas, remains unique. 'Astral' shapes include chipped-out circles, points and cups, and lines radiating out like sunbursts. A painted stone at Antelas appears to show the sun and the moon at the centre of a network of geometric motifs. A conical sculpted stone at Caramujeira near Lagos has finally been interpreted as a phallic emblem; of uncertain date, it is a betyl with a crowning bulge and wavy vertical lines.

It is debatable whether these different styles belong to the same period and the same form of expression: many motifs are both painted and engraved, some tend to be more often engraved, while yet others are always painted. The architecture of the tombs and the few confirmed dates nearly all point towards the second half of the fourth millennium; the deep floor layer of the decorated megalithic chamber of Carapito I in Portugal dates from 3300 B.C., corresponding with the dating for other monuments of the same type. The group of the Viseu region appears particularly homogeneous.

Iberian megalithic art has certain points in common with cave art, in particular the complex groups, still little known and poorly dated, in northern Portugal and Galicia. These contain several engraved or dot-outlined animals (Chão da Velha), anthropomorphic marks (Fratel), and spirals and concentric circles (Fratel and the Cambra valley). One block, at Marco de Canaverses in Portugal, has spirals and wavy lines similar to those on some Anglesey slabs. The stylistic resemblances between megalithic art and the art of the tombs' furnishings are less obvious: vessels, statuettes, idols and carved crosses all show symmetrical geometric designs that follow strict composi-

This bead-polisher, made of two pieces of sandstone with longitudinal grooves, was used for the production of hundreds of small cylindrical limestone beads, found in tombs on the Causses and in particular in Aveyron.

(Musée des Antiquités Nationales, Saint-Germain-en-Laye. Photo J.-M. Labat © Casterman)

Woman, the Stars, and Masculine Power

tional lines, contrasting strongly with the free decoration of megalithic stones. However, the themes of the two complement each other very satisfactorily.

In France the Breton group is by far the richest and most interesting. Megalithic artists adorned some 200 slabs set in thirty-five passage-graves and six angled chambers, as well as some fourth-millennium steles and seven very long chambers of the third millennium. Most of these monuments are near the coast, from the Loire estuary north to Perros-Guirec. The earliest motifs were drawn in with lightly chipped-out dots; the chipping-out became larger and deeper as time went by and sometimes produced false-relief effects, as in the crooks on the headstone of the Table des Marchands. In the very long chambers there are even bas-reliefs representing breasts.

There are five distinct styles. The 'plain' style was a fairly light decoration with relatively isolated motifs; thus before the year 4000 B.C. U-shaped signs appeared, with or without curved tips, together with crooks, broken lines shaped like a figure '7', and wavy lines. These can be seen in the oldest megalithic passage-graves, at Guennoc, Larcuste, and Mané Kerioned. The shield motif (the 'dishevelled idol'), the bow, and the axe are present in chamber H at Barnenez, and thus also belong to the oldest set of emblems. The magnificent Ile Longue monument at Larmor-Baden has images of bows and shields; the outline shield motif has been compared to certain engraved stone slabs such as the Guennoc steles, which are clearly anthropomorphic.

The 'monumental' style is best seen in the enormous (14 metres long) decorated monolith which probably originally stood near the Grand Menhir at Locmariaquer. (Today it takes the form of three blocks covering the burial chambers of the Tables des Marchands, Er-Vinglé at Locmariaquer, and Gavrinis.) The designs are, from bottom to top: an axe with handle, a crook, two oxen and an 'axe-plough' nearly 3 metres long. Three crescent signs remain unexplained, and the cattle motif is fairly unusual, although one has been noted on the Tremblais standing stone at Saint-Samson-sur-Rance.

The large 'axe-plough' appears again on the broken Great Menhir, where it measures 3.20 metres, on the Kercado covering stone at Carnac (which may also be a section of a standing stone), on one of the columns of the Penhape chamber, in the Ile-aux-Moines, and on two more columns of the Mané Rutual chamber at Locmariaquer. The stone covering this chamber is decorated with a large plain shield, 4.50 metres long and 3.36 metres wide. This monumental image of the idol resembles another anthropomorphic slab more than 5 metres high, set in the ground near the ancient Petit Mont mound at Arzon; the upper part was removed to·form part of a megalithic chamber.

These vessels and polished fibrolith axes from the Souc'h megalithic grave, in Finistère, are typical of the middle Neolithic era. The vessels, often very small, fulfilled a specifically ceremonial function. A decorated shard from a footed vessel (front), which may have been used as a perfume-burner or to contain offerings.
(Musée des Antiquités Nationales, Saint-Germain-en-Laye. Photo J.-M. Labat

The monumental style typical of the Carnac region is thus associated with large standing monoliths; it seems particularly well adapted to these enormous steles. Most of the broken blocks, were re-used in building megalithic tombs. The monumental style, which shares certain features with the plain style – axe, crook, shield 'idol' – appears to have been easily individualized. It dates from the middle of the fourth millennium. The discovery in 1983 of the covering slab at Gavrinis, decorated in this style and re-used, seems to prove that this type of expression pre-dates the 'baroque' style of its walls.

This baroque style developed at the end of the fourth millennium in the great monuments of Morbihan: Arzon, Locmariaquer, Carnac, and Gavrinis; in most cases the characteristically exuberant decoration covers the entire surface of the stone. The designs are marked out with dotted lines – either narrow (Arzon) or, more often, very broad (Gavrinis and Tables des Marchands). Classic designs from earlier periods are juxtaposed (Mané-er-Hroeck) or lead on from one to another (Gavrinis). A careful examination of the Gavrinis stones suggests that the stones may have been recovered from an earlier monument: and indeed several of these stones have plain style designs lightly dotted in, either on surfaces currently not exposed, or as a departure point for baroque decoration inscribed in broader dotted lines. These very free variations on simple themes give an impression of powerful creativity.

The head-stone of the Tables des Marchands, which is sculpted and decorated with the shield motif, carries four crook emblems arranged on each side of the central axis, and this crook theme occurs on other monuments. The triangular axe, with or without handle,

The chamber of one of the Knowth tombs in Ireland, discovered in 1968, contained in a side cell a sandstone bowl 1.20 metres in diameter. Its sculpted decoration, like that of the stone slab at the back, is characteristic of Irish megalithic art. Several deposits of burnt human bones were found on the floor of the chamber.

(Photo © Commissioners of Public Works, Ireland)

designs in curved sections or interlocking U signs, isolated or grouped wavy lines, and multiple chevrons, are typical of the baroque style. The bow appears at Gavrinis. The radiating wheel is only found on the Petit Mont monument where a cross, as at Carnac, perhaps represents a stylized axe with handle. On some stones the cup motif is repeated many times. The two feet side by side on the Petit Mont are unique in France; they recall the decorated stones at Calderstones near Liverpool, or Scandinavian Bronze Age cave art.

Archeologists have been much impressed by the baroque style, and have compared its flowering in southern Brittany with Irish megalithic art, and also with some Portuguese stones, such as the Bulhoa standing stone in the Alentejo. These resemblances still await study.

Geometrically decorated shields form a distinct style of their own. They are characterized by a tall, more or less rectangular figure, and are divided with motifs arranged on each side of its central axis: points (scoops), circles, interlinked U shapes, or butterfly-wing pattern segments. The upper edge is notched. This geometrically decorated design represents a variation on the 'shield' family which existed in earlier styles. It seems that the shields were all human representations, highly stylized: they are also known as 'idols'. They are only seen in the large angled megalithic chambers: Pierre Plates at Locmariaquer (with some twenty shields), Goërem at Gâvres, Mané Roullardé at La Trinité-sur-Mer, and Luffang at Crac'h. A few circles and crosses are sometimes associated with them.

Finally, there is the 'plastic' style. Achieved by the 'false relief' technique, it is seen clearly in the decoration of the very long Armorican chambers of the third millennium, in the form of linked protuberances representing breasts. Sometimes a necklace (another U-shaped protuberance) is associated with them, a design that can be seen on a stone at Tressé, at Bois-du-Mesnil in Ille-et-Vilaine, on two more stones at Kergüentuil at Trégastel, and on another at Prajou-

245

In the Maltese temple of Tarxien, this sculpted frieze probably represents rams. Animal motifs are rare in megalithic art and usually portray horned animals such as bulls, rams, or deer.

(Photo © Roger-Viollet)

Design carved on the edge of an oblong stone at Tarxien, in Malta. Insular individuality explains the rarity of this floral theme, in which it is possible to perceive the beginnings of a spiral.

(Photo © Roger-Viollet)

Menhir, at Trébeurden in the Côtes-du-Nord. This design also appears on a column of Crec'h Quillé at Saint-Quay-Perros, a long monument with a side entrance. These monuments and a few others are also decorated with axes with handles, again in false relief. In the Prajou-Menhir monument the axe – if indeed it is an axe – is shown surmounting a square dotted motif with parallel finer pin-head lines. This is repeated three times. Should this be seen as a development of the shield? One original motif is linked with this style: a long baton with wings and a long stem. Of the sixteen representations known, eight are on the Mougau Vihan monument.

The 'plastic' style reached its peak with two statue-menhirs, Laniscar at Trévoux in Finistère, and Kermené at Guidel in Morbihan, the latter dating from the middle of the third millennium. In each case the block is carved with a well-defined shoulder indication, a cylindrical head, separate breasts, and a clearly marked necklace; on the second stele arms are also indicated. Very similar work can be seen on the Catel statue in Guernsey, and two more anthropomorphic steles have been found in the same island, slightly different but of the same period.

What is the significance of these decorations on the Breton megalithic group? It is generally agreed that the shield may be an idol; it appeared at the same time as the anthropomorphic stone slabs in the fifth millennium monuments, and appears to have been depicted throughout the fourth millennium. In the third millennium it may have been replaced by distinctly female idols, in the 'plastic' style. This suggests that all the idols, even the oldest, were probably female. The few early fourth millennium terracotta statuettes found in France

The double spiral motif appears repeatedly on another oblong block in the Tarxien temple, covering the whole decorated surface. This is one of the most commonly found motifs in megalithic art.

(Photo © Roger-Viollet)

(outside Brittany) and in central Europe, confirm the essential role of the female image in neolithic anthropomorphic representation.

To what extent does the U-form, which in the 'plastic' style indicates the female idol's necklace, carry the same meaning in earlier styles? The question is a difficult one, for this very simple motif has several different meanings. When it is reversed to form interlinked hoops it appears to be a derivation or lateral extension of the shield, as seen at Gavrinis. In the fourth millennium the U-sign was frequently depicted with the tips curving back; was this intended to represent horns? The discovery of the Gavrinis ox with lyre-shaped horns may support this tentative hypothesis.

The polished stone axe, with or without handle, is a persistent theme in megalithic Breton art; at first long and triangular like the ceremonial axe found in grave-goods, it later became more compact. The axe-plough symbol is confined to Morbihan, although not identified with certainty; perhaps certain polished axes of this type were used as ploughshares. They are depicted with a handle on the upper part, and a long horizontal beam ending in a yoke or other form of attachment. One is associated with two oxen on the Gavrinis stone covering stone. On this evidence the identification appears reasonable, although there is no conclusive proof.

Crook emblems, almost as numerous as axes, must represent genuine objects, as do the axes with handles – substantial wooden objects, perhaps also rods of authority, symbols of political and religious power. The crook is the main motif of the head-stone of the Table des Marchands, and also on the large standing stone (6.50 metres high) of Kermarquer at Moistoirac in Morbihan. This sign of authority appears again on the late third-millennium menhir-statues in southern France, such as those at Rosseironne and Collorgues in the Gard. Some archeologists have linked the design of these crooks with genuine votive objects of similar shape made of polished schist, found in Portuguese megalithic passage tombs. In the third millennium Breton gallery graves the crook appears to have been replaced by a winged baton with a long stem.

The cross-shaped motif may be a stylization of the axe with handle, and the '7' motif that of the crook. A few rare circles, some surrounded by radiating lines and interpreted as suns, have been found at Tuchen Pol near Ploemeur and at Petit Mont. Although wavy and broken lines have been found in Portugal and Ireland, their significance is not known. At Gavrinis the wavy line motif appears to have a distinctive significance beyond simply padding out the design: perhaps they represent snakes, but there is no head. The vertical undulating motif has been thought to represent lightning, and the horizontal one water. Neither interpretation is entirely convincing.

247

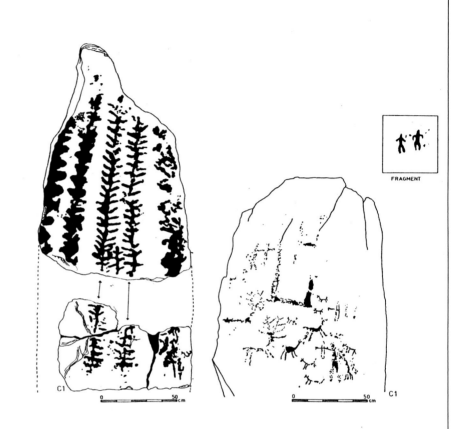

One of the stones in the Portuguese tomb of Pedralta is painted with red branching lines, characteristic of the area. Other red paintings on a stone at the Orca dos Juncais tomb near Viseu represent archers, surrounded by their dogs, aiming at a herd of deer.

(from *Megalithic Art of Western Europe*, by E. S. Twohig, Oxford, 1981)

In spite of so much uncertainty, an overall view of megalithic Breton art reveals some general tendencies. Two groups of motifs can be distinguished, which are complementary to each other: on the one hand, shields and female idols, on the other the attributes of political and religious power – the axe, the crook and the baton – which may rather be regarded as masculine. Studies of other French groups tend to confirm this general principle.

Decorative features in central western France are much less rich than in Brittany. They can be seen in certain megalithic passage tombs of the fourth millennium. There are crooks, the best known being at Ardillières at Rochefort in Charente-Maritime and at La Boixe at Vervant in Charente, and axes, some with handles like those at the Pierre Levée at Poitiers, and some without, as at the Grosse Pérotte at Fontenille in Charente. They stand out in false relief on the walls of the tomb. Three are decorated with a cross. Sets of sculpted 'hook' features are typical of Angoulême-style tombs, such as Bougon, the Grosse Pérotte, and Courcome at Magné in Charente. When seen in pairs, these protuberances resemble the plastic-style Armorican breasts; when isolated, they are more enigmatic. In any case, the crooks, the axes, and perhaps also the crosses, are in the mainstream of the Breton tradition. Much the same elements reappear in the Paris basin group. Designs on three flat stones at Saint-Piat, at Maintenon

MEGALITHIC ART IN THE IBERIAN PENINSULA

1 Aboboreira
2 Alijo
3 Almendres
4 Alpéris
5 Baiñas
6 Barrosa
7 Bulhõa
8 Castaneira
9 Codesas
10 Corão
11 Cubillejo
12 Dombate
13 Espiñaredo
14 Granja de Toninuelo
15 Lamoso
16 Lijo
17 Marzo
18 Montefrio
19 Nora Velha
20 Padrão
21 Pedra Coberta
22 Pola de Alande
23 Sallas
24 Santa Cruz
25 Solo
26 Vale de Rodrigo
27 Vega de Guadancil
28 Vilarinho
29 Zambujeiro
30 Zedes

Viseu Group

31 Antelas
32 Carapito
33 Chão Redondo
34 Cortiço
35 Cunha Baixa
36 Escariz
37 Fojbino
38 Fontão
39 Fories
40 Juncais
41 Lubagueira
42 Pedralta
43 Sobreda
44 Tanque
45 Vale de Fachas

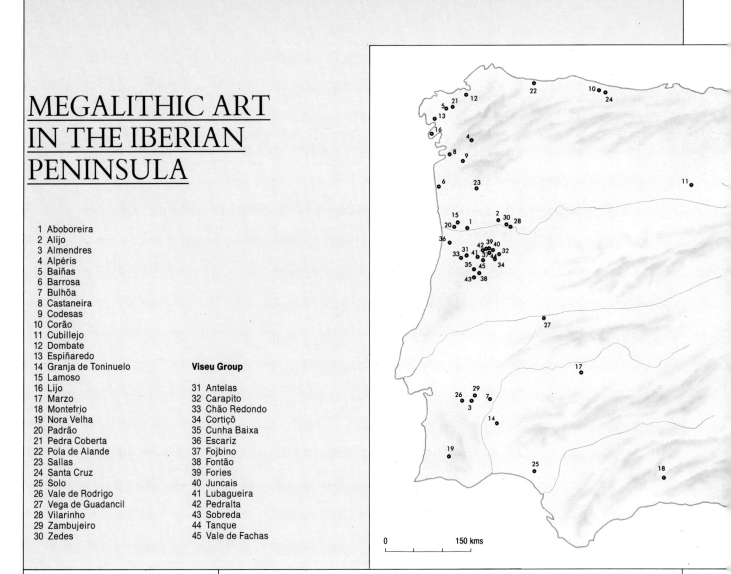

0   150 kms

Engraving, pecking, and painting were the characteristic techniques of western Iberian megalithic art but only a tiny part of its achievements has survived. Some links have been established between megalithic art and the cave art that gradually developed in mountainous regions, for example in the north of the peninsula.

in Eure-et-Loire, can be identified as simple shields, axes with handles, possibly crooks, and wavy lines marked out in dotted lines and placed in the same way as the baroque style of the Petit Mont.

The plastic style is quite well illustrated in the seven very long chambers and eleven hypogea of the Marne, which are all contemporaneous. At the entrance to the former there are, notably, representations of breasts surmounted by a necklace with one or more rows of beads: fine examples of this female idol exist at Dampsmesnil (Eure), at Boury-en-Vexin (Oise), at Guiry-en-Vexin, at Us and at Saint-Martin-du-Tertre (Val d'Oise). At Epône (Yvelines), in the antechamber of a gallery grave called the Trou-aux-Anglais, the notched entrance stone bears a representation of the same idol, this time with the features sketched in. In the Marne hypogea the most frequent motifs are the axe with handle in its deer-antler holder, and the female idol carved on the inner side of a hollow stone rib, with its 'owl face', necklace, and breasts. The two motifs are found together in the Courjeonnet and Coizard hypogea. Other motifs remain isolated: the perforated pick at Coizard, the pin with rays at its head at Chouilly. A few traces of painting have also been recorded.

The Irish group is one of the richest – forty-seven decorated stones have been discovered. These stones are in forty passage tombs in the north-east of the island, and a few blocks placed round the outside of the mounds of these same tombs. The most famous sites are in the valley of the Boyne, a small river of eastern Ireland: Newgrange, Knowth, Dowth, Tara, Loughcrew, Fourknocks. These are true necropolises with impressive and very elaborate monuments, dated by their surroundings to about 3000 B.C., with decorated stones showing a homogeneous series of dotted or incised signs on smoothed off surfaces. Some of the dotted lines were polished to soften the design, and at Fourknocks the inner surface of the motif was dotted, as well as its outline. In the Boyne valley incised lines resemble graffiti and are an adjunct to dotted motifs: they may be decorative, or they may indicate the preparation of the composition. A dozen geometric signs are visible, mostly in combination: there are isolated concentric circles, sometimes with a central point, also spirals, U signs (often interlinked), broken and wavy lines, parallel and radiating segments, triangles and lozenges, cups, and points. Despite the limited number of motifs, the expression is very varied and individualized from one site to another. It is, however, possible to make out two main styles.

The 'orderly' or 'official' Newgrange style, also known as the

Carvings and chipped-out designs cover some of the stones in the Mané-Kerioned tomb at Carnac in Morbihan. The shield-idol is clearly visible, also the axe with handle, reduced to an angled or cruciform motif.

(Photo © M. Sharp)

The shield-idol and axe with handle are also combined on a column of the Mané-er-Hroeck tomb at Locmariaquer in Morbihan. The snake-like motif is more difficult to interpret.

(Photo © Ed. Jos le Doaré)

Fourknocks style, is characterized by care in integrating motifs so as to produce a coherent decoration of the whole surface. Lozenges, broken lines and spirals are used to a considerable extent, in proportions that differ from site to site. This style appears on other stones at Knowth, Dowth, Clear Island in southern Ireland, Calderstones near Liverpool in England, and Barclodiad-y-Gavres in Anglesey.

The 'free', or Loughcrew, style, displays no apparent coherence. The motifs are either isolated in a corner of the stone, or combined in a somewhat confused composition. The principal elements are concentric circles, pointed circles, U-shapes, and wavy lines. Spirals, together with radiating and parallel segments, are common at Loughcrew and at Dowth.

The geometric motifs of Ireland, like their equivalents in Brittany or Portugal, are too consistently repetitive to have been simply decorative; but if they do signify something – and archeologists are agreed that they do – they remain difficult to interpret. The variety of circles, the favoured motif, appears to stress the importance of a celestial body such as the sun, and the obvious intention of the builders to orientate the monuments in relation to the sun tends to support this theory. Geometrical decoration represented the forces of nature, and realistic art – axe, crook, baton – religious or social power. Irish art has rightly been linked with the baroque art of the Gavrinis monument, which perhaps reflects the move from the portrayal of attributes to that of more abstract forces. The concentric circles, the semicircles combined to make full circles, the spirals – also seen in Ireland – subsume the representations of axes and crooks, encompassing at the same time the stylized image of the shield-idol. The other Irish motifs, such as lozenges and wavy or broken lines forming triangles, may be an expression of the natural elements (water, mountains, or fire, perhaps) animated by cosmic forces. This type of art certainly gives a strong impression of movement, and has been compared by some observers with Irish Celtic art at the beginning of the Christian era. Both emphasize the curving line linking the motifs and, with concentric circles and particularly with spirals and both express a type of perpetual motion.

In Irish megalithic art, as at Gavrinis, the impression of the idol appears to be outlined in the background in the shape of a very stylized anthropomorphic form. The shield sign, picked out several times on the Breton monument, presents a recognizable human shape, even though it is so stylized as to be almost abstract. In Ireland this indication is more subtle, and therefore less easily identifiable. The C1 stone at Fourknocks shows what has been accepted as a face: a double line in a crescent curve appears to indicate the lower outline of the face, with perhaps a necklace or a half-moon below and three lozenges above –

two for the eyes and one for the nose or the mouth. Other lines might
be arms and a belt. A block of the Barclodiad-y-Gavres tomb in
Anglesey bears a triangular composition and a series of lines underneath which might correspond to a face, arms, and a belt. Another
block in the same monument displays an original composition, probably anthropomorphic, with spirals (for the eyes?), broken horizontal

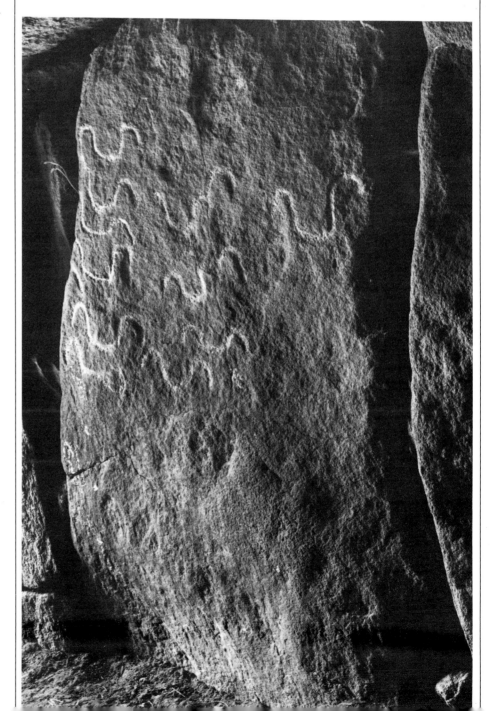

The head-stone of the Table des Marchands tomb at Locmariaquer is shaped to form a shield-idol monument. It is decorated with several rows of crooks, a masculine symbol similar to the axe.

(Photo © R. Estall)

lines, two central lozenges, and wavy vertical lines somewhat reminiscent of the Portuguese idol at Chao Redondo.

From the point of view of art the British groups are much less spectacular. To the north the Orkneys have only a very limited decorative range, of slanting segments engraved or dotted: the Skara Brae buildings have a uniform group of images in this style. In Scotland some of the megaliths carry cup designs which are difficult to interpret; some rocks are entirely covered with them. Bronze Age megaliths, which were used much less, were very little decorated; once again Stonehenge is the exception, for the hollows of the columns have been carved with a type of dagger and axe corresponding to early Bronze Age equivalents made of metal. Similar outlines of an axe with enlarged hammered blade exist in Scotland, on a rock in the Kilmartin valley in Argyll.

The megalithic art of Germany and the Nordic countries is quite varied. The hundreds of tombs in Denmark, southern Sweden, and northern Germany are for the most part undecorated, with the Hesse group of stone chests an apparent exception dating from the beginning of the second millennium – the early Bronze Age. Between Kassel and Marburg there are at least six decorated stones, while at Züschen the inner face of the cist's entrance stone carries a series of interlinked

253

This monumental drawing of an axe with handle – more than a metre long – on the covering stone of the Table des Marchands tomb. The outline of the axe itself, with pointed butt and curved cutting edge, also appears at Gavrinis.

(Photo © R. Estall)

broken horizontal lines, and what may be the outline of an ox. Inside, one stone shows oxen attached to a yoke, seen from above. The dotted style recalls Mont-Bégo in the Alpes-Maritimes, which dates from the same period. At Ellenberg there is a rectangular slab covered with six rows of dotted triangles, and a column with its upper part decorated with five rows of oblique lines. Another stone, at Wellen, displays the same type of decoration, but in columns. The Hesse chests have been compared with the Valais chest, while further north, near Halle, the stone Schafstädt stele dating from about 2000 B.C. displays a profile and necklace that brings to mind the female representations in the Paris basin.

The Kivik monument in southern Sweden is artistically exceptionally rich. There are two sequences of motifs; in one, realistic scenes show men and animals following each other, while the other shows a procession of women, musicians playing long trumpets, and one individual riding in a horse-drawn chariot. The four-spoked wheel evokes the solar symbol. Its style sets the monument apart from megalithic art; dating from about 1500 B.C., it was decorated during the middle of the Bronze Age, and can be seen as a final manifestation of a megalithism soon to be substantially changed.

The statue-menhirs scattered across Europe stand near megalithic monuments and sometimes form part of them. The female images on the tombs of the Paris basin have one element in common with the steles and statue-menhirs of the south of France, Italy and Sardinia: the mouth is never represented. These stone slabs were sculpted or carved at some time during the third millennium. In Provence the oldest steles display simple faces framed within a broad band with geometric chevron decorations. In the Rouergue group the lower limbs are represented. The feminine nature of the statue-menhirs is indicated by breasts, a necklace and a pendant, while the masculine character is linked with a bow, a crook, and an 'object' carried with the aid of a cross-belt. It has been debated whether this might be a flint or copper dagger: carved schist objects of similar outline have been discovered, which might be votive daggers in their protective sheath. Some stones have changed sex—some several times in succession: the Arribats stele at Murat-sur-Vèbre in the Tarn, masculine to begin with, was feminized by the addition of breasts, then masculinized again with the addition of the 'object', and re-feminized definitively with the incision of a wide necklace.

The context of these steles and statue-menhirs varies: the Provence steles appear to be connected with individual burials. Certain statue-menhirs in Languedoc have been found in collective tombs: the steles of Cazarils and Bouisset, in the Hérault, were associated with oval vaulted dry-stone tombs. The stone slabs of Foissac and

The polished stone axe motif is repeated several times on one of the columns of the Gavrinis monument. This does not represent a functional object axe, but one of the symbolic prestige objects, usually made of jadeite or chloromelanite, found in burial offerings.

(Photo © Phedon Salou-Artephot)

Collorgues in the Gard were found inside hypogea constructed in the galleries of former flint mines, and in the Ardèche, the Saint-Martin steles indicated the entrance to a natural burial hole.

Other Languedoc statue-menhirs have been discovered in open-air dwellings, as with Colombier at Euzet in the Gard and Montferrand at Saint-Mathieu-de-Tréviers in Hérault. Others again are isolated in the open countryside. It is probable that a substantial number, particularly in the Rouergue area, were originally set up deep in the forest.

Further to the north, the decorated steles of the Petit Chasseur were re-used in the late third-millennium funerary structures associated with bell-beaker vessels. Originally they must have been set up in front of barrows; their decoration displays bows, spiral jewelry, and a wealth of geometrical motifs.

255

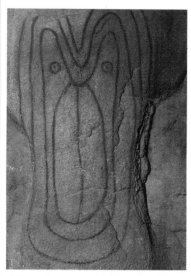

The anthropomorphic appearance of the geometrically decorated shield at Luffang at Crac'h in Morbihan indicates that the shield emblem is probably a stylized idol.

(Photo © Ed. Jos)

This stone displays a 'palette' design and (above left) two breasts complete with a curving line representing a necklace; it was found in the terminal cell of the long megalithic chamber of Prajou-Menhir at Trébeurden in the Côtes-du-Nord.

(Photo © B. Bréart)

Although the examples in the south of France form homogeneous groups, statue-menhirs are found from the Channel Islands and Brittany to Sardinia, most are female.

The ideologies which motivated megalith builders and users were not only expressed artistically; the search for other forms of expression, including offerings and ritual, should result in a deeper understanding of megalithic art – perhaps even a coherent overview.

The indications are that megalithic art represents only a limited form of expression; it is not always seen where megaliths occur, indeed far from it – the tombs of northern Germany, the Causses, and Los Millares in Spain are not decorated. The great decorated monuments occur in the richest and most dynamic areas of megalithic construction: Malta, Portugal, Brittany, and Ireland.

Certain motifs appeared at a very early stage (about 4500 B.C.) and developed over more than two millennia; the idol, the axe and the crook are linked with architectural forms as diverse as the passage tomb and the standing stone. Certain themes and styles belong to a single architectural form, however: this applies to the female statues in Maltese temples and the geometrically decorated idols of the angled Breton chamber, and also to the very distinctive art of the Irish cruciform chambers. Artistic groups, like architectural groups, each possess their own original elements, even if they share several widely known motifs. It is in fact these common motifs which give such an air of unity to megalithism in western Europe. Such similarities may be the result of convergence, particularly technological, but also of occasional links between the population groups.

Do the artistic themes reflect religious thought? This would seem to be the conclusion established by a combined analysis of decoration, offerings, and rites. The art of the tomb contents, seen in the objects deposited as offerings, is obviously complementary to the decoration on megalithic columns or blocks. In Portugal, for example, the grave-goods supply the idols and crooks that are missing, or almost absent, from the walls. In Ireland it confirms the importance of axes and the massed decorated weapons, prestige objects whose image does not appear on the stones. In most tombs the arrow heads placed as offerings demonstrate the high prestige of the bow in the rites practised at the megaliths, but the image of the bow itself does not normally appear. Placing three ox skulls at the foot of a long barrow in England was no doubt the equivalent of marking out the silhouette of an ox on a standing stone in Brittany; a similar relationship can be established between the deer-hunt painted on a Portuguese stone and the antler-wood pendants of the megalithic tombs in the Paris basin. There were certainly significant characteristics shared by reindeer and oxen. Sites with oxen are known which date back to the beginning of the Bronze

MEGALITHIC ART IN BRITTANY

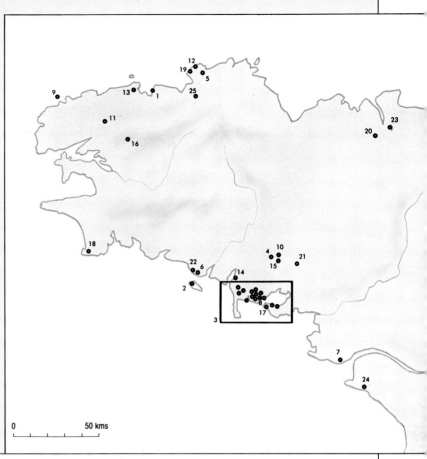

0   50 kms

Brittany's great artistic sites lie along the coastline, with Carnac a particularly rich centre, and were developed individually without any detectable pattern of style or period. Techniques used in Brittany include engraving, chipping out, and sculpture. Painting appears to have been unknown.

Several pairs of breasts are sculpted on one of the stones of the megalithic grave of Kerguntuil at Trégastel in the Côtes-du-Nord. The U-shaped motifs beneath them represent necklaces, often associated with female images.

(Photo © Ed. Jos)

Age, such as Mont-Bégo or certain Sardinian sanctuaries, and sites with reindeer such as the Val Camonica or Zalavrouga (near the White Sea). Starting from the same principle of animal strength and nobility, the result is on the one hand the image of agriculture, seen in the bull linked with the plough, and on the other hand the image of the hunter seen in the deer pierced with arrows.

Emblems such as the spiral and the cup appear in cave sites in the open countryside of north-west Iberia and Scotland, for example: they have been connected with observation of trees, which has not been proved but which appears reasonable.

Finally, the megalithic world presents three great universal themes. The first relates to the female, more specifically to the maternal body (the breasts) and to her ornaments (the necklace). Explicit in Maltese representations and on the Breton statue-menhirs, the female image becomes considerably more abstract with the engraved or sculpted shield, this abstraction, however, undoubtedly remains identified with the west. At this period the worship of terracotta female statuettes is well attested throughout the whole of temperate Europe, as far as the Paris basin, while the shield would represent the terracotta statuette transposed into monumental form, the underlying idea being reasonably clear in both. Often associated with this idol, the necklace motif reappears in concrete form as beads. The second theme common to art and religion combines the attributes of masculine power: bows, axes, crooks and batons; the male figure himself is very rarely represented, with a few exceptions in Portugal (the hunter). Reindeer and oxen are perhaps linked with this theme, as happened later in the Bronze Age. The third theme is an abstract one, including natural forms, with the moving celestial bodies (sun and moon) in the lead, as

257

Decorated block at the Irish necropolis at Knowth, with three motifs: plain circles, spirals, and concentric circles opening to one side.

(Photo © G Eogan)

An enormous block 3.50 metres long placed in front of the entrance to the passage in the Newgrange tomb in Ireland. It is entirely covered with carved linear motifs, forming spirals, chevrons, and lozenges.

(Photo © Bord Failte Photo D.R.)

Matching the entrance block, another block of similar dimensions was placed opposite the Newgrange tumulus in Ireland. This is also decorated; the composition and variety of styles is striking, and characteristic of the baroque dynamism of Irish megalithic art.

(Photo © Commissioners of Public Works/Ireland)

Decorated block in the Irish necropolis at Knowth; as well as the plain and concentric circles, the snake motif is developed here.

(Photo © G.Eogan)

The double spiral motif, perhaps symbolizing eyes, is chipped out on one of the surrounding blocks (K 67) of the Newgrange tumulus in Ireland. Two lozenges spring from the junction of the spirals, which may identify it as an anthropomorphic representation – the upper lozenge being the forehead, the lower one the nose and mouth.

(Photo © A. Weir/J. & C. Bord)

well as – perhaps – the earth's elements (earth, water, wind) to which may be added the snake symbol.

These themes may be interpreted as the response to the profound questionings of Neolithic cultures. To receive vital energies and legitimize the activities of earthly life, Neolithic peoples in western Europe turned to the maternal principle, representing the creative spirit. They also called on male authority, symbolized by attributes of the power of intercession. Finally, they sought the secrets of astral, solar and lunar cycles, thus seeking some form of participation in the dynamics of time and eternal renewal.

Although megalithic monuments were an integral part of the countryside and occupied important sites, their orientation in relation to the great solar, and perhaps lunar, axes is also not without significance. This search for reference to one axis or fixed point in the sky may reveal several concerns: not only the speculative need to locate the terrestrial monument in relation to the heavens, and to understand and master the paths of the great stars and their cycles through prediction, but probably also the metaphysical need to link the fate of dead ancestors with the natural forces revealed in solar and lunar

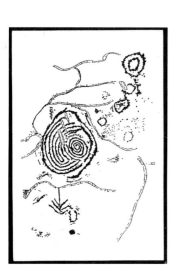

Megalithic art at Dowth in Ireland is less structured than at nearby Newgrange. Both employ the same motifs, plain or concentric circles, spirals, and chevrons, which undoubtedly have more than a simple decorative function.

(Photo © C. O'Kelly D.R.)

A column in one of the Loughcrew tombs near Newgrange in Ireland is decorated with a motif of rays (left) and a double spiral and lozenge (right), suggesting a face. Irish megalithic art was essentially abstract.

(Photo © A. Weir/J. & C. Bord)

rhythms. There are sites where the focus for ceremonial coincides with the focus of the great celestial axes. The orientation of megalithic burial chambers have been examined statistically; they are often a characteristic component of certain monumental groups. The passages of the oldest chambers of the Atlantic zone are orientated towards the south-east; the same applies to Angoulême-style monuments. The hundreds of megalithic graves spread across the Causses, between the Atlantic and the Mediterranean zones, invariably open towards the east or south-east. Only the Ardèche monuments display a few examples of orientation to the south and south-west; they share the preferred orientation of the southern Rhône valley group, and may have been influenced by them. In the Iberian peninsula the majority of megalithic tombs face south-east.

Other even more precise orientations are recognizable in monuments where the construction is particularly meticulous – at Dissignac and Gavrinis, for example, where on the day of the summer solstice the rays of the rising sun penetrate the passage of the tombs. At New-

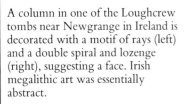

MEGALITHIC ART
IN IRELAND

0   100 kms

Ireland's artistic sites are concentrated in the north-east of the island, all decoration existing almost entirely in the passage tombs of the Newgrange type, which were not widespread. Techniques include engraving, chipping and sculpture.

Two Irish Bronze Age vessels, of the same date as the last megalithic expression in Ireland (c. 1500 B.C.)

(Photo © X.-D. R.)

grange, at the same moment, the sun's rays pass through a small opening set above the first covering stone of the passage, and light up the back of the chamber. This opening, which appears to have been designed for this purpose, is one clear architectural proof of the use of axes emphasized in megalithic rites. Another is the Heel Stone, used as a sighting point by the observer at the centre of Stonehenge's circle to observe the start of the solar path at the summer solstice. These precise orientations can be seen in monuments built in the fourth and third millennia. And from the standing stone on an artificial platform on the hillside of Kintrow in Argyll, in western Scotland, there is a remarkable view the sun rising in a dip in the skyline on the day of the solstice.

Other monuments appear to have been constructed with reference to lunar movement. Stonehenge might be one of these, but it is impossible to be sure. The monument is too complex to allow us to draw irrefutable conclusions, apart from the general solsticial orientation. The theories of Gerald Hawkins and Alexander Thom, broadly acceptable within certain approximations, nonetheless remain theories. But for monuments which are not unique but numerous, such as the circles of standing stones near Aberdeen which all include a horizontal stone placed to the south, statistical studies become possible and interpretations better founded. Thus the stone which is common to all these Scottish monuments must have been placed beneath the high point of the curving lunar path for an observer standing at the centre of the circle.

Such sites constitute reasonably convincing evidence for the precise orientation of megalithic monuments; but many others remain debatable, such as the Callanish group on Lewis, or once again the

261

This sculpted head, from Verrucola in Italy, belongs to a statue-menhir so similar in its owl-head stylization to certain specimens in southern France dating from around 2000 B.C. that it was first attributed to that era. Recent discoveries, however, have revealed that carving of these statue-menhirs continued for another thousand years, until the beginning of the Iron Age.

(Museo Civico, La Spezia. Photo © Artephot/Nimatallah)

Carnac alignments, linked entirely hypothetically with the broken Grand Menhir at Locmariaquer. As it happens, the monuments associated together in Alexander Thom's system of observation do not date from the same period; fuller chronological knowledge of the sites demonstrates in general terms that several centuries may separate the monuments. It is also true that before the construction of a tomb or a megalith, the existing monuments may already have been used as reference points. This set of theories is typical of the unverifiable statements that the 'archeo-astronomers' bring together to sustain some very bold hypotheses. We may be guided instead by the analytical critiques of Douglas C. Heggie, professor of mathematics at Cambridge University: although all evidence indicates that Neolithic peoples were concerned with astronomy, we have absolutely no way of judging its importance to them.

It certainly seems that this importance may be far from what Hawkins or Thom imagined. Such theoretical speculation on the subject of astronomy is improbable in these peasant civilizations. On the other hand, the clear signs of ceremonial, particularly the deposit of

A carved face within a large frame decorated with lozenges and chevrons, on the Lombarde stele 1 at Lauris-Puyvert in Vaucluse.

The Rocher-des-Doms stele at Avignon in Vaucluse depicts a face without a mouth; the significance of the starred cup mark (bottom right) is unknown.

The Mont-Sauvy stele at Orgon in the Bouches-du-Rhône is part of a fairly homogeneous group; only a carved face appears, within a large chevron-patterned frame.

(Photo © Musée Calvet at Avignon/ Casterman Archives)

offerings which are always found during excavations, indicate that the monuments were the setting for ritual practices which, in this world of cultivators, required sanctuaries orientated on some highly emphasized axes. The effectiveness of the rites was probably regarded as more important than absolute accuracy in the orientation; hence the approximations observed, which would result from simple empirical speculation. Thus although the orientation of megalithic monuments was important, it would be no more than a subordinate aspect of the ceremonial, and not the essential factor.

The diversity of cult sites confirms the ceremonial function of the monuments; as we have seen, the mounds covering tombs were not only places of burial but also ceremonial centres. Certain of these mounds in Wessex and central western France, moreover, do not hold graves; their function must have been essentially ceremonial. On the other hand the 'cult' sites of north-western Europe, which do not appear to have had links with death, are not without funeral references. At Stonehenge itself the remains of incinerated bodies have been found in the Aubrey holes. In sites with circular ditches, continuous or otherwise, it is not unusual to discover human bones.

Such enclosures appeared in Europe in the middle of the Neolithic age, that is, from 4000 B.C. onwards. Some are on the plains, others on high ground; some are completely surrounded with ditches, palisades, and walls, while others make use of natural defences, cliffs or rivers, adapted or complemented. Domestic, economic, social and religious functions have all in turn been suggested for these sites; some must have been inhabited, and the traces of flint trimming, pottery

263

The Mas d'Azaïs statue-menhir at Montlaur in Aveyron displays the shield-idol's anthropomorphic outline. The head is barely indicated; femininity is shown by the breasts and necklace. Representations of arms, legs, and a belt are traditional in the Rodez group.

A necklace with a large bead identifies the female gender of the Saint-Théodorit statue-menhir in Gard. The double lines carved beneath the eyes may be interpreted in two ways: either as tattooing, or as exaggerated 'owl' features.

(Musée des Antiquités Nationales, Saint-Germain-en-Laye. Photo J.-M. Labat ©️ Casterman. Museum d'Histoire Naturelle, Nîmes. Photo ©️ A. Aigoin)

manufacture, or cutting up of animals are frequent, as at Saintonge, where human bones have also been found. The presence of burials and terracotta statuettes at Noyen-sur-Seine in Seine-et-Marne, at Jonquières in the Oise, and at Fort-Harrouard in Eure-et-Loir are also indications of religious practices. Camps of the Windmill Hill type with discontinuous ditches, which appeared in England during the fourth millennium, are linked with other types of monument such as some of the long barrows near Stonehenge. In these areas of scattered dwellings the camps were centres for occasional assemblies, for fairs or festivals. The religious aspect is most clearly apparent at Hambledon Hill in Dorset, where human skulls were placed at the ends of the ditches, among some complete burials. Such camps would have been the origin for the cult sites built at the beginning of the third millennium, such as Avebury, with its impressive ditch and standing monoliths arranged in a circle, or Stonehenge itself which, in its first phase, included a small circular ditch, lined on the inner edge by the fifty-six Aubrey holes, which in later phases was linked with a ring of standing stones. The original of this layout has been sought in mounds such as that at West Kennet, bordered with enormous monoliths. Indeed it is not impossible that circular structures of standing stones may have existed independently of barrows. This would allow for the Carnac

264

alignments and their oval enclosures being quite old (fourth millennium). On the other hand, the stone circles which are so numerous in the north of the British Isles appear to be fairly late, contemporaneous with the later phases of Stonehenge – around 2000 B.C.

The construction of these cult sites – circular, elliptical or oval – has suggested that prehistoric builders had a very well-developed concept of geometry; all these figures, even the most complicated, appear to have been developed from the Pythagorean right-angle triangle. This theory, sustained in particular by Alexander Thom, is not improbable – but remains unproven. Douglas Heggie has pointed out how simple it is to construct a right-angle triangle in a circle, starting with a diameter; the builders of megalithic monuments could have done it easily with the aid of a cord. In the domain of geometry, as in astronomy, knowledge was no doubt more empirical than theoretical. Yet it was through studying the diameters of the stone circles of the British Isles, and particularly those of Scotland, that Douglas Heggie was able to use statistics to establish that a single unit of length and its multiples did genuinely appear to have been used. Alexander Thom's 'megalithic yard' (0.829 metres) and the 'fathom' of two and a half yards are thus based on reality. At Carnac, on the other hand, although there is some regularity in the distances separating the standing stones of the alignments, it is difficult to discern a system compatible with the theory of the megalithic yard. The Cojoux alignment is an example of a site altered at various times, and should encourage caution in seeking an interpretation; so too do the alignments of Mid Clyth in Caithness.

The view of English archeologists is that these cult monuments, which developed during the course of the third millennium and became so well integrated into the landscape, were conceived for ritual ceremonies in honour of the 'forces of nature' represented by the paths of the stars.

The polished flint axe was wedged into a horn sheath, pierced through to take the end of the wooden handle. This is a late Neolithic example; it is shown very realistically in one of the Coizard hypogea in the Marne, and is a symbol of masculine power.

(2 Photo J.-M. Labat © Casterman)

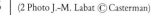

The 'Mother-goddess' figure, associated with many megalithic monuments in Malta, is depicted with unusual realism in this statue from the Hagar Kim temple. Its anatomical proportions are exaggerated, no doubt to express a concept which is larger than reality.

(Civic Museum of Natural History, Verona. Photo © Dagli-Orti)

SYMBOLS OF MEGALITHIC ART

Megalithic Art		Malta Sardinia	Iberian peninsula	Brittany	Paris basin	Ireland Brit. Isles		Offerings
Female	Silhouette 'shield' Idol							Idol
	Necklace Breasts							Necklace
Male	Silhouette							
	Bow Arrows							Bow Arrows
	Axes							Axes
	Crook							Crook Club
	Bull Deer							Bull
Abstract signs	Wavy line Zigzag							Vase
	Chevrons Triangles Lozenges							Vase
	U signs							Vase
	Moon Sun							Vase
	Concentric Circles							Gold ornament
	Spirals							Vase Stone mass

Looking from the centre of the circle at Stonehenge, the visitor can find his bearings from the Heel Stone, seen here through the central portico. It is aligned precisely with the spot where the sun rises above the horizon on the day of the summer solstice. This axis dominated all the successive modifications of the monument.

(Photo © M. Sharp)

Three Thousand Years of Religious Continuity

All these observations reveal a powerful religious atmosphere, which was expressed in a multitude of ceremonies. The smallest megalith was surrounded by rites of foundation and then worship. The reasons for such practices may have been simultaneously emotional, social, and religious; the knowledge of materials, of techniques, of seasonal cycles, remained essentially empirical and sustained by manifold rites. Megalithic cultures present a religious cohesion which was self-imposed and sometimes maintained through two or even three thousand years. The cult of ancestor worship appears to have been associated with devotion to a female divinity, linked with the sun and the moon. Their detail, architectural styles, offerings, iconographic themes, orientation, and finally the rites and ceremonies for which the megalith was the sacred setting, no doubt, represented the numerous local variations on these great themes.

THE ORIENTATION OF THE SITES

1 Lower-Rhone
2 Ardèche
3 Grands Causses
4 Languedoc
5 Quercy
6 Central-West France
7 Morbihan
8 Severn-Cotswolds
9 Clyde
10 Clava
11 Caithness
12 Shetland
13 Orkneys
14 Ross and Cromarty
15 Mayo
16 Clare
17 Boyne

Statistical studies show that the megalithic monuments were built according to well-defined orientations. Many face south-east or south-west depending on the region – in the direction of the rising and setting sun. It appears that certain important monuments such as Gavrinis, Newgrange and Stonehenge are orientated much more accurately, relating to the direction of the sunrise on the day of the summer solstice.

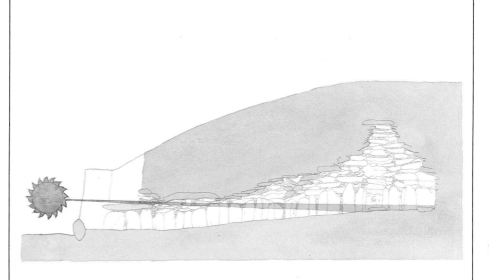

This plan of the Newgrange tumulus in Ireland reveals how the sun's rays penetrate to the back of the megalithic chamber at sunrise on the day of the summer solstice, through the small opening placed for this purpose above the passage entrance.

The End of the Megaliths

The impressive stones raised by human hands have become much more than mere stones – they have names, they are imbued with life; they are therefore capable of dying, through deliberate destruction or through neglect, as civilizations move on. The links between a group of megaliths and the multiple elements of their environment effectively imply the existence of a whole surrounding culture, with all its coherence and variety, both in the most ancient times, before the first great agricultural civilization of western Europe, and also to the later civilizations, mostly also agricultural, in India, China, Africa, Madagascar, or Easter Island. When a megalithic civilization dies, the megaliths themselves survive only in degenerate forms.

No one could fail to realize that the megalithic monuments did not appear purely accidentally or casually. Such constructions must be the result of a coherent and considered move, a careful plan; they imply elaborate conception, accurate skills, diplomacy, probably also great faith, even a certain mysticism. Overall surveys of the great megalithic centres of Europe have demonstrated to the full that each such centre combined these elements: geological, geographical and topographical, ecological and social, funerary and spiritual. In their diversity such constructions appear as the consequences of great cultural decisions, encouraged and inspired by the general context of neolithic, or more rarely protohistoric, civilization.

Stone was not the only material used in Neolithic architecture. In the Near East, bricks of sun-dried clay went to make the great buildings of Jericho and Susa possible. The use of unbaked bricks was impossible in the Atlantic climate of western Europe, but a mixture of loess and cut straw set in a wooden framework made sound and easily built walls for houses. The influence of this style of architecture is recognizable in both Scandinavian and British mortuary houses the stone megalithic construction of which have been thought by some to be imitations of houses made of timber and mud. Recently an example of a tomb made of great oak planks integrated into a megalithic monument was found.

In western France and the Iberian peninsula, however, stone slabs were used from very early times, apparently chosen to protect the dead. Wooden burial constructions were set up in northern Europe, but they had, naturally, a limited life. To preserve their memory, Neolithic peoples piled up mounds of earth or stone over the ruins, the stone edifices which have lasted until today. The choice of stone was no doubt linked with the search for permanence of the cult and for a enduring memorial. The great slabs were used at the same time as, by coincidence and perhaps through a taste for a challenge, the most imposing monuments were being conceived – and achieved where conditions were favourable. These conditions existed in the Neolithic

This copper-hafted battle axe, discovered in 1882 at Kersoufflet at Faouët in Morbihan, is an exceptional ceremonial weapon from the late third millennium, and one of Brittany's oldest metal objects. Copper and gold brought with them a new society with fresh implications for megalithic architecture.

(Musée des Antiquités Nationales, Saint-Germain-en-Laye.
Photo J.-M. Labat © Casterman)

societies of western Europe, and can be found in other megalithic societies of the world: a sufficiently large settled population, an often well-established social hierarchy, and a collective consciousness of ancestral powers.

As with any cultural phenomenon, megalithic constructions developed through several phases: archeologists have suggested the titles of early, middle, and late. Recent researches have made it possible to trace the very long life of western megalithism, which lasted for more than 3,000 years. It began with Mesolithic societies in the course of Neolithization, like that at Téviec in Morbihan, which in the sixth millennium were using the ancient style of mass burial – coffers, the prototype for megalithic tombs.

In the fifth millennium the funerary use of large stone slabs in the south of the Paris basin coincided with the beginnings of Neolithic attitudes in this area. The collective aspect was then more obvious in the effort required to set up the megalith than in the number of dead buried there, which was fairly small. Signs of this 'incomplete' megalithism are also apparent in the long monuments with individual grave in the Yonne and in the mass grave at Pontcharaud in Auvergne. In western France, however, the megalithic characteristics of monumentalism and of mass burial had already come together; in Normandy, Brittany, and Poitou, majestic mounds with multiple chambers were built at Fontenay-le-Marmion, Barnenez, and Bougon. In Brittany a female anthropomorphic outline was cut into some of the stones, and a few other decorations also appeared, including the axe and the crook. Megalithic tombs were probably built in Portugal at the same period, containing the remains of mass burials.

271

Excavated in 1939, the La Motta grave beneath a megalith at Lannion dates from the beginning of the Bronze Age. It contained the remains of one man, together with a veritable treasury: flint arrow-heads, a large polished stone, two axes, seven blades of daggers, swords, or halberds, and a gold box. The military and personal nature of these objects contrasts sharply with the collective offerings of Neolithic graves.

(Musée des Antiquités Nationales, Saint-Germain-en-Laye.
Photo J.-M. Labat © Casterman)

In north western Europe mounds which might be long or short, with a timber mortuary house or a small megalithic funerary chamber probably appeared before the end of this millennium.

The fourth millennium saw Neolithization ruling everywhere in western Europe. New great megalithic monuments were built. Standing stones and mounds with vast chambers and passage access have been discovered from Scandinavia to the Iberian peninsula and the Mediterranean basin. Some of the blocks used, such as the broken Grand Menhir at Locmariaquer, were of very considerable size. Europe's main megalithic centres developed their own individual styles, in Denmark, Ireland, southern England, Morbihan, central western France, Portugal, southern Spain, and Malta. Certain major sites such as Newgrange, Gavrinis, Bagneux, and Bougon date from the second half of this millennium, the period when distinctive architectural and decorative features became established. Irish, Breton and Portuguese megalithic art all featured the cult of a female deity and ancestor worship, represented by the symbols of power – the axe, the crook, and the bow. These figures were accompanied by motifs relating to an abstract symbolism, representing – it has been suggested – the 'forces of nature'. The megalithic societies of north-western Europe were egalitarian, although more hierarchical in Ireland and western France. Whether the monuments were of a closed design (tombs) or open (standing stones), they served as centres for religious ceremonial. There were geographical and iconographic links between them, as in the Mediterranean world where the tradition of artificial caves competed with open-air construction.

Megalithic monuments proliferated in the third millennium – in certain regions such as the Causses they are present in their hundreds.

A double pattern of evolution can be discerned; in northern Europe and the Paris basin tombs became longer and contained many more bodies, while in Ireland, the Causses, the Iberian peninsula and the Mediterranean islands they became smaller but also more numerous. Complex constructions appeared in Brittany, at Carnac, and above all in the British Isles, at Stonehenge and Avebury. The end of this millennium coincided with a crisis in society due to the introduction of new agricultural techniques – the swing-plough and manure – and above all to an economy based on quasi-industrial exchange which led to the first copper and gold metalworking in western Europe. The Neolithic Age was dying, and with it the megalithism of mass burial.

The end of megalithism in western Europe coincided precisely with the arrival of a new world, the Bronze Age world of metal which took over daily life, at the beginning of the second millennium. In fact the decline of the megaliths became evident even before the first development of metalworking, in the Iberian peninsula, France, Great Britain, and northern Europe alike. The change in civilization must

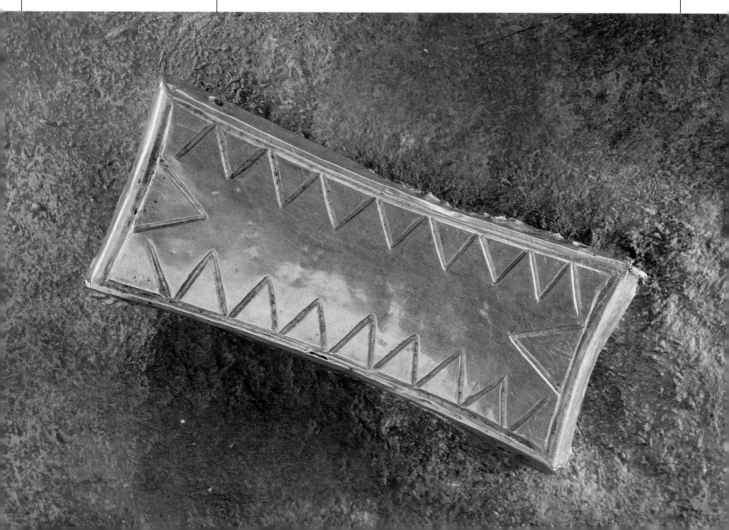

Breaking the Idols and Leaving the Great Sites

have been substantial, since it affected burial customs: the tombs with passages fell into disuse, and with them the practice of mass burial. But the megaliths came to an end in a variety of ways.

Romantic writers have attempted to explain the fall of the Grand Menhir at Locmariaquer, and its fragmentation into four sections, by lightning or an earthquake; but despite erosion of the rock, evidence has been found of deliberate cutting up, and the remains of a drawing of a large axe-plough like the one on the block covering the Gavrinis chamber. This block belonged to another large standing stone, of which a second section covered the chamber of the Table des Marchands, the remains of a tomb close to the broken Grand Menhir. This indicates a clear intention to bring down these great decorated monoliths and to re-use sections of them for new constructions. The 'breaking of the idols' suggests that a new religion may have replaced an older one. The same region offers another fine example, in one of the tombs of the Petit Mont cairn: a large anthropomorphic stone set in front of an initial mound was broken in half and the lower part, still upright, formed the head-stone, while the upper part was removed and used to pave a new chamber. Too many elements from destroyed monuments in Brittany were re-used during the third millennium for this to have been accidental; nor was it a simple technical convenience. Since the original designs are sometimes hidden, as at Gavrinis, we can easily see these sacred stones as offerings, not to the few of the living who penetrated to the interior of the tombs but to ancestors or gods. Even if beliefs changed, the intention of including these important blocks is evident. Other later examples can be seen in shapes prefiguring the end of the megaliths.

This end can be observed in other ways, such as the closed-off passage of a tomb or, above all, an interruption in the deposit of offerings in front of the exterior kerbs of a mound. Many monuments were completely sealed, buried beneath a thick covering of gravel which obliterated all architectural distinguishing features – anything that had played an important role in ceremonial rites. Such sealing has been recorded in Brittany and in central western France, sometimes several centuries after the construction of the tombs. Charles-Tanguy Le Roux's recent explorations at Gavrinis have clearly uncovered a conclusion of this type. In front of the majestic kerbs of the cairn, prehistoric people left artefacts in considerable abundance, although only shards, trimmed flints, dolerite chips, and polished axes now remain. In front of the passage entrance, long since sealed, a layer of ashes is all that is left of a wooden structure that was probably burned when the forecourt itself was finally sealed, covered with piles of gravel and sand concealing the architectural façade.

The tomb at Kivik in southern Sweden, as it appears today, looks very much like earlier megalithic graves, even though it was built in the middle of the Bronze Age.

This type of sealing is similar to that which in the British Isles and Scandinavia covered over the traces of the 'houses of the dead' beneath the mass of long barrows, marking the end of a period of ceremonial use. Other types still exist, for example in very long tombs. At La Chaussee-Tirancourt around 2000 B.C., lime and fire played a decisive role in the abandonment of collective burial.

After several millennia, the age of megalithic monuments in western Europe was coming to a close. At the beginning of the Bronze Age people returned to some of the great sites; at Bougon, a necropolis that had been in use from the beginning of the fifth millennium, the last burial was individual and dates from 2000 B.C.: the body was laid on its back with one vessel at its head and another at the feet on the debris of a chamber whose contents have been dated at 4500 B.C. In this region the last very large monuments were built around 3000 B.C., but old monuments were re-used throughout the third millennium to bury series of bodies, sometimes in considerable numbers. A sign of the times: the last use was for a single burial.

The Barnenez monument also shows traces of very long use, ending in the early Bronze Age, as indicated by a small deposit of shards in front of its façade. The latest object found near the mound at Gavrinis was a copper halberd from the beginning of the second millennium. In the Armorican megalithic tombs the final regular use of sites is indicated by some secondary adaptation. At the Parc Gurren sepulchre at Crac'h in Morbihan, the passage was modified at the same period by adding transversal stones. Coffers were arranged inside the megalithic mound of Bar-al-Lan at Portsall-Ploudalmézeau, in Finistère. The long Grée alignment at Cojoux was also in use for a very long period, until the deposit of a large corded ware jar dating from the early Bronze Age. Several large Neolithic standing stones were knocked down to construct the framework of the Giant's Tomb, the vast Bronze Age coffer in the forest of Brocéliande.

275

Ancestors Yield to the Prince

The megalithic tradition continued for several more centuries in the British Isles. Stonehenge underwent alterations until about the year 1500 B.C. The purpose of the site seems to have been fully developed from the late Neolithic age, and it may be supposed that its survival was due as much to its fame as to the universal character of its ceremonies, at least if its 'astronomical' function was to be retained. In fact no further mass megalithic tombs were built in the British Isles after the end of the Neolithic Age: they were replaced by enormous mounds and flat tombs for single burial. The megalithic forms that continued to be built and frequented were the more abstract 'cult' sites; stone circles in Scotland and Orkney, circles in England linked with circular ditches, and in particular the five most imposing groups were still being used – Durrington Walls, Mount Pleasant, Marden, Avebury, and Dorchester. The daggers and axes shown in dotted markings on the Stonehenge monoliths may represent bronze objects, which would support the suggestion that this Neolithic monument was assimilated into the new culture of the metal age; yet the move from one ideology to another is scarcely apparent. A possible manipulation by the leaders of this period has been debated: might they have adopted these traditional symbols to reinforce their authority over the new populations?

Although Breton megalithism was essentially Neolithic, certain of its characteristics have nonetheless been discovered from the beginnings of the Bronze Age, continuing up to about 1500 B.C. The passage from one period to another is marked above all by the abandonment of mass burial, a break which is clearly seen in the single burials with bell-beaker ware. Collective offerings also ceased: ancestors were superseded by the prince. The latter was honoured with an individual burial, sometimes megalithic, beneath a vast mound which required substantial collective effort. This work was therefore carried out for

The Kivik monument, discovered in 1748, consists of a megalithic chamber buried beneath a rubble mound. This late form of megalithism can be dated by the motifs on the wall slabs. The tomb was not built for mass burial, but probably for a single man buried with his metal weapons, one of the chieftains who introduced feudalism in the second millennium.

(Photo © Antikvarisk-Topographiska-Arkivet, Stockholm)

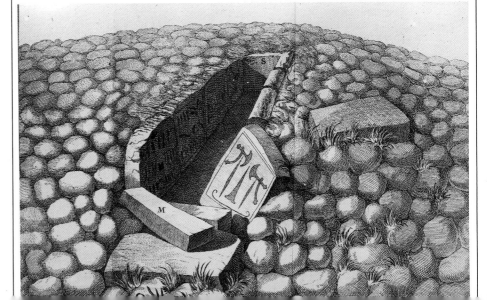

The slab stones of the Kivik tomb are decorated with representations of people, animals, and weapons, and even processions. The two-horse chariot certainly dates from the second half of the second millennium.

(Photo © S. Hallgren/Antikvarisk-Topographiska-Arkivet, Stockholm)

the glory of one individual, glory further exalted by offerings of great personal prestige, particularly gold. All this was new.

The megalithic tradition survived, however, in the construction of cists and funerary coffers beneath mounds. In addition, Neolithic stones were re-used, such as the great anthropomorphic stele covering the grave of Kersandry, at Plouhinec in Finistère. In the Valais one of the Petit Chasseur tombs was partly made of broken anthropomorphic steles, re-used around 2000 B.C. Large slabs of granite were used to build imposing Bronze Age caverns excavated in Finistère, such as the mounds of Kerlivit at Pouldergat, Kerhué-bras at Plonéour-Lanvern, and Kervastal at Plonéis. In the Côtes-du-Nord the rich sepulchre of La Motta at Lannion was set in a coffer made of schist slabs; like the Carnoët coffer, it contained the famous Armorican winged arrow heads with flint stem, large sword blades made of arsenious copper, and a set of gold jewelry. As in the Neolithic Age, some mortuary houses were built of wood: in one of the Saint-Judes-en-Bourbriac mounds in the Côtes-du-Nord, the chamber made of logs containing the skeleton was covered by a 'roof' of two sections, surmounted by the mass of earth. This double section is found again in the princely grave at Luben in Germany.

The same changes took place in the Paris basin and in northern Europe: around 2000 B.C. collective graves ceased to be used, and were therefore no longer built. The hundreds of megalithic tombs of the Causses and the Pyrenees also pre-date this period. The monument of La Halliade at Bartrès in the high Pyrenees, where the materials have been studied, shows how the traditional mound with megalithic tomb gradually changed in this area during the second and first millennia: first there were small coffers, then cists, and finally a simple deposit of cremations.

The same evolution occurred in the Iberian peninsula. Although most megalithic tombs, and in particular the circular corbel-roofed chambers, contained objects associated with bell-beaker ware and thus post-dated the Neolithic Age, the megalithic tradition itself continued through the second millennium in more or less degenerate forms. During the early Bronze Age cists were constructed which might be either rectangular and made of slabs, or circular and made of dry stones. In Portugal there are the rectangular Atalaia cists, for example, their low mounds bordered with stones laid flat. A later

277

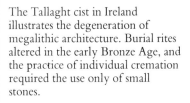

The Tallaght cist in Ireland illustrates the degeneration of megalithic architecture. Burial rites altered in the early Bronze Age, and the practice of individual cremation required the use only of small stones.

(Photo © National Museum, Dublin)

monument (end of the Bronze Age) at la Roça do Casal do Meio north of Lisbon displays a surprising survival of the circular passage tomb. Beneath a mound 11 metres in diameter, bordered with stones set on edge, the chamber is walled with dry stones covered with a well-preserved coating also present in the access passage. The grave contained two skeletons, and may have had a wooden covering.

In fact by the time the use of individual tombs became current, the tradition of megalithic construction had already almost vanished. In the great Scandinavian mounds with central burial only a circle of blocks, visible in front of the piled up earth, acted as a reminder of earlier monuments. The exceptional Kivik tomb in Scania (southern Sweden) may be seen as one of the final expressions of Nordic megalithism. In 1748 a burial chamber was discovered in a mound there, measuring 4 metres long and a metre wide: its walls were made of decorated stones set on edge. The dotted designs represented items such as an axe, human silhouettes in procession, two people blowing large trumpets, another on a two-wheeled horse-drawn chariot; such details make it possible to place the building of this tomb at the end of the second millennium. It was probably designed for a single important person, and it thus belongs to the fully developed Bronze Age.

The New World of Metals

When metal was introduced, it was no longer the collective effort required to work it that was emphasized, but the individuality of the person who wore it. This characteristic appeared from the fifth and fourth millennia onwards, in the Varna necropolis in Bulgaria, and more generally in megalithic tombs as soon as gold and copper were introduced beside the dead – that is, during the course of the third millennium: the rot had set in. And yet when copper extraction began at Chinflon in the rio Tinto area, in the south of the Iberian peninsula, the first metalworkers seem to have been the users, if not the builders, of the mass megalithic tombs of El Pozuelo. At Los Millares the situation seems to have been the same. The ritual of individual burial spread gradually. Already frequent in the bell-beaker ware period at the end of the third millennium, it became the general rule at the beginning of the second millennium, in the Bronze Age. The new funerary ritual was first seen in re-used collective megalithic tombs, and it appeared later only in megalithic cists beneath mounds.

In the early Bronze Age the large individual tombs beneath mounds for the princes of Wessex and Armorica were characterized by an abundance of metal objects, ornaments and personal weapons made of gold and arseniated copper. Brittany has the Carnoët group near Quimperlé, with its copper dagger blades and gold and silver rings, and the La Motta group at Lannion with axes and copper dagger blades, and part of a gold necklace. The man buried at Bush Barrow in Wessex wore a large gold lozenge plaque as a pectoral, and a golden belt buckle; near him lay copper and bronze dagger blades and a bronze axe, a mass of polished stone weapons and a sceptre of which fragments of ivory remained. The woman of Manton Barrow, wrapped in wool cloth, wore all sorts of ornaments including a necklace of lignite beads and pendants. One of these pendants, in the shape of a miniature halberd, had an amber handle and a bronze blade; she was covered with small gold plaques. An amber disc set into a sheet of gold has been compared to a similar piece of Cretan jewelry. Gold vessels such as those of Ploumillau in the Côtes-du-Nord and Rillaton in Cornwall, and silver vessels such as the Brun-Braz cup at Saint-Adrien in the Côtes-du-Nord, were also part of these very rich funerary furnishings.

A world was coming to an end. The megaliths were the major expressions of societies that were inventive in the realm of sacred architecture, linked with the death of ancestors or dedicated to ritual practices regulated by cosmology. These two complementary functions were often apparent in the same monument, with one of them perhaps more prominent than the other: the enclosed constructions more funerary, the open-air architecture more cosmological. The farming societies of the time settled around a monument that personalized the landscape and acted as a territorial marker. Certain megaliths, certain groups, seem to have been worshipped and frequented over more than 2,000 years: now they were condemned, destroyed, abandoned.

The social impact of the construction of these monuments had been profound, in accordance with their spectacular style and the worship of which they became the object. All this was associated with the need to legitimize the power of political and religious leaders, power which seems to have been proportional to the task undertaken or the sacrifice achieved. The social effort was not necessarily related to economic standards. The stars became an element of the ceremonial ritual rather than a pretext for abstract speculation, while the solar cycle of the seasons, and the lunar cycle, were observed as part of an empirical and practical concern to tame the universe. Certain megaliths seem to reflect a need to dominate terrestrial and celestial space – a great innovation, indeed one of the most important consequences of the neolithization in western Europe. Megalithic forms found elsewhere in the world display convergences that can be explained by common technical and social factors. They reflect various other powerful ideologies relating to the identity of each group of population, the most evocative and the most spectacular being the Easter Island group: the giant statues, overthrown in their hundreds, broken-necked and face downwards, are as impressive in their forcefulness and their genius – the work of an agricultural and fishing nation, manipulators of enormous stones – as in the brutality of their downfall, marking the collapse of the Easter Island civilization. There can be no doubt that the death of a group of megaliths represented, on each occasion, the death of a world.

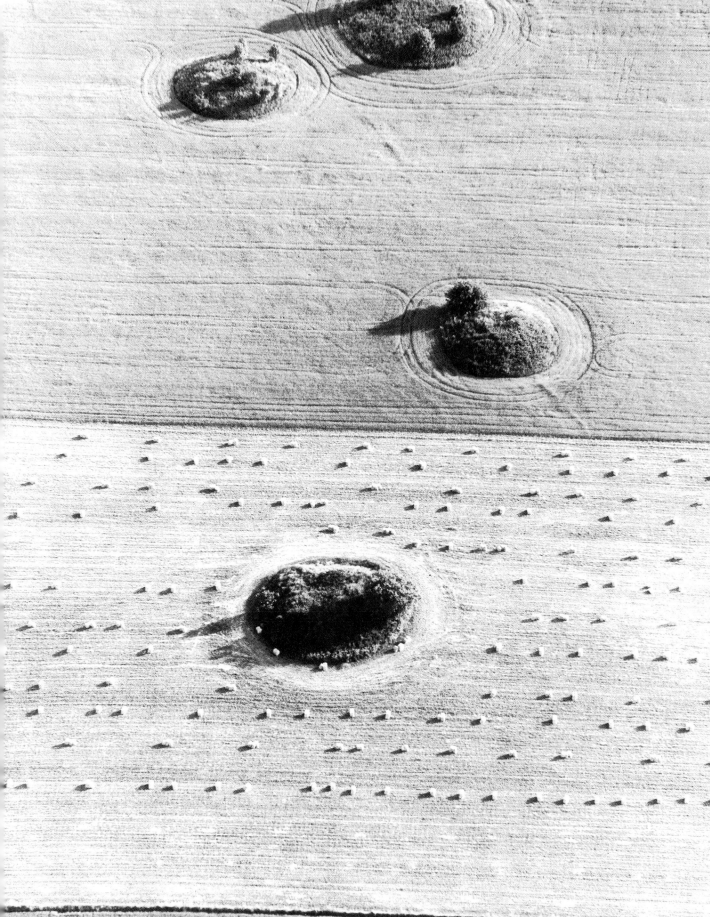

GUIDE

TO

MEGALITHS

CHRONOLOGICAL TABLE

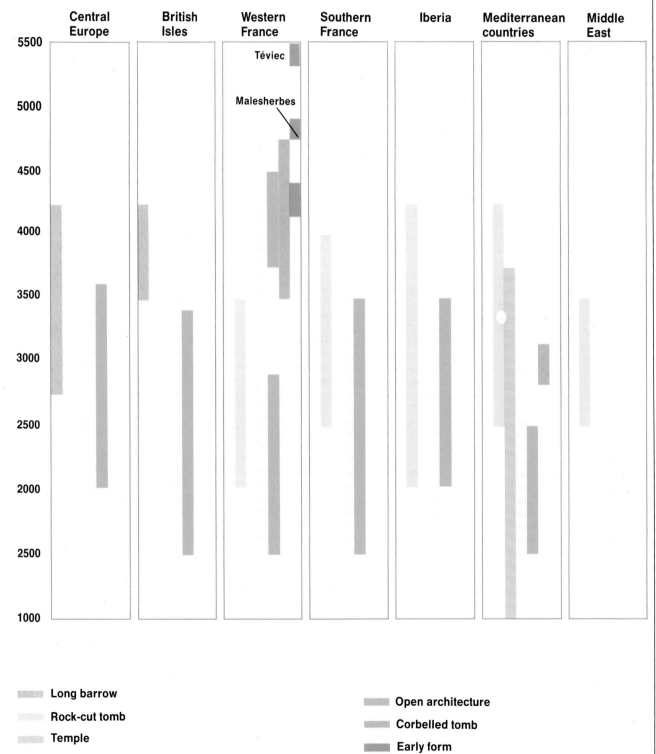

Central Europe · British Isles · Western France · Southern France · Iberia · Mediterranean countries · Middle East

Téviec

Malesherbes

Legend:
- Long barrow
- Rock-cut tomb
- Temple
- Megalithic tomb
- Open architecture
- Corbelled tomb
- Early form

TABLE OF CONTEMPORANEOUS MEGALITHIC CULTURES

Years BC	Central Europe	Near East	Central Mediterranean	Iberia	Southern France	West & Northern France	British Isles	Northern Europe
6000–5000	Karanovo I & II Starčevo Körös	Jericho Catal Hüyük Early Halaf Hacilar Obeid I	Proto Sesklo Sesklo Impressed ware	Cocina I Cocina II	Castelnovian Cardial	Téviec	Mesolithic Maglemosian	Mesolithic Maglemosian
5000–4500	Karanovo III Linear pottery Vinča A	Byblos Middle Halaf Obeid 2	Dhimini I Fiorano Stentinello	Cardial	Cardial Epicardial	Impressed ware	Mesolithic	Mesolithic Ertebølle
4500–4000	Linear pottery Karanovo IV Vinča B	Copper Obeid 3 Ghassoulian	Dhimini II & III Passo di Corvo Sasso	Cocina III Montbolo	Montbolo Chassean	Carn Cerny	Mesolithic	Mesolithic Ertebølle Early funnel-beakers
4000–3500	Tisza Roessen Grossgartach	Obeid 4	Ripoli Square-mouthed pot Dhimini IV & V	El Garcel	Chassean	Souch Cous Chassean	Early Neolithic	Early funnel-beakers
3500–3000	Karanovo VI Tripolje Cucuteni Gulmenitza Vinča D Michelsberg	Uruk Djemdet Nasr	Lagozza Zebburg Ozieri	Almeria Tabernas	Chassean Ferrières Treilles Copper	Chassean Kerugou Peu Richard	Windmill Hill	Middle funnel-beakers
3000–2500	Ezero A Pit tombs Carnavoda Collared bottles Baden		Copper Remedello	Los Millares I Zambujal Vilanova Copper	Fontbouisse Couronnian	Seine-Oise-Marne Corded ware	Windmill Hill Peterborogh	Late funnel-beakers
2500–2000	Cordé Ezero B Catacombs Vucedol Globular amphorae Bell Beakers	Agade Ur III	Gaudo Rinaldone Tarxien Bell Beakers	Los Millares II Bell Beakers El Argar	Veraza Bell Beakers	Artenac Bell Beakers	Rinyo Clacton Copper Bell Beakers	Collared bottles Individual graves Copper
2000–1500	Straubing Adlerberg Early Bronze Middle	Babylon	Early Bronze Middle Bronze	Early Bronze Middle Bronze	Early Bronze Middle Bronze	Early Bronze Armorican mounds Middle Bronze	Early Bronze Wessex Middle Bronze	Early Bronze Middle Bronze
1500–1000	Bronze Age mounds Late Bronze		Late Bronze	Late Bronze	Late Bronze	Late Bronze	Late Bronze	Late Bronze

Mesolithic   Neolithic   Metal Age   **Byblos** Town

Bibliography

General works on the Neolithic Age and the Bronze Age

The Bronze Age in Europe, John Coles and Anthony F. Harding, Methuen, London, 1979; St Martin's Press, New York, 1980

Introduction to British Prehistory, John Vincent Stanley Megaw and Derek D. Simpson, Leicester University Press, 1979

Neolithic Cultures of the British Isles, Stuart Piggot, Cambridge University Press, 1954

Le Néolithique et le Bronze Ancien Égéens, by René Treuil, École Française d'Athènes, De Boccard, Paris, 1983

Les Ors Préhistoriques, Christiane Eluère, Picard ('L'Age du Bronze en France' series), Paris 1982

La Protohistoire de L'Europe, Jan Lichardus, Marion Lichardus-Itten, Gérard Bailloud, Jacques Cauvin, P.U.F. (Nouvelle Clio), Paris, 1985

Megaliths in Europe

General

Antiquity and Man, John D. Evans, Barry Cunliffe, and Colin Renfrew, Thames & Hudson, London, 1981

L'Archéologie devant l'Imposture, Jean-Pierre Adam, Laffont, Paris, 1975

Les Architectures Mégalithiques, Jean-Pierre Mohen, La Recherche, 1984

Dolmens for the Dead: Megalith-Building Throughout the World, Roger Joussaume, Cornell University Press, Ithaca, 1988; Batsford, London 1988

Le Folklore de France, les Monuments, Paul Sébillot, Imago, Paris, 1906

The Megalith Builders of Western Europe, Glyn Daniel, Hutchinson, London, 1958

Megalithic Graves and Rituals, Glyn Daniel and Poul Kjaerum, Copenhagen, 1973

Megalithomania, Artists, Antiquarians and Archeologists at the Old Stone Monuments, John Michell, Thames & Hudson, London, 1982

Megaliths, Territories and Population, Colin Renfrew, Fourth Atlantic Colloquium, Gand, 1976

Les Monuments Mégalithiques et la Forme des Tumulus en Angleterre et en France, Glyn Daniel and Jean Arnal, Bulletin de la Société Préhistorique Française, 1952

Note sur la Terminologie Préhistorique de Bretagne, Commandant Alfred Devoir, Institut Finistérien d'Études Préhistoriques, 1926

Pauvres Pierres! Les Mégalithes Bretons devant la Science, Abbé Millon, Saint-Brieuc, Paris, 1909

Petit Lexique du Mégalithisme, Jean Arnal, Bulletin de la Société Préhistorique Française, 1956

Symbols of Power at the time of Stonehenge, David V. Clarke, Trevor G. Cowie, and Andrew Foxon, Edinburgh, 1985

Building the Megaliths

A Propos du Trilithon de Baalbek, le Transport et la Mise en Oeuvre des Mégalithes, Jean-Pierre Adam, Syria, 1977

Experimental Archeology, John Coles, Academic Press, New York, 1973; London, 1979

Aux Prises avec des Pierres de Plusieurs Dizaines de Tonnes, Jean-Pierre Mohen, Dossiers de l'Archéologie ('Revivre la Préhistoire'), 1980

Neolithic Engineering, Richard Atkinson, Antiquity, 1961

Studies in Ancient Technology, Robert James Forbes, Leiden, 1964 to 1972

Megalithic Art

Corpus des Signes Gravés des Monuments Mégalithiques du Morbihan, Marthe and Saint-Just Pequart and Zacharie Le Rouzic, Picard et Berger-Levrault, Paris, 1927

La Figure Humaine dans la Décoration des Allées Couvertes du Morbihan, Abbé Henri Breuil, Zacharie Le Rouzic, and Mary-Elisabeth Boyle, Leroux ('Préhistoire'), Paris, 1938

Les Idoles qu'on abat..., Jean L'Helgouach, *Archéologie Armoricaine*, Société Polymathique du Morbihan, 1983

The Megalithic Art of Western Europe, Elizabeth Shee Twohig, Clarendon Press, Oxford, 1981; Oxford University Press, New York, 1981

Quelques Dolmens Ornés du Morbihan, Abbé Henri Breuil and Mary-Elisabeth Boyle, P.U.F., ('Préhistoire'), Paris, 1959

Signes sans Paroles, Cent Siècles d'Art Rupestre en Europe Occidentale, Jean Abelanet, Hachette, Paris, 1986

Les Statues-Menhirs et Stèles Anthropomorphes du Midi Méditerranéen, André d'Anna, C.N.R.S., Paris, 1977

Les Statues-Menhirs, Hommes et Dieux, Jean Arnal, Les Hespérides, 1976

Science, Orientation

Megalithic Remains in Britain and Brittany, Alexander and Archibald S. Thom, Clarendon Press, Oxford, 1978; Oxford University Press, New York, 1967

Megalithic Science, Ancient Mathematics and Astronomy in Northwest Europe, Douglas C. Heggie, Thames & Hudson, London, 1981; Thames & Hudson, New York, 1982

Les Mégalithes, par Leurs Mesures, Nous Révèlent-ils une Science Inconnue? Père Le Carré, S.J., Ogam, 1964

La Préhistoire par les Étoiles, un Chronomètre Préhistorique, Doctor Marcel Baudouin, Librairie Maloine, Paris, 1926

Stonehenge Decoded, Gerald S. Hawkins, William Collins Sons, London, 1979; Hippocrene Books, New York, 1988

Regional Studies

Atlas der Megalithgräber Deutschlands, Ernst Sprockhoff, Bonn, 1966, 1967 and 1975

Ceramic Decoration and Social Organisation. Regional Variations Seen in Material from South Swedish Passage-Graves, Birgitta Härdh, Scripta min., Lund, 1986

Der Dolmen Trollasten in St Köpinge, Schonen, Märta Strömberg, Bonn-Lund, 1968

The Dutch Megalith Graves, Jan Lanting, Palaeohistoria, 1988

Die Funde aus Dolmen und Ganggräben in Schonen, Schweden, Axel Bagge and Lili Kaelas, Stockholm, 1950 and 1952

Hessische Steinkisten and Frühes Metall, Wolfgang Dehn and Josef Roder, Fundberichte aus Hessen, 1980

Ingelstorp, zur Siedlungsentwicklung eines Südschwedischen Dorfes, Märta Strömberg, Bonn-Lund, 1982

Die Mecklenburgischen Megalithgräber, Ewald Schuldt, Berlin, 1972

Die Metalithgräber von Hagestad, zur Problematik von Gräbbauten and Gräbritten, Märta Strömberg, Bonn-Lund, 1971

The Megalithic Tombs in South Scandinavia, Lili Kaelas, Palaeohistoria, 1966-67

Siedlungen und Gräber der Trichtrebecherkultur und Schnurkeramik bei Halle (Saale), Hermann Behrens and Erhard Schroter, Berlin, 1980

Totenhütten der Neolithischen Walternienburger Gruppe, Rudolf Fuestel and Herbert Ullrich, Altthüringen, 1965

The TRB West Group, Studies in the Chronology and Geography of the Makers of Hunabeds and Tiefstich Pottery, Jan Albert Bakker, Amsterdam, 1979

Wartberg-Gruppe and Hessische Megalithik, Winrich Schnellnus, Wiesbaden, 1979

The British Isles

The Age of Stonehenge, Colin Burgess, J.M. Dent & Sons Ltd, London, Toronto and Melbourne, 1980

The Chambered Tombs of Scotland, Audrey Shore Henshall, Edinburgh, 1963 and 1972; *The Chambered Cairns of Orkney*, Columbia University Press, New York, 1987

The Earthen Long Barrow in Britain, Paul Ashbee, University of Toronto Press, 1970

Excavations at Knowth, George Eogan, Royal Irish Academy, Dublin, 1984

Les Fouillages and the Megalithic Monuments of Guernsey, Ian Kinnes, 1983

Gwernvale and Penywyrlod: Two Neolithic Long Cairns in the Black Mountains of Brecknock, William Britnell and Hubert Savory, Cambrian Archaeological Monographs no. 2, 1984

The Prehistory of Orkney, Colin Renfrew, Edinburgh University Press, 1979; Columbia University Press, New York, 1987

Irish Passage Graves, Michael Herity, Irish University Press, Dublin, 1974

Knowth and the Passage-Tombs of Ireland, George Eogan, Thames & Hudson, London, 1986; Thames & Hudson, New York, 1987

The Megalithic Chambered Tombs of the Cotswold – Severn Region, Tim C. Darvill, Vorda, 1982

Monumental Function in British Neolithic Burial Practices, Ian Kinnes, World Archaeology, 1975

Newgrange, Archaeology, Art and Legend, Michael J. O'Kelly, Thames & Hudson, London and New York, 1982

Prehistoric Anglesey, Frances Lynch, The Anglesey Antiquarian Society, 1970

Prehistoric Avebury, Aubrey Burl, Yale University Press, Newhaven and London, 1979

The Stone Circles of the British Isles, Aubrey Burl, Yale University Press, Newhaven and London, 1976

Stonehenge Complete, Chris Chippindale, Thames & Hudson, London, 1985; Cornell University Press, Ithaca, New York, 1987

Stonehenge, Richard Atkinson, Penguin Books, 1979

Survey of the Megalithic Tombs of Ireland, Ruaidhri de Valéra and Sean O'Nuallain, Dublin, 1961

Tomb of the Eagles, a Window on Stone Age Tribal Britain, John W. Hedges, John Murray, London, 1984; New Amsterdam Books, New York, 1987

Trefignath and Din Dryfol, the Excavation of Two Megalithic Tombs in Anglesey, Christopher Smith and Frances Lynch, Cambrian Archaeological Monographs no.3, 1987

France, Belgium, Switzerland

L'Architecture des Dolmens entre Languedoc et Centre-Ouest de la France, Yves Chevalier, Bonn, 1984

Au Pays des Mégalithes, Carnac, Quiberon, Locmariaquer, Michael Batt, Pierre-Roland Giot, Yannick Lecerf, Joël Lecornec, and Charles-Tanguy Le Roux, Édition d'Art Jos le Doaré, Châteaulin, 1983

Barnenez, un Grand Cairn Mégalithique, Pierre-Roland Giot, Jos, Châteaulin, 1987

Le Complexe Mégalithique du Petit-Mont, Arzon (Morbihan), Joël Lecornec, Revue Archéologique de l'Ouest, 1985

La Corse avant l'Histoire, Roger Grosjean, Klincksieck, Paris, 1981

Les Dolmens du Département de l'Hérault, Jean Arnal, Préhistoire, Paris, 1963

Fouilles Récentes de Quelques Dolmens du Quercy, Bernard Pajot, *Mémoires de la Société Archéologique du Midi de la France*, 1987

Les Grottes Sépulchrales Artificielles en Languedoc Oriental, Albert Colomer, *Archives d'Écologie Préhistorique*, Toulouse, 1979

Megalithic Brittany, Aubrey Burl, Thames & Hudson, London and New York, 1985

Inventaire des Mégalithes de la France, 1 – Indre-et-Loire, Gérard Cordier, Gallia Préhistoire, C.N.R.S., Paris, 1963

Inventaire des Mégalithes de la France, 2 – Aine-et-Loire, Michel Gruet, Gallia Préhistoire, C.N.R.S., 1967

Inventaire des Mégalithes de la France, 3 – Loir-et-Cher, Jakie Despriée and Claude Leymarios, Gallia Préhistoire, C.N.R.S., Paris, 1974

Inventaire des Mégalithes de la France, 4 – Région Parisienne, John Peek, Gallia Préhistoire, C.N.R.S., Paris, 1975

Inventaire des Mégalithes de la France, 5 – Lot, Jean Clottes, Gallia Préhistoire, C.N.R.S., Paris, 1977

Inventaire des Mégalithes de la France, 6 – Deux-Sèvres, Georges Germond, Gallia Préhistoire, C.N.R.S., Paris, 1980

Inventaire des Mégalithes de la France, 7 – Aveyron, Jean Clottes and Claude Maurand, Gallia Préhistoire, C.N.R.S., Paris, 1983

Inventaire des Mégalithes de la France, 8 – Puy-de-Dôme, Sylvie Amblard, Gallia Préhistoire, C.N.R.S., Paris, 1983

Mégalithes et Environnement en Bretagne Intérieure, Jacques Briard, Documents d'Archéologie Française, Paris, 1988

Les Monuments Mégalithiques du Morbihan, Causes de leur Ruine et Origine de leur Restauration, Zacharie Le Rouzic, Bulletin de la Société Française, 1939

La Nécropole de Chanon, Étude d'un Ensemble Dolmenique Charentais, Edmond Gauron and Jean Massaud, Gallia Préhistoire, C.N.R.S., Paris, 1983

La Nécropole Mégalithique de la Clape (Laroque de Fa, Aude), Jean Guilaine, Carcassonne, 1972

Le Néolithique dans le Bassin Parisien, Gérard Bailloud, Gallia Préhistoire, C.N.R.S., Paris, 1964

The Prehistoric Chamber Tombs of France, Glyn Daniel, Thames & Hudson, London, 1960

Préhistoire de la Bretagne, Pierre-Roland Giot, Jean L'Helgouach, and Jean-Laurent Monnier, Rennes, 1979

La Préhistoire du Morbihan, le Vannetais Littoral, Yannick Rollando, Société Polymatique, Vannes, 1961

Les Sépultures du Vaucluse du Néolithique a l'Age du Bronze, Gérard Sauzade, Institut de Paléontologie Humaine, Études Quarternaires, Paris, 1983

Les Sépultures Mégalithiques en Armorique, Dolmens à Couloir et Allées Couvertes, Jean L'Helgouach, Rennes, 1965

Les Sépultures Mégalithiques en Belgique, Inventaire et Essai de Synthèse, Éric Huysecom, Société Royale Belge d'Anthropologie et de Préhistoire, Brussels, 1982

Le Site Préhistorique du Petit Chasseur (Sion, Valais), 1 et 2, le Dolmen MVI, Olivier-Jean Bocksberger, Cahiers d'Archéologie Romande, Lausanne, 1976

Le Site Préhistorique du Petit Chasseur (Sion, Valais), le Dolmen MXI, Alain Gallay and Louis Chaix, Lausanne, 1985

Les Tumulus d'Armorique, Jacques Briard, Picard ('L'Age du Bronze en France' series), Paris, 1984

Southern Europe

Asmamoas de Furnas (Serra da Aboboreira), Vitor Oliveira Jorge, Arqueologia, 1987

Civiltà Nuragica, Ferrucio Darreca, Fulvia Lo Schiavo, and Ermanno A. Arslan, Electa, Milan, 1985

Die Megalithgräber der Iberischen Halbinsel, 1 – der Suden, Georg and Vera Leisner, Römisch-Germanische Forschungen, Berlin, 1943

Die Megalithgräber der Iberischen Halbinsel, der Western, Georg and Vera Leisner, Madrider Forschungen, Berlin, 1956-1959-1965

El Poblado y la Necropolis Megaliticos de Los Millares, Martin Almagro and Antonio Arribas, Bibliotheca Praehistorica Hispana, Madrid, 1963

Secuencia Cultural de la Prehistoria de Mallorca, Manuel Fernandez-Miranda, Bibliotea Praehistorica Hispana, 1978

Tholoi, Tumuli et Cercles Funéraires, Olivier Pelon, De Boccard, Paris, 1976

Zur Relativen Chronologie Portugiesischer Megalithgräber, Philine Kalb, Madrider Mitteilungen, Mainz, 1981

Eastern Europe

Dolmens du Caucase Occidental, Vladimir Markovin, Sovietskaia Archeologia, 1973

Megalithi Thraciae, Alexander Fol and Ivan Venedikov, Sofia, 1976

Megaliths Outside Europe

Aku-Aku, The Secret of Easter Island, Thor Heyerdahl, London, 1958

Aux Origines de la Berberie, Monuments et Rite Funéraires Protohistoriques, Gabriel Camps, Paris, 1962

La Civilisation Mégalithique de Bouar, Prospection et Fouilles 1962 – 1966, Pierre Vidal, Paris, 1969

Dolmens for the Dead: Megalith-Building Throughout the World, Roger Joussaume, Cornell University Press, Ithaca, 1988; Batsford, London, 1988

L'Ile de Pâques et ses Mystères, Dr Stephen Chauvet, Paris, 1935

Le Mégalithisme en Éthiopie, Roger Joussaume, Museum National d'Histoire Naturelle, Paris, 1974

Les Monuments Mégalithiques de tous Pays, leur Age et leur Destination, James Fergusson, Haton, Paris, 1878

The Mystery of Easter Island, Mrs Scoresby Routledge, Sifton, Praed, & Co Ltd, London 1919

Nouveau Regard sur l'Ile de Pâques, Jean Dausset, André Valenta, and Marie-Charlotte Laroche, Moana Éditions, 1982

Recent Archaeological Discoveries in India, Bal Krishen Thapar, The Centre for East Asian Cultural Studies, UNESCO, 1985

Recent Archaeological Discoveries in Japan, Tsuboi Kiyotari, The Centre for East Asian Cultural Studies, UNESCO, 1987

Recherches Préhistoriques en République Centrafricane, Roger de Bayle des Hermens, Nanterre, 1975

Rude Stone Monuments in All Countries, James Fergusson, John Murray, London, 1872

Sépultures Mégalithiques à Madagascar, Roger Joussaume and Victor Raharijoana, *Bulletin de la Société Préhistorique Française*, 1985

Glossary

ALIGNMENT: a series of standing stones set in a straight line. There may be several parallel lines, as at Carnac (France). The alignment may be linked to an oval or rectangular enclosure also marked out by standing stones.

ANTECHAMBER: front section of a megalithic tomb or hypogeum, separate from the chamber but of the same width and height; this distinguishes it from the portico and passage. (See PASSAGE, PORTICO.)

ANTHROPOMORPHIC: in the form of a human silhouette; the shouldered outline of some Breton stones, for example, recalls the shield idol (see SHIELD).

ANTHROPOMORPHIC SLAB: a large stone, at least 1 metre across, carved in low relief on one surface only to represent a face and some features, or more simply carved into the form of an anthropomorphic silhouette with shoulder-indications and a point to indicate the head.

AVENUE: grand ceremonial way bordered by ditches and banks of earth leading to a ceremonial centre such as at Stonehenge.

BETYL: small carved standing stone, with broad circular base and rounded top.

BARROW: a TUMULUS (q.v.). A round or elongated mound. A *long barrow* is an extended tumulus, an *unchambered long barrow* is a long tumulus without a burial chamber, and a *chambered barrow* is a tumulus containing a tomb, generally megalithic.

BLOCK: a stone with bulging or irregular surfaces, as distinct from a flat stone slab.

BURIAL or INHUMATION: strictly, internment. However, the term has come to be used in a broader sense to refer to the deposition of a corpse or human bones in a tomb by any means, even if not covered over with earth. It is thus differentiated from CREMATION (q.v.).

BURIAL CHAMBER: the burial or funerary chamber, sometimes called a CELLA (q.v.), is a stone or wooden construction with dimensions greater than 2 metres by 1 metre externally, and 1 metre high internally – these measurements distinguish it from the COFFER and the CIST (q.v.). The chamber usually contains collective graves, either inhumations or cremations; a single interment is much rarer. It may be built above ground and set inside a barrow, or completely or partially dug into the ground, as with the very long chambers of the Paris basin or rock-cut caves (q.v.). Its passage may be long or short, central or off-centre, straight or angled; the chamber may be circular, polygonal, trapezoidal, square, or rectangular, with breadth:length ratios of

between 1:1 and 1:3. The chamber is said to be long when the ratio is greater than 1:3 and very long when it exceeds 1:4.

CAIRN: a mound of stones constructed for a megalithic tomb, often used as a synonym for BARROW (q.v.).

CARNACIAN: referring to the Carnac region in the French département of Morbihan in Brittany. Applied to a series of giant tumuli and a particular category of grave-goods including rings and large polished axes made of semi-precious stones.

CELLA: enclosed and sacred space within a temple or burial chamber. The term is sometimes used in a more restricted sense to indicate a small auxiliary chamber like those behind the head-stone of certain Armorican monuments with a very long chamber.

CHAMBER TOMB (Frenc, *chambre simple*, Danish, *dyss*, Swedish, *dös*): a closed burial space, underground or inside a mound, with internal dimensions greater than those of a cist or coffer, i.e. 2 metres long by 1 metre wide and 1 metre high. The chamber tomb was generally used for mass burial. It could be reached in various ways which are not always easily recognizable: removal of a stone, or of rubble, for example. Glyn Daniel distinguishes between megalithic, rectangular, polygonal and oval chamber tombs, and circular chamber tombs with dry-stone work walls, sometimes roofed with wood.

CHE-PIN: the Chinese term for a megalithic chamber, meaning literally 'stone table', the equivalent of dolmen (q.v.).

CIRCLE: general name for any circular structure, most frequently applied to a circle of standing stones, bordered with or without a ditch, a bank of earth, or a pali-

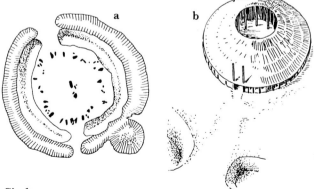

Circles
a Circle of standing stones surrounded by a ditch and mass of earth broken by two entrances: Arbor Low (Derbyshire, England).
b Circular and covered timber structure, built to south of an area surrounded by a ditch: Durrington Walls (Wiltshire, England).

sade. The terms CROMLECH and HENGE (*q.v.*) were often wrongly used to denote forms of circle; they were thus applied to a whole range of ceremonial sites – Stonehenge, Arbor Low, and Durrington Walls in England, and Quenstedt at Schalkenburg in Germany, for example.

CIST: from the Latin word meaning 'small basket with lid', and used to denote a small construction made of dry stones or with vertical and horizontal stone slabs sheltering an individual grave, which distinguishes it from a COFFER (*q.v.*). The cist may be found in a pit or beneath a tumulus, and may contain a burial or, more rarely, cremated ashes. Although usually smaller, it may be confused with a coffer when the lack of bones makes it impossible to know whether the burial was single or collective. The word 'cist' has also taken on a wider meaning in certain expressions such as 'long cist' or 'long stone cist', used to designate a long megalithic chamber.

COFFER: a burial construction of stone or wood, of modest size, with access generally from above. It is not usually larger than 2 metres by 1 metre, and 1 metre inner height – this distinguishes it from a burial chamber. Unlike the CIST it was built to receive collective burials. Its setting was in a pit or beneath a mound. In the absence of bones, the terms CIST or COFFER are interchangeable, except that a coffer is generally larger than a cist.

COLUMN: Block or slab supporting the covering stone of a megalithic chamber or its passage. The column may be either integrated into the wall or central, forming part of the compartmentalization of the chamber.

COMPARTMENT: part of the ground space of a megalithic tomb which can be subdivided into sections marked out by rows of pebbles, small stones, or sometimes stone slabs, which thus formed part of the basic structure of a chamber described as 'compartmentalized'.

CORBELLING: ' "oven" vaulting achieved by stones cantilevered forward on each other until opposite sides meet or a stone slab acts as keystone' (Jean Arnal, 1956). The vaulting used in tombs of the Barnenez type in Brittany, Newgrange in Ireland, using the Cueva de Romeral in Spain is in fact false corbelling. These tombs should not be confused with the Mycenian THOLOS (*q.v.*).

COURT-CAIRN: a tumulus with a court giving access to the burial chamber. In Ireland the court may be internal, and completely surrounded by the mound. It may be external, bounded simply by a concave façade; this is closer to a FORECOURT (*q.v.*), which is found in the Car-

lingford group in Northern Ireland and the Clyde group in south-west Scotland.

CREMATION: this burial practice of burning the dead is often difficult to recognize, though it seems to have been more wide-spread than was once thought. Frequent in Ireland, it was probably practised sporadically in megalithic tombs elsewhere as well. The crematorium found beneath the Hoguette tumulus at Fontenay-le-Marmion in Calvados may be connnected with the monument itself.

CROMLECH: the Welsh name for a stone slab supported on blocks – equivalent to a dolmen – and later, more broadly, the circle formed by the blocks surrounding a barrow that covers a megalithic chamber; such blocks form a peristyle. Some writers have used the term to designate any stone circle or megalithic enclosure. (See CIRCLE, DOLMEN, ENCLOSURE.) Consisting of a series of standing stones set in a circle, an oval, or a square, the cromlech differs from the alignment with which it may be associated, as at Carnac. The Scottish observatory circles, which are fairly numerous, are sometimes described as cromlechs, as are the great monuments of Avebury and Stonehenge. The word is in fact obsolete and now covers too many different styles to carry a precise meaning. It is better to use neutral terms such as stone circle, oval or square, and standing stones, which all belong to the category of open structures.

CROOK: a motif of megalithic art, seen in the tombs of Brittany and on the statues or menhirs of southern France. Its outline recalls the votive crooks carved in schist and placed in Portuguese megalithic tombs, as

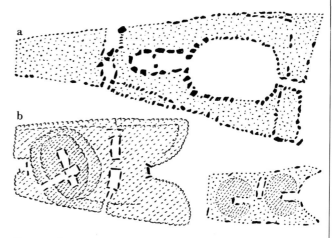

Court-cairn
a Internal court: Creevykeel (Co. Sligo, Ireland).
b External court or forecourt: left, Ty Isaf (Powys), right, Mid Gleniron I (Wigtownshire, Scotland).

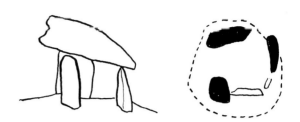

group, which must be considered as a whole. The general term of 'megalithic monument' appears preferable, and 'megalithic tomb' to cover the very wide range of chambers (dolmens in the strict sense of the word), mounds, and other structures of very different shapes and materials. This simple analytical and descriptive approach helps to achieve an understanding of the different functions of each part of the monument.

DRY STONE: style of construction using flat stones piled up on each other without bonding, clay, or mortar, to form walls and kerbs. The latter may reach several metres in height, usually leaning slightly towards the outside of the construction.

ENCLOSURE: closed structure, which may be circular, oval, or quadrangular; sometimes very large, it may consist of a ditch, a wall, a series of standing stones, or several of these elements together. (See also CIRCLE.)

ENGRAVING: engraved (carved) megalithic art appears in the Atlantic zone of southern Spain, Portugal, central western France, Brittany, the Paris basin, and Ireland. The most frequent themes are highly stylized representations of a female figure, symbols of male power such as the axe, the crook and the bow, and abstract motifs that appear to represent the great forces of nature.

FALSE ENTRANCE: certain tumulus façades, particularly of the Severn-Cotswold group, display at the centre a blocked dummy entrance to a non-existent passage. The significance of this feature is not known.

FORECOURT: the space (French, *parvis*) in front of the concave façade of certain British or Iberian mounds see COURT-CAIRN *q.v.*).

FUNERAL RITES: the overall term for ceremonies indicating the attitude of the living towards their dead. Primary rites, such as the ossuary and cave rituals, should be distinguished from secondary rites such as reliquary ritual.

GALLERY-GRAVE or LONG STONE CIST (French, *allée couverte*; Spanish, *galeria cubierta*; German, *Steinkiste, Westeuropaische Steinkiste*, or *Galeriegrab*): this term is employed somewhat loosely in reference to a wide variety of structures, and care is required in its use. The only generally applicable feature is the disproportionate length of the slab-lined chamber passage: monuments which differ considerably from each other may therefore all be described as gallery-graves.
The Armorican gallery grave is built above ground, covered by a row of slabs, then buried beneath a long barrow: it contains an antechamber and a terminal cella which is sometimes decorated. In a buttressed

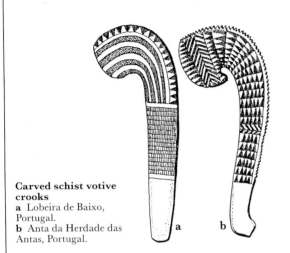

Carved schist votive crooks
a Lobeira de Baixo, Portugal.
b Anta da Herdade das Antas, Portugal.

well as that of a wooden club found at Auvernier-Saunerie on the shore of Lake Neuchâtel in Switzerland.

CULTURE: archeologists' term for a homogeneous group of material effects (tools, weapons, ornaments, dwellings, or funeral rites, for instance) the traces of which they study. A culture is defined by its geographical and chronological boundaries and within a single culture various features such as pottery or building styles are distinguishable. Several cultures may combine to form a civilization, such as the Neolithic civilization of western Europe, or that of Greece or Rome. The chart of cultures contemporaneous with megaliths is on page 285.

CUP or SCOOP MARK: small circular depression on a stone or rock; often grouped together, they are the result of a repeated ritual gesture of unknown significance.

CWM: welsh term for tumulus.

DOLMEN: Welsh term (now obsolete in English) for a 'stone table', the most frequent relic of the burial chamber of a megalithic monument. 'Although the place-name *Tolmaen* may appear on a plan or monastery record in Landevennec, to designate any unknown place, it was Th. M. Corret de Kerbeauffret de la Tour d'Auvergne who popularized the barbarism *dolmin*, also used by Legrand d'Aussi, and *dolmen*, used by J. Cambry (instead of *taolven*, the correct term for a stone table). Following this elastic use of the word it has now become the very generalized term for any megalithic place of burial.' (Pierre-Roland Giot, 1979). In Jean Arnal's 1956 definition, 'A dolmen is an open burial chamber, generally megalithic, covered with a tumulus and designed to contain several burials.' The definition thus always focuses on the central part of a monumental

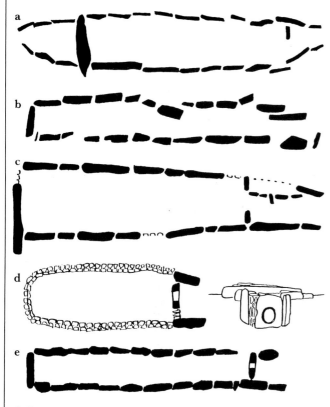

Gallery graves
a Armorican type: Prajou-Menhir, Trébeurden (Cotes-du-Nord)
b Aquitaine type: Roquefort, Lugasson (Gironde). **c** Aude type:
Saint-Eugène (Aude). **d** Paris basin type, with dry stone walls:
Guiry-en-Véxin (Val d'Oise). **e** Westphalian and Hesse type:
Lohne-Züschen (Hesse).

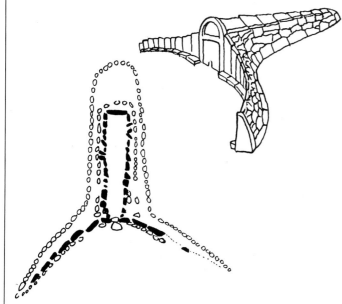

The Li-Mizzani Giant's grave, Sardinia.

gallery-grave the wall slabs lean inwards and support each other.

The Aquitaine gallery-grave is also built above ground. Its side columns increase in height from the entrance towards the head-stone.

In the Aude gallery-grave, the height of the antechamber and the chamber decreases with distance from the entrance.

The Paris gallery-grave is built in a trench, with an antechamber which may be decorated; some graves of this type are lined with dry-stone walling, others with wood. In many cases the covering does not appear to be megalithic. There are iconographic and ritual links between these monuments and the Marne hypogea.

The entrance to the *Westphalia and Hesse* gallery-grave is axial. The monuments with side entrances, such as the series of tombs in Denmark, northern Germany, the Netherlands, and Brittany, are not known as gallery-graves.

The *Loire gallery-grave* is now regarded as an Anjou-style of megalithic tomb with a portico.

The *segmented cists* of the British Manse group and the Giants graves (*Giganti*) in Sardinia are of an independent style with a tendency to a longer burial space. The general evolution towards passage chambers of increasing length was combined with changes in funeral rites, but there is no reason why the general basic terminology should change. This book therefore uses the expressions 'long' or 'very long' tomb, as appropriate, rather than 'gallery-grave' – retaining the term for the geographical groupings listed above, however. See also PASSAGE GRAVE (*q.v.*).

GIANTS' GRAVE: (Italian, *tomba di giganti*), a very long third-millennium megalithic tomb built in Sardinia, covered with blocks and with two wings on either side of the curved façade. Access to the monument is via a low entrance in a large sculpted stone.

GIANT TUMULUS: these mounds, which may be circular or elongated, have in common their considerable size (more than 100 metres in length or width, and more than 5 metres in high), modest (or absent) funerary references, and obvious connection with megalithic monuments (kerbs, orientation, shape of graves, a degree of contemporaneity). The giant tumulus must have constituted a specific tradition of the northern half of western Europe, in countries bordering the English Channel and the Atlantic Ocean as far as central western France.

GRAVE-GOODS: funeral offerings placed inside or near a tomb. They are often the only means of establishing the chronological sequence of the various uses of the burial place. The oldest remains, taken as being the nearest to the time of construction, help to date the monument.

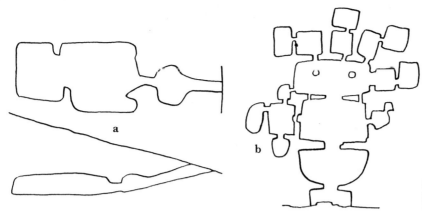

Hypogea
a Les Mournouards II, Mesnil-sur-Oger (Marne).
b San Andrea Priu, Sardinia.

HEAD-STONE: the head-stone (or apsidal stone) of a megalithic chamber is the stone slab in the wall of the tomb which faces the entrance. Perhaps the finest head-stone can be seen in the Table des Marchands tomb at Locmariaquer in Morbihan. It has an anthropomorphic profile and crook decoration.

HENGE: traditional English name for a circular structure, which may consist of a ditch, usually beside an earth bank, and/or a series of standing stones – Stonehenge exemplifies this type of open construction. The term no longer has any precise meaning and has been avoided in this work; its etymology offers no indication of a circular structure, but refers to supported stones, such as the trilithons at Stonehenge. Since these Stonehenge trilithons are arranged in a circle or arc, the term has been extended to include any circular prehistoric structure. (See CIRCLE.)

HYPOGEUM: a particular form of rock-cut tomb, consisting of a burial chamber preceded by a smaller antechamber, reached from the outside by a sloping passage. The group of hypogea at Coizard, in the Marne, is characteristic; the Arles hypogea in the Bouches-du-Rhône are distinctive in being covered by stones. Other hypogea can be seen in the Mediterranean islands – Malta and Sardinia – and in Egypt, where the term is also applied to graves in the Valley of the Kings. Round the Tagus estuary in Portugal they form a homogeneous group characterized by a domed chamber.

IDOL: name given to anthropomorphic representations, covering both statuettes, often stylized, made of terracotta, bone, or stone, and designs carved or chipped out on the stone slabs of megalithic tombs. One such design, called the 'shield' (See SHIELD) or 'dishevelled' idol, is highly abstract.

KERB: piled up stones forming a retaining wall surrounding the various elements of a tumulus. The kerb may be internal, hidden beneath the body of a mound, or visible and external, with offerings at the foot. Kerbs are sometimes built up in steps, enabling the monument to be built to a greater height.

KISTE: German name for a cist. When used in the form of *Steinkiste* the word indicates a megalithic chamber, usually a long one; this term is not used by the present writer, however, who prefers the greater precision of the word 'cist' (*q.v.*).

KO-IN-DOL: Korean word for a megalithic chamber; literally, 'supported stone'.

LATERAL CHAMBER: small annexe chamber opening into the main chamber or passage of a megalithic tomb.

MEGALITH: a large block of stone (from the Greek *mega*, large, and *lithos*, stone), which has given its name to the type of construction in which it is used as an integral part. Megalithic architecture is 'simple' when it consists of a standing stone placed in relation with the natural elements of a landscape. It is 'open' but more complex when several standing stones are placed in aligned rows or in a circle: Stonehenge is the most remarkable example of this type. It is 'closed' when the blocks are used to construct the cella of a temple (in the temples of the Maltese islands) or a burial chamber (tombs in the Atlantic zone). In such cases·megaliths are often associated with dry-stone kerbs, with banks of earth or rubble, and sometimes even with wooden structures; a mound covers the tomb. There are many forms of megalithic architecture throughout the world. (See also CELLA, KERB, TUMULUS.)

Megalithic building has sometimes been associated with other forms of architecture, such as the cyclopean constructions of Mycenae and Peru. These are built from stone blocks some of which are extremely heavy, with surfaces cut and polished for perfect fitting. These constructions, thought to have been the originals of megalithic monuments, appeared in various contexts: they have been found in some of the western Mediterranean islands, such as the Balearics and Corsica. The ancient colossus figures, and the more recent statues of Easter Island, though their settings are very different from those of megalithic monuments, share some of

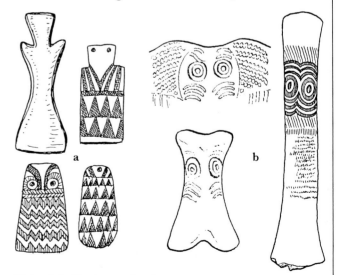

Idols of the Iberian peninsula
a stone **b** bone

294

their features, and their extraction from quarries and their transport gives some indications as to what these operations must have meant for megalith builders. Anthropomorphic STELES and STATUE-MENHIRS (q.v.) likewise represent a specific category of monoliths some of which show interesting links with megalithic construction, in particular Brittany, the Valais of Switzerland, and the south of France. The design and function of hypogea and rock-cut tombs, and the iconography of their carved motifs, similarly evoke many aspects of megalithic monuments.

MEGALITHISM: a worldwide phenomenon using large blocks of rough-cut stone (see MEGALITH). They may be standing or rounded stones, isolated or gathered together in constructions of greater or lesser complexity, sometimes with kerbs of dry stones, earth banks, and wooden structures. Megalithism is one of the most important characteristics of the Neolithic Age in western Europe, appearing there in the fifth millennium in its monumental form, and represents the world's oldest known form of stone architecture. It is the major social and religious expression of peoples who developed an agricultural way of life and became settled. Other regions worldwide also experienced megalithism in specific chronological and anthropological contexts. It has for instance been identified through oral tradition in eighteenth and nineteenth century society in Madagascar, and even as late as 1900 in Borneo. Megalithism is studied by comparative methods, based on unique or convergent features.

MENHIR: this term (in the form of *minhir*, meaning 'long stone') came into use through the writings of Celtic enthusiasts in the late eighteenth century. It is not certain that the word originates in popular usage, although it appears in many place-names (Kermenhir, for instance). In his 1732 dictionary, Dom Grégoire de Rostrenen gave as an equivalent of *menhir* the word *peulvan*, meaning a standing stone. (See PEULVAN and STANDING STONE.)

MONOLITH: a single stone (from the Greek *monos*, one, and *lithos*, stone). A standing stone is a monolith; so is a single slab of stone covering a chamber.

MORTUARY HOUSES (or HOUSES OF THE DEAD): in Denmark, a small wooden edifice of wood, mud and straw, used for the deposit of a corpse – occasionally several and offerings; the structure also served as the starting point for a large tumulus. This type of construction occurs also in the British Isles and elsewhere.

MOUND: the funerary mound is synonymous with the TUMULUS (q.v.)

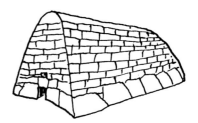

Naveta at Els Tudons, Minorca.

NAVETA; in the Balearic island of Minorca, a long burial chamber covered with blocks. The slightly concave façade reveals the low entrance to the grave. It dates from the second millennium B.C.

NECROPOLIS: a 'city of the dead' (from the Greek *necros*, dead, and *polis*, city), implying two concepts, that of its architecture and that of its burial purpose. The necropolis differs from the cemetery in its architecture; some became sanctuaries when no longer used for burial.

NURAGHE: in Sardinia, a tower built in Cyclopean style, either simple or complex. It is the equivalent of the Corsican torre or the Balearic talayot, and dates from the third millennium B.C.

OFFERING: any object placed as a gift for an ancestor or a deity, found in tombs and at the base of standing stones. The offering may be individual, but more generally appears to be collective.

ORTHOSTAT: slab of stone set up to form the wall of a megalithic tomb or an element of a wall.

OSSUARY: burial place for a large number of bodies brought together after massacre, epidemic, or natural death.

PASSAGE (FRENCH, *couloir;* German, *gang;* SPANISH, *corredor*): 'The passage is narrower and lower than the burial chamber, allowing access from the edge of the mound' (Jean Arnal, 1956). The sides are usually parallel, made of dry stones or columns supporting the covering stones. The passage entrance is often sealed by piled-up stones. The existence of a passage characterizes a category of tombs known as 'passage graves'. The passage should not be confused with either the PORTICO or the ANTECHAMBER (q.v.).

PASSAGE GRAVE (Danish, *jaettestue;* French, *chambre à couloir;* German, *ganggrab,* Spanish, *camera de corridor;* Swedish, *ganggrift*): burial chamber with a passage providing access from the outside of a tumulus to the place of burial within it. The passage grave is often all that

295

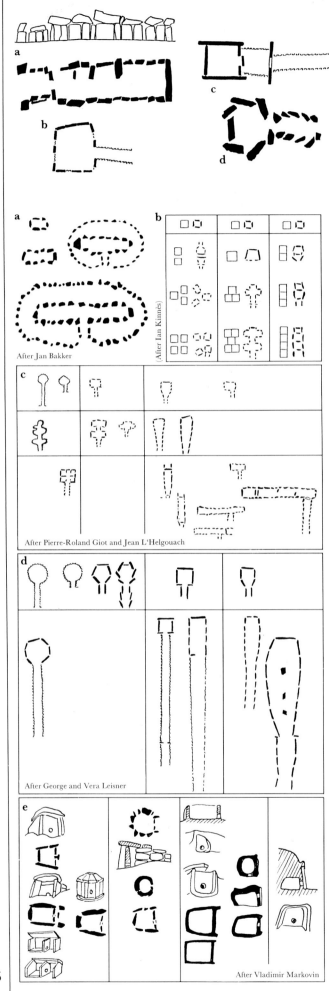

Passage graves – Some specific types
a Anjou-type with portico: La Roche-aux-Fées, Essé (Ille-et-Vilaine).
b Angoulême-type: Chamber F2 at Bougon (Deux-Sèvres).
c Languedoc-type: Lamalou, Rouet (Hérault).
d Portuguese type: Remendo I (Evora).

Passage graves – Evolution of the principal types
a Netherlands, North Germany and Denmark. b British Isles: from left to right: dispersed system, concentrated system, linear system. c Brittany. d Iberian peninsula. e Western Caucasus.

After Jan Bakker

(After Ian Kinnes)

After Pierre-Roland Giot and Jean L'Helgouach

After George and Vera Leisner

After Vladimir Markovin

remains of a tomb when the tumulus has been eroded. The chamber may be circular, polygonal, trapezoidal or rectangular. Tombs with square or rectangular chambers may have a portico (Anjou type) or ante-chamber (Languedoc type), while in Angoulême-style tombs the passage is slightly off-centre; there is also a Portuguese style with seven overlapping stone pillars. Other chambers are transepted with small side compartments; still others are long – some with a passage entering at an angle – or very long indeed (see GALLERY-GRAVES) of which several styles can be identified: Armorican; flying buttress; Aquitaine; Aude; Parisian; Westphalian and Hesse.

PAVING: flat stone slabs covering the ground. In a megalithic tomb, paving stones superimposed on each other may indicate several phases of use.

PEULVAN: an ancient Breton name for a standing stone in the Audierne region. The plural form, *peulvanet*, uses the characteristic ending for animate objects, indicating the life of such stones.

PIT: these are normally holes dug in the ground, usually filled in. There are foundation holes, the well-known 'post-holes', and holes dug to take the base of columns, walling stones, or standing stones, in which wedging stones are often found. Some foundation pits, for example those of certain standing stones, contain offerings sanctifying the monument. Burial pits were dug for the internment or remains of the dead, or of their ashes after cremation. Such remains may be of single or collective burials.

PORTAL DOLMEN: a type of megalithic chamber found in Ireland and Wales, which in its ruined state looks like a great portico with a vast covering stone supported on two columns at the front and a lower stone at the back.

PORT-HOLE SLAB: a perforated slab placed at the entrance of certain burial chambers. The opening, usually round, was closed by a stone or wood plug. Some writers refer to 'the hole of the spirit' to indicate the symbolic function of the porthole through which the souls of the dead could come and go.

PORTICO: megalithic trilithon at the entrance of certain tombs such as those of the Anjou type.

RELIQUARY: place where sacred relics were deposited – all or part of a skeleton, or an embalmed body.

RE-USE: megalithic tombs often reveal several successive phases of use, indicated by the specific placing of bones, by small stone annexe structures, and by grave-goods from various cultures. Re-use was sometimes in line with the original rite, using the same entrance and

296

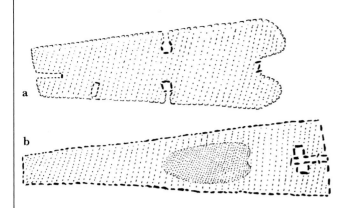

a

b

Severn-Cotswold tombs
a Belas Knap (Gloucestershire, England).
b Wayland's Smithy (Berkshire, England).

Shields
a Barnenez, Plouézoch (Finistère). b Ile Longue, Larmor Baden (Morbihan). c Le Rocher, Le Bono (Morbihan). d Les Pierres-Plates, Locmariaquer (Morbihan).

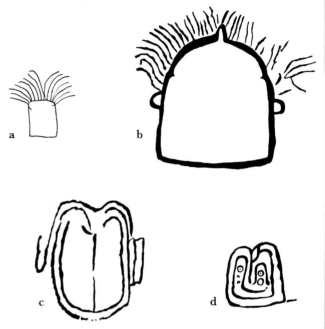

a   b

c   d

following the same pattern (with the body laid in a crouching position, for example). In such cases the older skeletons might be rearranged to provide space and the bones set out along the sides of the chamber. Re-use might occur quite a long time after the original construction, a thousand years later or even more, and might involve the construction of a new entrance, perhaps directly below the summit of the mount, ignoring the original entrance with its long-sealed passage; there might be additions, such as a coffer with a single skeleton and bell-beaker ware.

ROCK-CUT TOMB or ARTIFICIAL CAVE: an underground monument hollowed out of solid rock, and generally designed to take a collective burial. Rock-cut tombs are frequently found in the Mediterranean basin. The general term includes a particular form with antechamber, called a HYPOGEUM (*q.v.*), and can reasonably be grouped with megalithic monuments since the two have many points in common, including their chronology, function, and iconography.

ROUGH-HEWING: smoothing of the megalith surface or carving of features such as notches, hooks, or grooves, carried out by crushing the block persistently with a stone hammer, which left characteristic shallow scoop marks. The latter have frequently disappeared with the erosion of the megalith.

SANCTUARY: a construction designed for ceremonial rites in accordance with religious and spiritual beliefs. A necropolis may become a sanctuary once its burial function has ceased. A sanctuary could exist without any burials; this appears to have been rare, however, since death appears to have been the starting-point for all metaphysical ideas.

SEALING OFF: when a megalithic tomb had received its funeral deposits and offerings it was often sealed. First the access passage was blocked by broken stones and hidden by a stone facing or slab; next the monument, particularly the façade area, was covered by a mass of gravel. Sometimes it appears that certain wood or stone structures were deliberately destroyed, for example by fire. Although sealed after the first use, the monument might still be venerated, as indicated by later re-use.

SEVERN-COTSWOLD TOMB: long barrows found in the British Isles containing various types of megalithic chamber tomb, often constructed at different periods.

SHIELD: a design carved or chipped out on the slabs of Breton tombs, it is a highly abstract version of an anthropomorphic figure, interpreted as an IDOL (*q.v.*). Occasionally, as at the Table des Marchands at Loc-

mariaquer, it is integrated into the outline of an ANTHROPOMORPHIC SLAB (*q.v.*).

SLAB: a large flat stone, usually not very thick. Smaller slabs may be used for paving or for dividing up into compartments.

STANDING STONE: any stone used by human beings to mark a place, as a memorial or sign of respect, or for veneration. It may also be called a MENHIR or PEULVAN (*q.v.*), and may either be isolated or form part of an ALIGNMENT or a CIRCLE (*q.v.*)

STATUE-MENHIR: monolith representing 'the human body as a whole, on the anterior and the posterior surfaces, sculpted in *bas-relief* or sometimes carved. The height varies between 75 centimetres and 4 metres. The shape is generally rectangular or subrectangular, but the top may be rounded or pointed.' (André d'Anna, 1977.)

STELE: monolith of modest size (less than 75 centimetres high) with one face only decorated with cut-away carving (excised) or low relief sculpture.

TABLE: in the traditional concept of the 'dolmen', the term denotes the single covering stone of the megalithic tomb.

TALAYOT: in the Spanish island of Minorca, a second-millennium cyclopean-style tower with one or more chambers inside it.

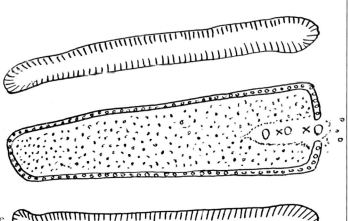

Unchambered barrow
Fussell's Lodge (Wiltshire, England).

TAULA: in Minorca, a massive column dating from the second millennium, supporting a block balanced on its top and surrounded by a circular stone wall.

TEMPLE: megalithic temples on the islands of Malta, Gozo and Sardinia are fourth- and third-millennium buildings with fairly large internal spaces, not designed specifically for funerary use. There are various styles.

THOLOS: a term wrongly used in referring to Mycenean tombs to denote a circular vaulted chamber with passage entrance. The widely varying contexts and designs of prehistoric tombs indicate that this is a term to be avoided.

TOMB: from the Latin *tumba*, meaning a burial stone, simple or monumental. In this context it is used in very broad terms to denote megalithic graves.

TORRE: a Cyclopean style tower in southern Corsica, the equivalent of the Balearic talayot. The torre, dating from the second millennium, has only one chamber, roofed by vaulting with niches.

TRANSEPT: a megalithic passage tomb may have two or even four lateral compartments, forming a transept or double transept. This style is characteristic of the Loire estuary region in France and the valley of the Boyne in Ireland.

TUMULUS (See also MOUND, FUNERARY MOUND, BARROW, CAIRN; German, *Hugel*; Italian and Spanish, *tumula*; Portuguese, *mamos*; French dialect names include *butte, clapas, galgal, hougue, mané*, and *motte*): all denote an artificial mound covering a burial deposit, ranging from a simple pile of burned bones to a megalithic tomb; hence the expression 'megalithic tumulus'. The exterior of the tumulus is rarely a simple mound of earth (tumulus proper) or of stone (cairn); it is often surrounded by a series of blocks or a kerb of dry stones, and there may even be an additional wooden structure. A façade is sometimes built round the entrance to the grave. Again, the upper part of the tumulus may be supported by rows of facing stones set in concentric rings. Depending on the design and size, a tumulus may be referred to as circular, long, or giant (see GIANT TUMULUS).

UNCHAMBERED BARROW: a tumulus without a burial chamber, although the tumulus, which may be elongated or round, usually has some burial reference (a simple deposit of bones, for example).

VAULT: burial place used for depositing a dead body.

VIOLATION: It is not unusual to find evidence of intrusions into megalithic tombs. These occurred in Neolithic times and also later, during the Bronze and Iron Ages and during the Roman era. They were accompanied by some degree of destruction or disturbance, as well as leaving traces by which the intrusion may be dated. The 'violation' may have taken various forms, such as fresh burial use, intrusion with deliberate or accidental deposit of offerings or remains, or criminal intrusion to steal offerings.

Wedge-shaped gallery grave: Island (Co. Cork, Ireland).

WEDGE TOMB: a very long Irish megalithic tomb, with the covering sloping downwards towards the further end.

WINDOW: a gap cut in the upper section of a column, which may be connected with a secondary entrance into the tomb or to a symbolic feature.

WINGS: Many megalithic mounds in the southern Iberian peninsula (at Los Millares, for example), Sardinia, and the British Isles present a concave façade with its two extremities ending in extensions known as 'wings' or 'horns'. They define a partly enclosed space described as the 'forecourt of a horned cairn'. Some Scottish barrows are thus façaded at both the front and back of the mound. (See also COURT-CAIRN and GIANTS' TOMB.)

Geographical Index

This index lists the great megalithic sites of the world. Page numbers in italic refer to photographs, maps or illustrations.

ABERDEEN, Scotland, 261
ABKHAZIA, Caucasus, Soviet Union, 46
ABOBOREIRA, Portugal, 123;
AILLEVANS, Haute-Saône, France, 146; 216;
Three megalithic monuments from the late Neolithic Age, each with a chamber and vestibule, stand a few hundred metres apart. The first grave was originally protected by a round barrow, which was then converted into a trapezoidal mound nearly 80 metres long. The post holes of an unidentified structure remain. At least twenty-three bodies were placed in the first chamber, and about a hundred in the second. Some multiple offerings were found on each side of the chamber entrance: flint arrow heads with wings and pendant, a flint dagger blade from Le Grand Pressigny, a copper bead, and bones of pigs sheep, oxen and dogs.
AL-KHURAYS, Yemen, 50
ALA PRAIA, Portugal, 236
ALA-SAFAT, Jordan, 47
ALBORG, Jutland, Denmark, 197
ALDEIA DA MARTA, Grato, Portugal, 123
ALFRISTON (barrow), England, 85
ALMERIA, Spain, 71; 124; 152; 234
ALSBERSG, Denmark, 110
ALTENDORF, Hesse, West Germany, 146
ANCRESSE (dolmen), Guernsey, 16
ANDLEYSTOWN, Ireland, 90
ANGERS, Maine-et-Loire, France, 161
ANGHELU RUJU, Alghero, Sardinia 155
The Anghelu Ruju necropolis comprises thirty-five tombs; some of its carvings simulate door-lintels; others are of bulls' heads, like those found in the eastern Mediterranean. This area has been suggested as the origin of cycladic style statuettes (Senorbi, Porto Ferro). Samples from the Del Guano cave have been carbon-dated at 2950 and 2880 B.C., which links this culture with that of the Ozieri hypogea.
ANGLESEY (isle of), Wales, 24; 241
ANNAGHMARE, County Armargh, Northern Ireland
This mound of stones was excavated in 1963 and 1964; it has a concave façade marking out a fairly large forecourt, and has been dated at 3170 B.C.
ANTA DOS GORGINOS, Upper Alentejo, Portugal, 122
ANTA GRANDE DA COMENDA DA IGREJA, Alentejo, Portugal, 124
ANTELAS, Oliveira de Frades, Viseu, Portugal, 240
ANTEQUERA, Spain, 43; 94; 125; 125; 198, 223
    North of Malaga, this megalithic group includes several important monuments:

– the Cueva de Menga, beneath a mound 50 metres in diameter, a long trapezoidal chamber with a 25 metre access passage, built of stones that weigh up to 180 tonnes;
– the Cueva de Viera, under a tumulus 60 metres in diameter, consists of a passage 25 metres long ending in a port-hole, a square chamber, and a small cella.

– the Cueva de Romeral lies beneath the most impressive tumulus, which is 90 metres in diameter and 9 metres high. It consists of a double circular chamber (the larger is 4.50 metres across) roofed with corbelling and reached by a long passage.
The grave-goods have long since disappeared, making it impossible to date these monuments with certainty to the Neolithic age.
ARALAR (chamber), Pays Basque, France, 151
ARDILLIÈRES, Rochefort, Charente-Maritime, France, 20; 24
ARGENTEUIL, Val d'Oise, France, 142; 217
The multiple megalithic grave at the Vivez factory is some 20 metres long by 2.10 metres wide, and walled with dry stone. To the north, behind the head-stone, a terminal 'cupboard' 50 centimetres deep contained several hundred perforated discs, pendants, bone and stone tools, an intact vessel, and a skull. The archeological layer 25–30 centimetres deep had been paved over. Within it were found human bones, including trepanned skulls, quantities of bone-working accessories, awls, polishers, two double-pointed bone instruments, perforated shells, roundels linked together, pierced teeth, a polished ivory head of a 'crutch-headed' pin, stone beads and pendants; a copper bead and a copper awl were also found, a bead and an awl, as well as shards from the late Neolithic and early Bronze ages.
ARGUENON, Jugon, Côtes-du-Nord, France, 17
ARLES, Bouches-du-Rhône, France, 21; 132; 133

ARLES-FONTVIEILLE, Bouches-du-Rhône, France, 148; 234

Four hypogea were dug out in the Cordes mountain near Fontvieille, each consisting of a long chamber and antechamber roofed with stone slabs and covered by an oval or circular mound. The largest, the Grotte des Fées, or "Épée de Roland", is 43.40 metres long. The Castellet cave contained 100 skeletons, twenty-six arrow-heads, two axes, six bone awls, 110 variscite beads, 571 steatite beads, five shell beads, a gold bead, some pottery (possibly of the Chassey culture), ribbed shards, and fragments of bell-beaker ware. The Grotte de la Source yielded four arrow-heads, a stone axe and amulet, a large copper bead, eight steatite beads, and shards of bell-beaker vessels. Arrow-heads, buttons with V-shaped perforations, a copper dagger, and a cup with decorated base were found in the Bounias cave.

ARRAN, Isle of, Scotland, 208; 210
ARRÉE hills, Côtes-du-Nord, Brittany, France, 194
ARRIBATS (stele), Murat-sur-Vèbre, Tarn, France, 254
ARRIZALA, Pays Basque, France, 150
ARZON, Morbihan, France, 107; 231; 244
ASCOT-UNDER-WYCHWOOD, Oxfordshire, England, 222
ASWAN (obelisk), Egypt, 158; 166
ATALAIA (chests), Portugal, 277
ATAUN (chamber), Pays Basque, France, 151
ATRIDES, tombs of the, Mycenae, Greece, 45
ATTELN, Westphalia, West Germany, 146
AUBERGENVILLE, Yvelines, France, 143
AUVERNIER, Lake Neuchâtel, Switzerland, 169
AVEBURY, Wiltshire, England, 30; 116; 129; 144; 162; 173; 264; 273

This late Neolithic site consists of a massive bank 400 metres in diameter, lying outside a broad ditch. Near the inner edge of the ditch is a large circle of standing stones inside of which there were originally two smaller tangential circles, also of standing stones; the north-eastern circle was probably a double ring. There must originally have been four entrances, diametrically opposite each other. To the south, a double avenue of megalithic stones leads to the small 'Sanctuary' circle two kilometres away, made in the first place of wood later rebuilt in stone. To the west was another avenue described in the eighteenth century by William Stukeley.

BAALBEK, Lebanon, 12; 58; 158
BAGNEUX, Maine-et-Loire, France; 94; 95; 119; 272

The 'Great Dolmen' of the Roche-aux-Fées, the largest megalithic cavern in France, is an Anjou-type of court-cairn. The rectangular chamber is 17.30 metres long by 4.25 metres wide; each side consists of four slabs, similar to the covering stone which is 2.50 metres above the present ground level. Traces of the covering barrow were still visible in 1847, but the burial deposits and offerings were long since scattered and lost, and nothing is known of them.

BAHRAIN, 50
BAIÀO, Portugal, 240
LA BAJOULIÈRE, Saint-Rémy-la-Varenne, Maine-et-Loire, France, 119
BALLYGLASS, County Mayo, Ireland, 90; 202
BALLYMACDERMOT, Ireland, 98
BALLYMARLAGH, Ireland, 90
BALLYNAGILLY, County Tyrone, Ireland, 195; 202
BAR-AL-LAN (barrow), Portsall-Ploudalmézeau, Finistère, France, 273
BARCLODIAD-Y-GAVRES, Isle of Anglesey, Wales, 111; 236; 251; 252

A large megalithic passage tomb of transept design, excavated in 1953. Some of the stones are decorated; the motifs include some described as 'anthropomorphic'.

BARKVIEREN, Rostock, Mecklenburg, West Germany, 83
BARNENEZ (Cairn), Plouézoc'h, Lanmeur, Finistère, France, 65; 72; 72; 73; 74; 75; 79; 99; 104; 107; 181; 182; 185; 193; 198; 242; 271; 275

The oldest part of this double tumulus, 70 metres long by 25 metres wide, contains five gallery graves in its east side and six more chambers to the west. Most are round and covered by dry-stone corbelling; some are clearly megalithic, however, such as tomb H with its vaulted antechamber and a column at the entrance carrying two axe motifs. Remains from the first phase of use – round-based pots, trimmed flints and polished stones – have been carbon-dated at 4700 B.C. The second monument appears to date from three centuries later.

BARRANGQUETE (El), Spain, 154
BARUMINI, Sardinia, 149
BAUME-BOURBON (Cave), Cabrières, Gard, France, 190
BEAGHMORE, Ireland, 132
BECKHAMPTON ROAD, Wiltshire, England, 85; 236; 268
BECKUM-WINTERGALEN, Westphalia, West Germany, 146
BÉGADAN, Gironde, France, 16
BEHY, Ireland, 112
BELDERG BEG, Ireland, 197
BENON, see CHAMP-CHALON
BERNET (tumulus), Saint-Sauveur, Gironde, France, 80
BISCEGLIA, Italy, 154; 154
BJERRE, Jutland, Denmark, 197
BLOMESKOBBEL, Denmark, 139
LES BOILEAU, Vaucluse, France, 148; 214; 227
BOIS-DU-MESNIL, Tressé, Ille-et-Vilaine, France, 245
LA BOIXE, Vervant, Charente, France, 117; 118

A necropolis and sanctuary consisting of five large complex monuments. The first structures, built at about 4700 B.C., were round burial chambers roofed with corbelling (tumulus E and FO), with contents attributable to an early phase of the Cous group. Later followed small megalithic rectangular chambers with off-centre passages (tombs B1, B2, and C1), with contents characteristic of the pre-Chassey culture of the middle Neolithic era. Two large rectangular Angoulême-type chambers (mounds A and F2) were built at the end of the fourth millennium; the vessels found there were part of the Chassey culture, with bases decorated in what has come to be known as the 'Bougon' style. Most of these chambers were re-used from the third millennium until the late Neolithic age (Peu-Richardian and possibly early Bronze). Some burial sites were embellished with spectacularly massive constructions (mounds C2 and F1) with functions that were ceremonial rather than funerary. The Neolithic zone of Bougon is defined by the megalithic monuments spread across an area about 10 kilometres broad, based on dwellings and the quarries supplying the various stones used. In 1979 Bougon was the scene of a series of experiments designed to test theories about the techniques used by megalith builders.

This megalithic grave, excavated at the beginning of the twentieth century, reveals successive phases of use. The chamber, measuring 6 by 1.60 metres, is bounded by two parallel rows of four uprights supporting three large blocks. Human bones were found on the paved floor, as well as pottery with deeply engraved decoration of the Funnel beaker culture. Shards of similar vessels and burnt bones were scattered over another paved area. There may have been a later burial, accompanied by a vessel dating from a time when individual burial was practised. The final phase of use is identified by the presence of a bell-beaker jar, and of 'giant'-type vessels.

A mound of stones surmounted by a ring of slanting slabs. It stands in an area that is especially rich in Neo-

lithic and Bronze Ages monuments.
This large round barrow lying south of Stonehenge belongs to the Normanton burial group, and dates from the first half of the second millennium. It is the most famous of the barrows of the Bronze Age princes of Wessex, because of the richness of the offerings found in its central coffer, which include copper axes and dagger blades, quantities of stone weapons, ivory items, and a decorated sceptre.

This long fourth millennium tumulus reveals several phases of adaptation:
  – a trapezoidal enclosure within a palisade, with a mortuary house built on top of a pit grave;
  – two further mortuary houses and a pit grave in the same enclosure, partly covered by a long barrow;

Les CHATELLIERS-DU-VIEIL-AUZAY, Vendée, France, *219*; 229

CHAUMES (plateau des), Exoudun, Deux-Sèvres, France, 166

La CHAUSSÉE-TIRANCOURT, Somme, France, 142; 218; *224*; *225*; 228; 273
Late Neolithic mass grave, built in a trench ending in a small compartment. The rectangular chamber, built of massive slabs, is 11 metres long, 3 metres wide and 1.70 metres high. Access is via a small antechamber defined by two vertical blocks; the nature of its covering is unknown. The tomb was originally divided into three sections by small sandstone slabs and contained the remains of 350 individuals. Other similar small compartments were later identified higher up; one of them contained the bones of six children. The whole monument was sealed with a layer of limestone slabs.

CHENON, Charente, France, 118
A vast group of seven megalithic tombs, extending over 134 hectares; six of the monuments remain, each containing one or two square or rectangular passage graves, beneath a round barrow. The grave-goods date from the middle (Chassey) and late Neolithic age.

CHERMIGNAC, Charente-Maritime, France, 16

CHINFLON, Andalusia, Spain, 279

CHOUILLY, Marne, France, 249

CHUSENJI, Japan, 53

La CLAPE (necropolis), Laroque-de-Fa, Aude, France, 106

CLAVA (type of monument), Scotland, 132

CLEAR ISLAND, Ireland, 251

CLYDE (group), Scotland, 89

CODDU VECCIU, Sardinia, 137

COHAW, Ireland, 101

COIZARD see Le RAZET

COJOUX, (alignment), Saint-Just, Ille-et-Vilaine, France, 122; *122*; 225; 230; 266
One of the most important megalithic sites of inland Brittany. The main alignment of standing stones is the classic example of open architecture whose complex history has been reconstructed. The first monoliths were set up in about 4500 B.C. contemporaneous with a set of small stone-filled hearths. Schist blocks and stakes were added later, followed by a low mound concealing a small burial cist containing a bell-beaker jar and an urn from the second half of the third millennium. Finally, a small circular tomb with two coffers was constructed. Nearby is a group of three stones, the remains of another monument, and a mound crowned with a row of white stones which remains a mystery, as well as other megaliths.

COLL DE CRUES, Spain, 152

COLLORGUES, Gard, France, 247; 255

COLOMBIER (Le), Euzet, Gard, France, 255

COLOMBIERS, (menhir), France, 19

COLOMBIERS-SUR-SEULLES, Calvados, France, 79

COLPO, Larcuste, Morbihan, France, 94; 105; 242
A necropolis of four monuments, of which three have been studied though only two remain visible. The mounds with architectural kerbs were constructed successively. The first mound covers a round passage grave, containing Carn-type goods. The second is oval (13 by 10 metres) and contains two passage graves associated with Carn- and Souch-type material. The last cairn, also oval (15 by 13 metres), contains a megalithic transepted chamber with a long access passage, contemporaneous with the Chassey culture; charcoal from the passage has been carbon-dated to 3540 B.C.

La COMENDA, Reguengos de Monsaraz, Portugal, 101; 102

CONGUEL, Morbihan, France, *244*
This megalithic passage tomb near Quiberon contains two archeological levels separated by stone paving. Vessels patterned with horizontal broken lines recall the 'Conguel' type found in the Gulf of Morbihan and dated between 2500 and 2300 B.C.

CORATO, Italy, 154; 169

CORSEUL Côtes-du-Nord, France, 20

COURCOME, Magné, Deux-Sèvres, France, 248

COURJEONNET, Marne, France, 249

COUS (Les), Bazoges-en-Pareds, Vendée, France, 117; 182
A round tumulus, 15 metres across, covering a central circular chamber 4.50 metres in diameter and a slab-lined passage 5 metres long. About fifteen globular pots were found there, all dating from the middle Neolithic Age.

COVA D'EN DAYNA, Romanya de la Selva, Spain, 152

CREC'H QUILLÉ, Saint-Quay-Perros, Côtes-du-Nord, France, 141; 246

CREEVYKEEL, Ireland, 90; *91*

CRO-MAGNON (site), Les Eyzies-de-Tayac, Dordogne, France, 91

CROH-COLLÉ, Morbihan, France, 194

CRUCUNO, Erdeven, Morbihan, France, 121

CRUGUELLIC, Ploemeur, Morbihan, France
This megalithic tomb with double transept was discovered in a subrectangular mound 20 metres long by 12 metres wide. Two of the slabs are decorated with carving, one with a highly stylized anthropomorphic figure, the other with a sharply-cut 'shield'. The primary grave-goods, and the most plentiful, are associated with the Chassey culture and especially with that of the south Armorican or Cruguellic type. A substan-

tial secondary deposit is identified by late Neolithic vessels associated with the Seine-Oise-Marne culture to which can be added three rimmed bottles. A Chalcolithic bell-beaker jar indicates a third phase of use of the grave.

A subcircular cairn, built in about 4500 B.C., is surrounded by a row of large stones and covers two megalithic passage tombs. One of the roofing slabs is carved with crooks and axes with handles. In its later phase the monument was enlarged, the passages were lengthened by 4 metres and new outer walls were built, forming a tumulus 30 metres across and 6 metres high. The discovery of microliths beneath the mound suggests a possible interrelationship of this ancient industry with the first phase of the monument's construction.

Long megalithic cavern, measuring 11 by 2 metres, containing 573 flint arrow-heads, 185 lignite and amber beads, copper ornaments, and 1200 vessels with deeply incised decoration.

Double circle of standing stones, the first containing about fifty stones and the second thirty. The two circles are tangential to a large monolith which was originally 7 metres high. Traces of Chassey culture may be associated with hearth structures or with small coffers near the circles.

A late Neolithic age grave, consisting of a large block covering a half-buried oval chamber with sides made of slabs and low stone walls, and a mound covering the whole construction. The remains of ninety individuals, including sixteen children, were found there, and shown to belong to two intermarried genetic groups. One skull had been trepanned. The grave-goods included arrow-heads, two small perforated axes, stone and bone beads, perforated canine teeth, bone awls, between twelve and fifteen vessels, and several animal bones.

This is a complex Neolithic and Bronze Age site, in which traces of dwellings and graves lie side by side. Recent excavation has uncovered a small structure, approximately 6 by 6 metres, bounded by ditches dug into the gravel and post-holes. This may have been a house or a small sanctuary; flints and undecorated pottery from the first half of the third millennium were found there. Four Neolithic skeletons were found in an irregular pit 120 metres away; one had an arrow-head at chest level, which must have been the cause of death.

Four megalithic monuments beneath barrows have been found on this plain, and one has recently been excavated. Beneath the semicircular pile of in-fill from sealing the monument lay a walled, trapezoidal mound, containing a rectangular chamber with a short passage. This type of monument was built during the first half of the third millennium, and was in use until its end, as shown by the wealth of grave-goods in the tomb inside the second tumulus.

The megalithic chambers and standing stones were constructed at the end of the Neolithic age. The standing stones with their anthropomorphic outline, which becomes better defined as the Bronze Age progresses, are the most famous element of this magnificent site. It is possible to make out swords and warriors. Some steles were used at the end of the Bronze Age for the construction of a torre.

The Neolithic tumulus of La Hogue is 40 metres long, 30 metres across, and 2 metres high. It contains twelve circular multiple graves, roofed with dry-stone corbelling, with access passages between 5 and 10 metres long and a fair number of skeletons and offerings dating from the first half of the fourth millennium. Six hundred metres from the mound is a second similar tumulus, La Hoguette, 30 metres long and 20 metres wide. It covers seven, perhaps eight, circular corbelled chambers with access passages. Shards found at the base of the mound are decorated in the late Danube style.

One of the most impressive decorated monuments stands on the island of Gavrinis in the Gulf of Morbihan. Of the twenty-nine slabs forming the burial chamber and its passage, twenty-three are decorated from top to bottom. Some are decorated on their hidden side; these have probably been re-used. In 1984 part of a drawing of an ox was found, of which the other part was on the covering stone of the Dolmen des Marchands at Locmariaquer (Morbihan). These blocks originally came from a menhir 14 metres high; a sample has been dated at between 3480 and 2950 B.C.

Long Neolithic tumulus orientated east-west, bordered with large blocks. At the centre it has a rectangular megalithic chamber, 8 metres long by 2 metres wide, divided by small slabs into five compartments in which bones were arranged according to ethnic or social criteria.

A chamber beneath a tumulus consists of stone slabs decorated with incised motifs painted in red and black, representing a battle-axe, a bow, and a quiver with arrows. The grave-goods consisted of a bevelled axe, a flint knife, and a late Neolithic amphora.

Four mounds were built in about 4720 B.C. on the island of Guennoc; one contains six round chambers roofed with dry-stone corbelling. The wall slabs in tumulus 3 are anthropomorphic in shape. The round-based pots are associated with an old style found in Carn Island and at Barnenez.

This round tumulus, 25 metres in diameter, contains two graves which share a passage. A large quantity of human bones was found on the paving of the rectangular chambers, as well as ornaments, weapons, and late Neolithic tools.

A Neolithic complex with several burial monuments and dwelling sites, including four megalithic tombs. A passage tomb beneath a mound called 'Carlshögen' contains the remains of fifty people; its oval chamber is subdivided by low walls into nine paved compartments, each containing bones. Pits also contain human bones and some offerings.

Large archeological complex covering 60 hectares. The group consists of an inner enclosure of three discontinuous ditches at the top of the hillside, outer ditches dug further down the slope, and another small enclosure on another spur of the hill. Two long barrows were built around 3000 B.C., one between the ditches of the inner enclosure and the other on top of the neighbouring spur to the north. Recent excavations indicate that the various structures had different functions: the outer ditches may have been defensive. Although the central enclosure contained traces of occupation, the filling-in of the ditches suggests ritual activity, since skulls and other human remains were found in them. The secondary enclosure might have been a dwelling site, however: skeletons and large numbers of arrow-heads and burnt items from the ramparts were found in the ditch, and may be the remains of the storming of the settlement.

A rectangular monument, 6 by 27 metres, edged with standing stones and subdivided into three compartments. One enclosure has been extended twice. The burial function appears to be indicated by the deposit of two items of pottery at the beginning of the third millennium, but there is no trace of a chamber or a coffer, nor of a mound.

A megalithic passage tomb, with a chamber divided into two lateral compartments. It gives its name to Kerugou style of pottery, round and flat-based vessels decorated with three or four vertical ribs on the upper part of the bulge. Many of these pots were found in the grave; they are found everywhere along the southern coast of Brittany, and date from about 3000 B.C.

The valley contains several monuments, including the Neolithic chambered tomb of Nether Largie South, Bronze Age mounds – like Nether Largie North with its carved stones, and Ri Cruin – and the Temple Wood stone circle, isolated standing stones, and carved rocks.

Megalithic monument discovered in 1748 beneath a mound. There is a long coffer, 4 by 1 metre, made of decorated stones set on edge, which appears to have been constructed for a single burial. The great point of interest of this tomb is the internal decoration which shows in particular a Bronze Age ceremonial · procession.

Lying 1500 metres from the famous Newgrange group and on the same bank of the river Boyne, the

Knowth necropolis has recently been excavated. An enormous central mound, almost 90 metres across at its broadest point, is surrounded by seventeen smaller mounds. The main mound contains two small chambers, one long and quadrangular and the other of transept form, with a long passage opening to the west and another to the east, and a border of decorated blocks at the same level. The smaller mounds contain similar megalithic chambers, also quadrangular or transepted, but with shorter passages. The offerings found and some carbon-14 datings yield indications of use around 3000 B.C.

Megalithic monument lying beneath a circular barrow of classic Languedoc type of passage grave with antechamber, dating from the third millennium B.C. The three slabs forming the walls of the trapezoidal chamber support a large roof slab; the entrance is formed by two portal stones, and the antechamber and dry-stone-walled passage are separated by a stone shaped like a furnace door.

The site of many megalithic remains, among them the Table des Marchands, Er-Vinglé, and the Pierre Plates monuments. The most famous is the broken Grand Menhir, known as Men-er-Hroeg (the 'Fairy Stone'), France's most imposing megalith. Broken into four pieces in prehistoric times, it was originally 20.30 metres long and weighed about 350 tonnes. The motifs chipped out on it link it with another monolith, also broken, of which sections have been re-used as covering stones for the Gavrinis chamber, and for the Table des Marchands and Er-Vinglé at Locmariaquer itself. It was probably erected at the end of the fourth millennium. Some writers, including Alexander Thom, suggest that because of its height it probably served as a reference point for astral observations. [See GREAT MENHIR, PIERRES PLATES, TABLE DES MARCHANDS.]

A double burial chamber beneath ground level, without tumulus. It consists of two rows of stones 19 metres long, set at intervals of 2.50 metres; at the centre a port-hole slab is set transversely. Some of the stones are decorated. The remains of forty-five people were mixed with tools made of flint, polished stone, and bone, as well as ornaments and late Neolithic vessels.

The thirty mounds of this necropolis are spread over four hills, about 40 kilometres west of Newgrange. The chambers are transepted, and some of their slabs carry a type of rich free-style decoration to which Loughcrew has given its name: the motifs are mainly chevrons, bows, zigzags and wavy lines, spirals and sun emblems, pointed circles and lozenges. Petit Mont at Arzon (Morbihan) is similarly decorated.

One of Europe's finest megalithic monuments. It is a

passage tomb constructed with small slabs laid flat to form the walls and corbelling, and is covered by a tumulus surrounded by a ditch. The monument dates from 2670 B.C.

Two Neolithic graves with megalithic stone covering have been discovered at Les Marsaules and La Chaise. A single crouched skeleton was found in a pit lined with rubble. A fragment taken from the La Chaise monument was carbon-14-dated to 5600 B.C.

In the late Neolithic age, the islands of Malta and Gozo developed a unique civilization that gave rise to the construction of a series of funerary and religious monuments. Several phases have been identified: the

Zebbug phase, about 3000 B.C., is characterized by tombs hollowed out of the rock; the Mgarr phase produced the first hypogea and temples, apparently at about 2700 B.C.; the great megalithic temples and most elaborate hypogea belong to the later Ggantija and Hal Safliéni phases, while the complex megalithic temples were built in the final Tarxien phase, abruptly interrupted at about 2000 B.C. when, it is thought, metalworking was introduced. Some of the stone tombs are very imposing; many of them carry the image of a woman, probably a goddess.

A very long megalithic tomb containing two rows of compartments. Excavated in 1932 and 1933, it was restored so that it could be opened to the public.

On a high plateau between two rivers in deep ravines, this complex site includes a town surrounded

by a rampart and flanked by towers and three ditches, a necropolis, and, further away, ten bastions. It was occupied during the second half of the third millennium. The graves are multiple; some have a passage grave burial (a round chamber covered with corbelling and a dry-stone-walled passage); in others with the same layout, shaped stones are laid against the chamber walls, or perforated stones in the passage. Some are partially buried. The finds are varied. Some are made of stone: polished axes, leaf-shaped and triangular arrowheads with concave bases, flint knives and daggers, alabaster vessels, limestone idols and betyls, and beads, mostly of limestone but also of jadeite, turquoise, and variscite. Polished bone is common, in the form of tools and idols, and ivory combs and amber beads have also been found. The pottery includes biconical bowls, spherical vessels, bottles, some vases with several openings, and others shaped like animals; many are decorated with incised, printed or painted motifs of chevrons, suns, houndstooth patterns, and occasionally animals (deer). Many cast copper goods were found – flat axes, knives, saws, awls, scissors, and triangular daggers – showing that copper-working was important in this agricultural society.

A 50 metre-long tumulus, 24 metres broad, covering probably five megalithic passage tombs of which the first, polygonal in shape, has a sculpted stone doorframe of 'furnace-door' design.

Two hypogea have been discovered, hollowed out in the chalk. The second, extensively excavated in 1960, yielded information on late Neolithic burial rites. The burial cavern had an access passage, an antechamber, and a chamber 5 metres long, 3 metres wide, and 1.15 metres high, subdivided into two compartments, in which the bodies of forty adults and twenty children had been laid over the years. The grave-goods appeared to date from the first burials: a polished flint axe and adze, horn scabbards, bone awls and polishers, a chisel made from the sharpened incisor tooth of a pig, ninety-five sharpened arrows, thirty-eight flint knives, beads of limestone and shell, a perforated fragment of amber, mollusc shells, pigs' teeth pierced with holes, and pendants of bone, horn and schist.

More than thirty monuments are grouped in a four-kilometre area of the Boyne valley; the largest are Dowth, Knowth, and Newgrange. The Newgrange tumulus, about 80 metres in diameter, is surrounded by a circle of stones, some pf which carry non-figurative designs, either pecked or carved – this decoration is one of the richest of all megalithic art. The body of the cairn is supported by a large kerb, now reconstructed through the work of Michael O'Kelly. A long passage lined with stone slabs leads to a cruciform chamber covered by corbelling. The funeral ritual consisted of cremation and partial burial. The monument appears to have been in use in the first half of the third millennium.

Collective megalithic chamber grave with an antechamber, consisting of a double row of large blocks, 10 metres long and 3.20 metres apart. Ten layers of human bones lying on the paved floor included the remains of 177 individuals – men, women and children – mingled with arrow heads, flint tools, a few late Neolithic shards amd copper, amber, and dog-tooth jewelry.

The collective Paradis grave is late Neolithic in date. It is elliptical in shape, and recesses have been dug into the walls; a well 5 metres deep has been sunk in the chamber floor. The rectangular antechamber has a 'false door' consisting of a sandstone slab between two limestone columns; two intact skeletons were found there, and the remains of seventeen others, including seven children, lay in the chamber itself.

A buried funeral chamber, 6 metres long by 4.20 metres wide with a short lateral passage. The dry-stone structure contained the bodies of fifty people, arranged in three rows, and funerary offerings of pottery, shaped flints, and dogs' teeth.

A tumulus and grave, with a chamber 8.70 metres long by 1.55 to 2.10 metres wide. The first burial layer was associated with Neolithic vessels decorated with deeply impressed patterns; the second, separated from the first by stones, contained bell-beaker ware and 'giant' cups from the Chalcolithic era .

Four rock-cut tombs, north of Setubal, contain circular chambers between 4.50 and 5 metres in diameter, approached through an antechamber. The undecorated vessels were spherical or hemispherical, and belonged to the local late Neolithic tradition; the decorated ones were hemispherical bowls, large cups, and some beakers ornamented with horizontal, vertical and oblique dotted lines created with a comb. Stone artefacts included trapezoidal microlith plates, concave based arrow-heads, large blades of flint, and several polished axes. Limestone cylinder idols, plaques of engraved schist, bone buttons of various shapes with V-shaped perforations, and stone beads were also found on the site. The copper items were small awls, a spatula, a dagger, and the famous Palmella point (an arrow head with a near-circular blade and long tang) of which examples have been found in the south and south-west of France, and as far away as Brittany. Recent excavation of a dwelling site at Malhadas, near Palmella, have shown the importance of copper-working in this early second millennium culture.

By the end of the fourth millennium a village was established here, close to a cemetery of graves consisting of cists marked by an alignment of standing stones. Later a dozen megalithic coffers and chambers were built. Monument 6, dating from the late Neolithic era, includes a chamber built at the end of a triangular paved area 16 metres long. Steles may have been erected across the front of the monument; they were re-used at the end of the third millennium for construction of chamber 11, which appears to be associated with bell-beaker jars of the Chalcolithic era. These large steles

were fully decorated, with a recognizable dagger and double spiral copper pendant; they were one of the most original features of megalithic art.

PETIT-MÉNEC (alignment), Carnac, Morbihan, France, 37

PETIT MONT (mound), Arzon, Morbihan, France, *98*; *99*; 100;103;107; 231; *231*; 244; 245; 247; 274

Several phases of construction have been identified beneath this impressive mound, which is 60 metres across. Nothing beyond its mere existence is known of the first mound, which was oblong and is now completely levelled. Its site was partially covered by another mound which was almost quadrangular; a dip appears to indicate a still unexcavated chamber, with retaining walls more than 2 metres high. These have been protected by material from the enlargement of the monument, which includes on the south-east a passage tomb constructed of several decorated and re-used blocks, one of them a large anthropomorphic slab. The addition of supporting walls made it possible to enlarge the cairn again, and two more passage tombs were created on the east side, one of which is artistically very rich; the second was destroyed during the Second World War to build a blockhouse. Archeological remains date back to the middle Neolithic and Chalcolithic ages, and to Gaulish and Gallo-Roman times.

PETIT MORIN (valley), Marne, France, 144; *228*; *239*
PEYRE LONGUE, Dax, Landes, France, 20
PEYROLEBADO, Aveyron, France, 20
PIERRE AUX MARIS, La Baroche, Haut-Rhin, *25*
PIERRE-BISE, Boissy-le-Sec, Eure-et-Loir, France, 16
PIERRE-DE-CHANTECOQ, Eure-et-Loir, France, 17
PIERRE DE DAVID, Cangy, Indre-et-Loire, France, 16
PIERRE DE GRIBÈRE, Sabres, Landes, France, 18
PIERRE DE MINUIT, Pontlevoy, Loir-et-Cher, France, 16
PIERRE DES DEMOISELLES, Le Mesnil-Hardray, Eure, France, 16

A row of three Neolithic mounds, 170 metres long. The first mound contains six megalithic tombs; the second, 70 metres long and 30 metres wide, has not yet been explored; the third, Les Mousseax, has been studied recently. It is a subrectangular tumulus measuring 20 by 24 metres, and contains two megalithic graves in transepted passaged chambers. Two vessels were found in front of the passage entrance, as well as Chassey vessel bases from the middle Neolithic age.

Lying six kilometres north of Sintra, this double collective grave has a sequence of domed passage chambers. The oldest, dug into the rock, is between 2 and 2.50 metres across, with vertical slabs lining the sides. The passage has two small lateral cells connected with the second chamber. The latter, which is circular (6 metres in diameter), is built of dry stones and covered by a corbelled vault; two narrow points in the passage define a kind of antechamber, 1.90 metres across, which was closed off by a pile of stones. Between 150 and 200 individuals were deposited in this grave, with some offerings: arrow-heads, smooth pots, and copper items – Palmella pins and dagger blades. Two carbon-14 analyses point to dates of 1700 and 1690 B.C., indicating 2000 B.C. in absolute chronological terms. The first grave has been dated at 2300 and 2210 B.C., (i.e. 2800 B.C.), and contained a great many concave-based arrow-heads, large flint blades, decorated schist plaques, bone pins, beads, and two vessels. The juxtaposition of these two monuments is particularly interesting since it makes it possible to distinguish between the late Neolithic and Chalcolithic periods in Portugal.

Excavated in 1965 by Jean L'Helgouach and then restored, this very long gallery-grave, 9.50 by 2.40 metres, was built with slabs of local granite. The antechamber lies to the south-east, and on the opposite side there is a terminal cell with four decorated stones; four more lie in the chamber itself. 'Shield-idols' are visible, with breasts (with an added necklace in one case), palettes and an axe. The offerings – polished axes, trimmed flints, and rimmed vessels – belong to the late Neolithic age.

This monument on the largest of the Orkney islands is a large oval stone cairn, kerb-edged. A passage leads into a corbel-roofed transepted chamber. Only one part of the grave has been explored. Fragments of human bones were found, some of them partly burnt, together with pots, small objects made of hard stone, flint, and bone, and animal bones. Carbon-14 analysis dates the monument between 2600 and 1900 B.C.

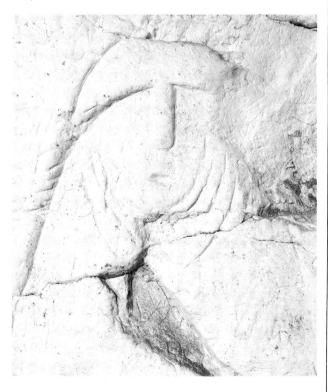

This late Neolithic necropolis consists of thirty-seven rock-cut tombs dug out of the limestone; the oldest part is probably a square chamber with a simple passage at the centre of the burial area. The tombs furthest from this point are the most recent, and have the most clearly defined antechambers. The decoration of two of the hypogea with motifs of axe with handle and the female deity is particularly interesting.

There are three levels within the Crottes hypogeum. In the oldest, dating from 2150 B.C., most of the skeletons were disarticulated. The offerings included quantities of jewelry – 2,300 beads of mollusc shell or limestone, 185 of steatite, a few made of variscite, one of glass, and another of copper. In the next layer, dating from 2090 B.C., thirty-five complete skeletons were piled up haphazardly – presumably following a massacre, for arrow-heads were embedded in the bones. Finally, within the top layer were found more than fifty skulls, laid out in a row along the back wall.

The finest dolmen in France, in the opinion of the Breton archeologists. The large rectangular megalithic chamber (14.30 by 4 metres) is approached through an antechamber and portico, linking the tomb with the Anjou monuments. It consists of forty-one blocks, of which the heaviest weighs some 50 tonnes. The tumulus which must have completed the construction has long since disappeared, and any offerings within the chamber have vanished without trace. The construction of the Roche aux Fées has been dated at about 3000 B.C.

The mound of small stones, 21 by 12 metres, is edged with a kerb hidden by the embankments used to seal off the monument. The double grave within faces west; the original coffer was surrounded by a subrectangular tumulus and closed with a slab, but later a second, larger, coffer and mound were built. Among the ten skulls discovered, three showed traces of post mortem cutting of strips of bone. Some shards and a long trimmed flint blade indicate use during the second half of the third millennium.

A tumulus covering a wooden burial chamber; the skeleton has not been preserved. Offerings include a battle axe with knob, a rimmed bottle, a decorated beaker, amber beads, and sharpened arrow-heads. Near the tumulus, a horseshoe-shaped outline indicates the remains of a tomb or cult building.

A long tumulus covering a pit grave 2.50 metres by 80 centimetres, surrounded by stones. It contained two axes and four flint arrow heads with cutting edges, amber ornaments and a disc of sheet copper with repoussé decoration.

SAN ANDREA PRIU (hypogeum), Sardinia, 132; 136

The San Andrea Priu hypogeum belongs to the Ozieri culture of the late fourth millennium. It consists of two main chambers with recesses built round it for bodies and offerings.

SANGAPP-NI-KOCHANG, Korea, *53*

SANTU ANTINE (nuraghe), Sardinia, 138

SANTU PEDRU (rock-cut tomb), Sardinia, 137; 239

SAO PEDRO DO ESTORIL (cave), Portugal, 152

On the Atlantic coast not far from the Tagus estuary, two rock-cut tombs were excavated in 1944, part of a regional series of Chalcolithic graves. The chambers of these caves, hollowed out of the rock, are circular (the first is 4.70 metres across, the second 4.50 metres), with a hole at the top of the dome. A sloping passage gives access from the surface to the grave. Burials were fairly numerous – there were at least sixty-five skulls in the first chamber, in several layers, and twenty in the second. The offerings in the first are by far the most interesting: polished axes, archers' brassards, limestone cylinders, flint blades, beads, buttons with V-shaped perforations, bone pendants, pins and tubes, copper awls and daggers, four gold spirals; quantities of polished pottery vessels, cups and bowls, some decorated with horizontal grooves, and some with handles, contrasting with bell-beaker ware mostly decorated in international or Palmella style. Offerings were probably deposited in several phases, with the last around 2000 B.C.

SARNOVO, prov. Wloclavek, Poland, 82

A necropolis of nine trapezoidal mounds measuring between 38.50 and 83 metres across; there are from one to five burial places in each. Traces of Neolithic dwellings have been found beneath mounds 7 and 8.

SARUP, Odense, Funen, Denmark, 197; 210

These two camps, surrounded by a double ditch and fencing with multiple openings, cover 9 and 2 hectares respectively. There is no trace of dwellings inside, but late Neolithic material has been found in pit dwellings nearby.

LA SAUZAIE, Soubise, Charente-Maritime, France, 199

SCHAFSTÄDT, East Germany, 254

SCHWASDORF, Mecklenburg, East Germany, 110

SCHWÖRSTADT (type), 147

SEINE-OISE-MARNE (culture), 143; 144; 235

SENNORI (tomb), Sardinia, 137

LES SEPT CHEMINS, Bougon, Deux-Sèvres, France, 120

SERPENT MOUND, Ordams County, Ohio, U.S.A., 30; 62

SETTIVA, Corsica, 135

SEVERN-COTSWOLD (group), 98; 116; 216

SÉVÉROUÉ, Ille-et-Vilaine, France, 186

SHANBALLYEDMOND (tumulus), County Tipperary, Ireland, 139

SHEIKH ABDALLAH QUARRY, Baalbek, Lebanon, 166

SHIMOSUKE, Japan, 53

SILBURY HILL, Wiltshire, England, *110*

SION see LE PETIT CHASSEUR

SKARA BRAE, Orkney, Scotland, 114; *198*; *199*; 200; 209; 253

This outstanding late Neolithic site to the north of Scotland, open to the public, consists of extremely well-preserved stone houses separated by passage-ways, surrounded and partly covered by piles of rubbish. Carbon-14 dating indicates that they were inhabited from approximately 2400 to 1800 B.C. The stone houses of the first phase of occupation are square or subrectangular; their remarkable interior features include central hearths, and beds or lateral compartments. The second, and principal, phase, consists of eight more solidly-built and better preserved houses; the walls of some of these have survived to a height of 3 metres. There are central hearths, lateral beds, cupboards in the walls, and even shelving, made of a local stone that is easily split. The main passage-way was covered. One house – perhaps a workshop – is separate from the others, which stand close together. The site has yielded plentiful finds of domestic pottery and a great many stone and bone tools. Cattle- and sheep-rearing is much in evidence; so is barley cultivation, while sea fishing was also important. Orkney has at least two other similar sites, Rinyo in the island of Rousay, and Links of Noltland on Papa Westray. Some of the megalithic tombs in this region, such as Maes Howe, and circular enclosures such as the Ring of Brogar and Stenness, may date from the same period.

SLEWCAIRN, Scotland, 89

A trapezoidal tumulus 20 metres long with, at the base of the concave façade, a very long burial structure

315

with three pits in a passage leading to two recesses.

SODDO TIYA, Ethiopia, *50*

SON BAULO, Balearic Islands, 133

SONDERHOLM, Denmark, 83

SORGINETXE (chamber), Arrizala, Pays Basque, France, 151

SOTO, Spain, 126

SOUC'H (Le), Finistère, France, *243*

SOUTH STREET, Wiltshire, England, 85; 197

SPIENNES, Belgium, 163; *169*

STAR CARR, England, 204

STEIN, Netherlands

The grave consists of a paved area 5.50 metres long and 1.75 metres wide, with two lateral post-holes. The cremated remains of skeletons were mixed with the grave-goods, a beaker and a rimmed pottery bottle, an adze, ninety-six flint arrow-heads, and eleven bone ones. These items have been dated to the end of the third millennium.

STENNESS, Orkney, Scotland, 114; 132; 200; 210

Excavated in 1973 and 1974, the circle of standing stones is surrounded by a ditch and has an unidentified feature at its centre. Two radiocarbon datings place its construction at about 3000 B.C. A little to the north lies another stone circle, the Ring of Brogar.

STENO (tumulus), Ithaca, Greece, 44

STERN, Belgium, 144

STONEHENGE, Wiltshire, England, 12; *16*; *17*; *18*; *19*; 30; 32; 35; 36; 37; 38; 39; *39*; 40; 42; 43; 65; 107; 108; *128*; *129*; *130*; 131; 132; *133*; 159; 162; 163; 165; 175; 178; 180; *183*; 185; 186; 195; 198; *201*; 210; 211; 214; 226; 233; 238; 261; 263; 264; 265; *268*; 273; 276

This classic site is part of a whole complex of ritual monuments on Salisbury Plain. It dates from the late Neolithic times and the Early Bronze Age. Excavations by W. Hawley in 1919-26 and Richard Atkinson in 1952 - 58 indicate several phases of development. In about 2750 B.C. the side was a modest enclosure with a ditch and inner rampart, with an entrance. Fifty-six pits set around the inside face of the rampart contained earth and the remains of human cremations, and at this period wooden structures probably occupied the centre of the site. The entrance was later modified by adding two large sandstone monoliths, of which the famous Heel Stone still exists, and an avenue of banks and parallel ditches. A double circle of holes found in the centre of the site was apparently destined to receive the blue-stones, blocks of unusually hard stone brought from south-west Wales. The monument is orientated towards the point on the horizon where the sun rises on the day of the summer solstice. The third phase of construction at Stonehenge left the monument much as it stands today, with its five central trilithons set in a horseshoe, surrounded by a circle of standing stones supporting lintels. An outer circle of low stones was set up during the fourth and last phase.

STRALENDORF, Kr. Schwering, Mecklenburg, East Germany, 82

A funeral structure, 125 metres in length, containing several graves made of small stones and covered with slabs.

STREET HOUSES, England, 203

STRENSTRUP, Denmark, 110

STROBY EGEDE, Denmark, 86

SU-CUVECCU-BULTEI (tomb), Sardinia, 137

SUSA, Iran, 270

SWEET TRACK, Somerset, England, 231

SYROS (island), Greece, 44

TABERNAS, Spain, 154

LA TABLE DES MARCHANDS, Locmariaquer, Morbihan, France, 103; 107; *172*; 242; 244; 247; *253*; *254*; 274

TAGARP, ö TOMMARP, Sweden, *104*; *211*

TAHITI, 59; 62

TAIZÉ, Deux-Sèvres, France, 106

TAKAMATSUZUKA, Nara, Japan, 53

TAKCHARA, Fukuoka, Japan, *55*

TALLAGHT, Ireland, *278*

TAMULI, Sardinia, 239

TANANARIVE, Madagascar, 58

TANUM TEGNEBY, Sweden, 197

TARA, County Meath, Ireland, 250

TARAJAL, Spain, 154

TARXIEN, Malta, 133; *142*; 198; 238; 239; *246*; *247*

TATETSUKI, Okayama, Japan, 53; *54*

TAUZAC (dolmen),Charente, France, 16

TCHELENKO, Ethiopia, 49

TE PITO TE KURA (moai), Easter Island, 160

TERRIER DE LA FADE, Anglade, Gironde, France, 20

TÉVIEC, Morbihan, France, 72; 104; 194; 206; 271

This long barrow with passage grave near Windmill Hilland Avebury in southern England, is built of earth, chalk, and small blocks of sandstone. It is nearly 90 metres long and trapezoidal in shape, containing at its broaders and higher end, a corbel-roofed transepted passage tomb made of stone slabs with dry stone walling. The passage from the tomb opens onto a convex megalithic façade, facing east. Some 50 people were buried here; most of the bones were disarticulated, with skulls arranged together with the long bones. The very few offerings were fragments of vessels and flints. The monument was probably built at about 3000 B.C., but it remained open for a long period after its construction. The passage was finally filled in with earth and chalk at the beginning of the second millennium, the façade was built with four enormous sandstone monoliths.

WINDMILL HILL, Wiltshire, England, 116; 129; 264

Traces of a large enclosure covering 10 hectares, inside 3 discontinuous ditches. the first phase of occupation of the original enclosure left remains ins ome of the ditches beneath the ramparts, dating from the en dof the foruth millennium. The ditches of the second occupation are rich in Neolithic remains, also from the late fourth millennium, and in the upper layers there are substantial remains from the third millennium. These indicate that cereals were cultivated and that livestock, mainly cattle, were kept. The presence of imported hard stone axes is evidence of contact with distant cultures. The ditches were later re-dug; they intersect in several placcs, but contain no important indications of occupation. There may have been deliberate deposits in the ditches – animal bones for example – and the site may have had a ritual significance, but this remains debatable.

WOODHENGE, Wiltshire, England, 233
YAYOI (culture), 52
ZALAVROUGA, U.S.S.R. 206; 257
ZAMBUJAL, Portugal, 153; 214; 234